D1799938

Hardy's Geography

Hardy's Geography

Wessex and the Regional Novel

Ralph Pite

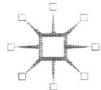

Published by
PALGRAVE MACMILLAN
Houndmills, Basingstoke, Hampshire RG21 6XS and
175 Fifth Avenue, New York, N.Y. 10010
Companies and representatives throughout the world

PALGRAVE MACMILLAN is the global academic imprint of the Palgrave
Macmillan division of St. Martin's Press, LLC and of Palgrave Macmillan Ltd.
Macmillan® is a registered trademark in the United States, United Kingdom
and other countries. Palgrave is a registered trademark in the European
Union and other countries.

ISBN-13: 978–0–333–98774–2
ISBN-10: 0–333–98774–8

This book is printed on paper suitable for recycling and
made from fully managed and sustained forest sources.

A catalogue record for this book is available from the British Library.

Library of Congress Catalog Card Number: 2002025237

Printed and bound in Great Britain by
Antony Rowe Ltd, Chippenham and Eastbourne

Contents

List of Illustrations

Acknowledgements

Thanks to Hester Jones for her constant support and durable willingness to be interested; to Adrian Poole for his thoughtful reading of these chapters in early versions; to Marilyn Butler for discussing this project with me on several occasions; to my colleagues at the University of Liverpool, especially Tony Barley, Nick Davis, Andrew Hamer and John Lansley, for their many comments and suggestions; to Tinho da Cruz, the map curator in the University of Liverpool, for his generous help; to Eric Woehrling for ideas and conversation; and to Jonathan Coe for directing me towards Henry Fielding and William Cooper. My reader at Palgrave Macmillan made many very helpful suggestions. I greatly appreciate his or her thoughtfulness and care.

Also to the Department of English Literature at the University of Glasgow, especially David Pascoe and Adam Piette, where part of this study was given as a paper; to Timothy Webb for organising the conference 'Bristol: Romantic City' held in Bristol, September 1998; to Michael Baron for organising the conference on 'Literature and Regionalism', University of London, November 1998, and to Josie Billington and her colleagues for inviting me to speak at the Centre for Victorian Studies, University College, Chester.

Much of the work for this book was prompted by teaching an undergraduate course on 'Hardy and his Successors'. I have been fortunate in having such enlivening students. Research for the book and its composition have been made possible by the Leverhulme Trust's award of a post-doctoral research fellowship. I am most grateful for their generous support.

The book is written in loving memory of Solomon, an African Grey:

> *Better blankness day by day*
> *Than companion torn away*

RALPH PITE

The map on page xi of turnpike roads and railways in and around Dorset, drawn by John Britton, is reproduced by kind permission of the publisher, Phillimore & Co. Ltd, Shopwyke Manor Barn, Chichester, West Sussex, PO20 6BG, from Cecil Cullingford's *A History of Dorset* (3rd edn, 1999).

Abbreviations

Hardy, *DR*   Thomas Hardy, *Desperate Remedies*, edited by Mary Rimmer (Harmondsworth: Penguin, 1998)

Hardy, *HE*   Thomas Hardy, *The Hand of Ethelberta: A Comedy in Chapters*, edited by Tim Dolin (Harmondsworth: Penguin, 1996)

Hardy, *Jude*   Thomas Hardy, *Jude the Obscure*, edited by Dennis Taylor (Harmondsworth: Penguin, 1998)

Hardy, *Laodicean*   Thomas Hardy, *A Laodicean; or, The Castle of the De Stancys. A Story of To-Day*, edited by John Schad (Harmondsworth: Penguin, 1997)

Hardy, *Madding Crowd*   Thomas Hardy, *Far from the Madding Crowd*, edited by Rosemarie Morgan and Shannon Russell (Harmondsworth: Penguin, 2000)

Hardy, *Mayor*   Thomas Hardy, *The Mayor of Casterbridge: The Life and Death of a Man of Character*, edited by Keith Wilson (Harmondsworth: Penguin, 1997)

Hardy, *PBE*   Thomas Hardy, *A Pair of Blue Eyes*, edited by Pamela Dalziel (Harmondsworth: Penguin, 1998)

Hardy, *Return*   Thomas Hardy, *The Return of the Native*, edited by Tony Slade; introduction by Penny Boumelha (Harmondsworth: Penguin, 1999)

Hardy, *Tess*   Thomas Hardy, *Tess of the D'Urbervilles*, edited by Tim Dolin (Harmondsworth: Penguin, 1998)

Hardy, *Well-Beloved*   Thomas Hardy, *The Pursuit of the Well-Beloved and The Well-Beloved*, edited by Patricia Ingham (Harmondsworth: Penguin, 1997)

Hardy, *Withered Arm*   Thomas Hardy, *The Withered Arm and Other Stories: 1874–1888*, edited by Kristin Brady (Harmondsworth: Penguin, 1999)

Hardy: A Biography   Michael Millgate, *Thomas Hardy: A Biography* (Oxford: Clarendon Press, 1982)

Hutchins, *Dorset*   John Hutchins, *The History and Antiquities of the County of Dorset [. . .]*, 3rd edn, 4 vols (Westminster: John Bowyer Nichols & Sons, 1861–73)

IR   *Thomas Hardy: Interviews and Recollections*, edited by James Gibson (Basingstoke and New York: Macmillan – now Palgrave Macmillan, 1999)

Letters   *The Collected Letters of Thomas Hardy*, edited by Richard Little Purdy and Michael Millgate, 7 vols (Oxford: Oxford University Press, 1978–88)

Life   Thomas Hardy, *The Life and Work of Thomas Hardy*, edited by Michael Millgate (London and Basingstoke: Macmillan – now Palgrave Macmillan, 1984)

Literary Notebooks   *The Literary Notebooks of Thomas Hardy*, edited by Lennart A. Björk, 2 vols (Basingstoke: Macmillan – now Palgrave Macmillan, 1985)

Poems   Thomas Hardy, *The Complete Poems*, edited by James Gibson, The New Wessex Edition (London: Macmillan – now Palgrave Macmillan, 1976)

Poetical Works   Thomas Hardy, *The Complete Poetical Works*, edited by Samuel Hynes, 5 vols (Oxford: Clarendon Press, 1982–95)

Personal Writings   *Thomas Hardy's Personal Writings: Prefaces – Literary Opinions – Reminiscences*, edited by Harold Orel (London and Melbourne: Macmillan – now Palgrave Macmillan, 1967)

'Studies, Specimens &C' Thomas Hardy's *'Studies, Specimens &C.' Notebook*, edited by Pamela Dalziel and Michael Millgate (Oxford: Clarendon Press, 1994)

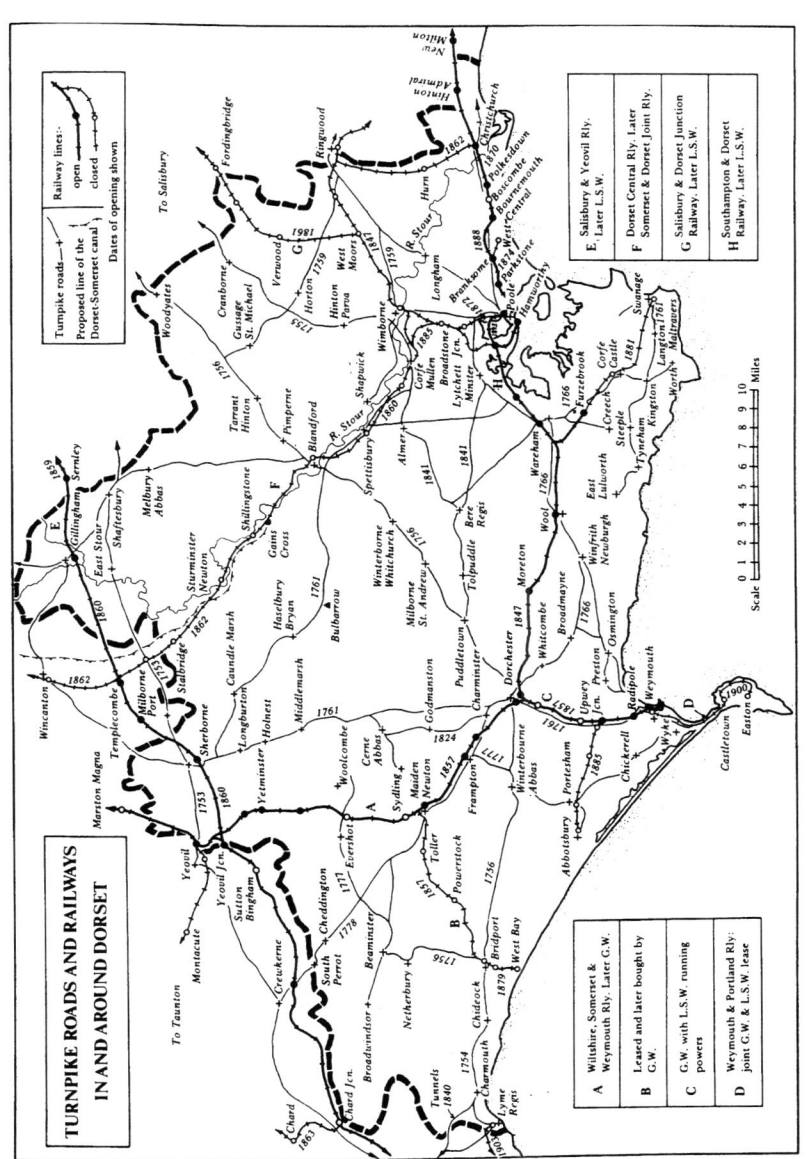

Figure 1 Turnpike Roads and Railways in Dorset

Figure 2a Near Dorchester

Figure 2b Near Poorstock

Figure 2c Near Bockhorn Weston

1
Introduction

Place is frequently seen as of great importance in Hardy's fiction. The famous opening chapter of *The Return of the Native* epitomises the emphasis he apparently lays in all his novels on particular geographies and the influence they wield over their inhabitants. 'Novels of Character and Environment' seems such a well-chosen generic title because it reflects the way that his books join character and environment together, making the two appear equivalent to one another. 'Story' in Hardy, as John Bayley remarked, 'isn't to be read in isolation from context.' And despite Hardy's writing about London and other urban centres at points throughout his career, this context is nearly always seen as rural. Michael Irwin has recently called him 'that rare thing a landscape novelist' and lists the items in Hardy's landscape as 'hills, rivers, trees, animals, birds, clouds, stars, sunsets, weather' plus 'a scattering of man-made objects: buildings, roads, walls, fences'. In other words, Hardy's is 'a landscape context', 'a particular natural environment'.[1]

So far, so uncontroversial perhaps. The presence of a rural landscape is hard to avoid or forget when reading Hardy's novels. Morever, this landscape is not only a generally 'rural' one but 'particular', specific to 'Wessex' – that is, to Dorset and the surrounding counties. As Simon Gatrell points out, this is something as hard to forget as Hardy's rural settings:

> So powerful and widely disseminated has been Hardy's imaginative creation that, even during his lifetime, Wessex was being used to denote a region of vague extent in south-western England. Now, at the end of the twentieth century, a glance at a directory to any town to the south and west of Oxford will probably throw up a business or two with Wessex in its name; and this is Hardy's doing.[2]

Because Wessex forms so large a part of readers' experience when reading Hardy, he has become identified with this aspect of his achievement: he is to many the historian of Wessex, the Wordsworth of Dorset. And, as Gatrell's essay very carefully shows, Hardy was aware of this: he adapted himself and his work to his readers' perception of him. Moreover, partly developed because his novels were already attracting what Hardy called 'explorers' – people on the hunt for equivalents between fictional and actual places – Wessex has continued to attract them. Anne-Marie Edwards, *Discovering Hardy's Wessex* (1978), Desmond Hawkins, *Hardy's Wessex* (1983) and *Thomas Hardy's England*, edited by John Fowles, text by Jo Draper (1984), are only a few of very many books inviting an exploration of Dorset which will reveal the world of the novels.

More harmfully, I think, treating Hardy as someone who records particular places and times, using invented names as only a thin disguise, leads people to read the novels too literally. Gatrell regrets this with respect to Egdon Heath, which was unclearly located when *The Return of the Native* was first published and incorporated into the Wessex topography later: 'What was once of mysterious extent and shifting definition is now a limited tract of land any tourist can tramp over.'[3] And the confident, blinkered tourist can use not only guidebooks but critical writing if s/he wants to find an exact correspondence between fictional and real worlds. When the match is absent or faulty, such critics condemn Hardy for inaccuracy. Keith Snell, for instance, states that the harsh conditions of nineteenth-century Dorset have been replaced in Hardy's novels 'by a romanticising and pastoral gloss which, from the viewpoint of the social historian, is simplistically misrepresentative [and] reveals its political partiality in all that it deliberately omits and discounts'.[4] This judgement seems to be missing something important in the books but rejecting it may lead to an opposite position where 'Wessex' is entirely fictional:

> Artists don't copy landscapes, they make them in the discourses of their work. 'Truth to Nature' may be preceptive, but 'the landscape' is constituted and exists only in its artificial image. So we may say that Hardy 'the poet' creates an English landscape – 'Wessex'.[5]

Peter Widdowson is employing doubtful oppositions here – copying and making often overlap; 'Truth to Nature' may be possible only via an 'artificial image'. He uses them to insist that Hardy 'creates' in Wessex a world independent of anything to which it may apparently refer.

Hardy's locations still tend to be understood in these ways, within either a realist framework or an anti-realist one. Both are mistaken, I believe. The difficulty lies in describing exactly how Hardy and his locations are linked together – how they interact with one another. This is what the following chapters attempt to address, in Hardy particularly and more generally, too, as a theoretical question for literary studies. It is an unusual project because, broadly speaking, Hardy criticism has in recent years set aside the question of his depiction of Wessex and concentrated instead on other issues: his portrayal of women, his subversiveness, the innovativeness of his narrative forms, his relation to Victorian popular fiction and to Victorian scholarship.[6] Among other things, this work has revealed that Hardy was not a straightforwardly realist novelist and by no means a simple historian of his time and place. It has also shown his preoccupation with contemporary issues – a preoccupation which makes it difficult to see him as the creator of a self-contained, fictional world. Other approaches to Hardy have, in other words, brought out qualities which cast into doubt received accounts of Hardy's Wessex and it is partly in the light of them that I am attempting to characterize that 'partly real, partly dream-country'[7] – one which is recognizably the West of England and, at the same time, a transformation of that real place into something different.

In his novels' use of dialect and their maps Hardy startlingly juxtaposes a real and a dream-country. His maps put fictional names and fictional places into an immediately recognizable map of south-western England. His novels present dialect in such a way that it is both easily intelligible and strange. His rustics speak a language that is not simply and quaintly rustic; rather, it is at once English and not exactly English. These strategies mean that the artist as recorder and artist as creator are made to coexist. Consequently, the presentation of Wessex illuminates Hardy's understanding of how imagination and observation are combined in perception. His sense of place informs, in other words, his sense of mental operations and of personhood (male and female). Secondly, the maps and the dialect – along with other comparable features of the novels – argue against provincialism: Hardy's Wessex emerges as a world unto itself within the world of England, even though most readers would have considered (and perhaps still consider) Dorset to be a somewhat backward province, remote from the centre. Societal differences, leading to political disagreements, are both implied and addressed by the novels' portrayal of a particular region of England. Dominant cultural geographies are acknowledged and countered. Issues central to Hardy, then, arise out of how and where he places Wessex and as a result a study of his geography helps make sense of some of his most pressing concerns. Naturally, Hardy's understanding of geography is governed to some extent by the practice of the discipline in his lifetime. More peculiarly, twentieth-century critical readings of his geography and his work are linked to changes in that practice.

Hardy's geography

Hardy boasts mildly in his autobiography about being good at geography: at his first school 'he worked at Walkingame's *Arithmetic* and at geography, in both of which he excelled'; visiting Hertfordshire with his mother when aged eight or nine, he was 'mercilessly tyrannized over by the bigger boys whom he could beat hollow in arithmetic and geography' (*Life*, pp.21–2). Hermann Lea reports that, much later in life, Hardy loved maps:

> It always gave him intense pleasure to map out the route a day or two before we started, and many an hour have we spent over the ordnance maps spread out on the table at Max Gate planning each road, and so arranging that we took in any place he wanted to see, or to show Mrs Hardy, that lay not too far off the actual route.
>
> (*IR*, p.55)[8]

These journeys were made in 1914–16. When Hardy was at school, in the 1840s and 1850s, geography was largely the domain of eight-year-olds, being thought too elementary for older children; it was taught in a catechetical, mnemonic way and involved little more than memorizing detailed lists of a country's rivers, counties and principal towns.[9] By the time, sixty or seventy years later, that Hardy was travelling around the West Country by car, geography had risen enormously in prestige and was being taught as a complex 'science of synthesis' which linked together the sciences and the humanities.[10] It was established as a degree subject in Oxbridge in 1887–8 not least because it was seen to be 'a matter of imperial importance that no reasonable means should be neglected' of training the nation's youth in 'sound geographical knowledge'. Anglo-German rivalry and German's perceived excellence in geography may have contributed to its 'imperial importance'.[11]

The emergence of geography occurred in Hardy's lifetime, therefore, and it follows a pattern which is paralleled in his career and his reception. Of particular importance, I think, are the liberal claims for the subject made by its early advocates. Archibald Geikie, at one time professor of geology in Edinburgh, recommended geography to school-teachers in 1887 on the grounds that:

> even among the youngest children and in every rank of life, an intelligent interest may be awakened and stimulated in the world around them; [. . .] they may be encouraged to look at things with their own eyes, and draw from them their own conclusions, and [. . .] in this way their conceptions of their immediate surroundings, of their country, and of the whole globe may, from the very outset, be made vivid, accurate, and enduring.[12]

Geikie constantly recommends the avoidance of 'mere pages of definitions and statistics mechanically learnt by rote' which, he says, will be forgotten soon enough. Instead, geography should offer a training in observation and in reflection upon what is observed. Analysis constantly leads outward from 'immediate surroundings' to the country beyond and from there to the whole world. Chapter 11 of his book is entitled: 'Relation of the School Locality to the Rest of the Country, and of the Country to the Rest of the Earth'. Geikie suggests that study should begin with a large parish plan of the local area, move first to a county map, then a wall-map of the country and, lastly, a globe. 'And thus, by a continuous chain of illustration, the minds of the learners are led upward and outward from their school surroundings to realise the shape and dimensions of the earth.'[13]

Children start on this movement 'upward and outward' by being prompted to notice the connections between their home territory and the world outside – roads and railways converging on a point off the local map show the presence and influence of 'some great town in an adjoining county'; streams and rivers crossing the map can be traced to their source and their mouth: this will reveal the watersheds and the drainage basin of the local and surrounding areas. Secondly, Geikie urges teachers to use maps imaginatively: journeys outside the local area are usually not practicable; a map makes possible 'imaginary ones, the teacher acting as leader and guiding the scholars in traverses across the map'. This method is 'more lively than mere narrative'; and, in addition:

> pupils are incited to find out for themselves what the map can teach them, their eyes are kept on the alert, their powers of observation and reflection are continually appealed to, and recognising feature after feature, they experience something of the zest of personal discovery.[14]

Seeing the place of the 'immediate surroundings' in the world as a whole is coupled in Geikie's work with seeing the present day in an extending historical context. Local place-names show the traces of Saxon, Roman and, further back still, Celtic occupation; roads, coins, even telegraph poles can be used to lead the pupils' minds to places outside their knowledge and to times when communications were more difficult, coins less commonplace or when roads were being built along lines which have been followed since.[15] Geikie's geography combines many kinds of knowledge – historical, geological, scientific – in order to depict the part within the whole and the whole within the part. Through studying and thinking geographically, moreover, collections of dry, received information can be instantiated and the pupils given 'the zest of personal discovery'.

Geikie is by no means the only geographer making such claims and practising the subject in this way. Around mid-century, Francis Galton and Thomas Arnold also saw geography uniting different disciplines,[16] and T.H. Huxley's popular success, *Physiography* (1877) shares with Geikie the view that students of the subject must start from experienced particulars and understand them in the widest context possible:

> I endeavoured to show that the application of the plainest and simplest processes of reasoning to any one of these [particular and local] phenomena, suffices to show, lying behind it, a cause, which again suggests another; until, step by step, the conviction dawns upon the learner that, to attain to even an elementary conception of what goes on in his parish, he must know something about the universe; that the pebble he kicks aside would not be what it is and where it is, unless a particular chapter of the earth's history, finished untold ages ago, had been exactly what it was.[17]

By the end of the century, however, this emphasis had been replaced by a less expansive account of region and of geographical practice. Influenced by the work of the German geographer, Ratzel, and particularly that of the French geographer, Paul Vidal, the Oxford school of regional geography developed. Regions began to be treated as autonomous areas, determined by the features of their natural landscape. Within them, human culture was seen as reflecting the qualities of the local environment. Holt-Jensen in his history of the subject points out the conservative impulse underlying Vidal's work:

[His] method [. . .] was best suited to regions which were 'local' in the sense of being somewhat isolated from the world around them and dominated by an agricultural way of life. These circumstances favoured the development of local traditions in architecture, agricultural practices and the general way of life.[18]

Similar priorites govern H.J. Mackinder's *Britain and the British Seas* (1902) even though it was increasingly perceived that autonomous regions of this kind no longer existed in England. This perception clashed with a desire, especially marked after the First World War, to institute political decentralization. Mackinder and C.B. Fawcett both argued for political and economic devolution to regional centres. This would help to restore regional autonomy and so would counteract the harmful consequences of uninhibited *laissez-faire* capitalism.[19] Mackinder and Fawcett divided Britain into different regional areas but both seek to encourage local loyalty and regional identity in order to prevent local differences from being eroded any further.

The Oxford school of regional geography, then, identifies distinct, self-sufficient regions even where they barely exist any longer. It invokes Hardy in its cause; Fawcett writes:

Wessex is a well-marked natural region, with a very considerable regional consciousness and patriotism, which in its modern revival owes much to the writings of Thomas Hardy.[20]

Critical writing on Hardy from around the same period refers constantly to his depiction of country life and customs in Wessex.[21] Moreover, this Oxford school account of geographical region (as opposed to that of Geikie and Huxley earlier in the nineteenth century) has continued to influence readings of Hardy. It has been until recently an unquestioned assumption that Hardy portrays Wessex as an Oxford school regional geographer would, treating it in isolation and as a whole unto itself.[22] The actual geography of Hardy's novels, though, resembles Huxley's and Geikie's much more closely. His writing constantly and in many different ways emphasises connections between places, their interdependence with other places and other times. Also, like Geikie, the books welcome maps because they are seen as a means of access to experience.[23]

Critics have recently attacked Hardy's supposed regionalism, seeing it as a version of his work imposed on him late in his career by conservative interests who supported a national culture founded on a 'pastoral myth of rural England'.[24] His regionalism must be stripped away, such critics argue, before his real subversiveness and radicalism can emerge. My own view is that Hardy's radicalism occurs within his regionalism. Certainly, his concentration on one rural area gives him points of contact with the conservative 'Englishness' of his Edwardian admirers and with Oxford school geography. The similarities, though, are superficial. Hardy's writing resists the idea that Wessex is a separate, autonomous region and thinks of region much more as Geikie and Huxley do. Arguably, in attacking Christminster (Oxford) in *Jude the Obscure* (1895), Hardy is attacking, among other things, the emerging Oxford school idea of regions which ignores economic interconnectedness and personal mobility. That novel and its predecessors, however, also see such a perspective on regions as encouraging outsiders to idealise, stereotype or condescend to the inhabitants. Where the region is predominantly rural, Hardy's readers employed a set of ruralist assumptions, which derived from the Romantic picturesque and were pervasive in mid-century. These assumptions rendered the countryside and its people idyllic or barbaric according to their degree of cultivation. Overall, therefore, Hardy's writing of Wessex seeks to give a sense of region which avoids becoming regionalist and seeks to present the rural without making it ruralist. His work corresponds to the geography of the 1870s and 1880s, when most of the novels were written.

The following chapters attempt to articulate Hardy's distinctive sense of the local and the regional. They do so by first discussing how Dorset was perceived in his day – where it was placed on the map(s) of England drawn by the economic, cultural and imaginative geographies of the Victorian period. In Hardy's response to the associations of particular places (Dorset, the West Country, the Thames Valley) and particular kinds of place (the countryside, the provinces), we can see him reacting to and modifying his period's dominant understandings of locality. These responses colour several of his novels, especially the more 'pastoral' ones such as *Far from the Madding Crowd* and *The Return of the Native*. They can also be seen at work in less familiar texts where, in addition, Hardy's own, personal relation to his home territory is of particular importance. Combined, these readings aim to show the development of Hardy's personal, independent geography of Wessex, a geography which countered provincialism, ruralism and the nationalism which underpinned both as well as differing from the regional geography of the late nineteenth century.

The geography of Hardy's novels indicates his distinctive sense of interconnected place; one that has parallels in the geographical thinking of his day (Huxley and Geikie) and has been (mis)understood according to a slightly later geographical model (Oxford school regionalism). Modern geography runs up against similar questions about the relation between locality and region, region and nation. Geographical studies of region constantly test the relation between empirical and theoretical, struggling to describe how material and abstract interact. Moreover, the critical divide over Hardy's regionalism is representative of a wider division within English studies, one again which is repeated within geography. The local in geography has the same elevated and questionable status as 'minute particulars' have in the study of literature. It either stands apart from the wider world or is irrelevant to the working out of general principles in the same way that literature's formal and linguistic intricacies either tend to be read in isolation from what is external to the text or are ignored by theory.

It is currently fashionable to draw geography and literary criticism together; this book is dependent upon and in part a response to that interest.[25] Literary studies influenced by geography, however, often prove to be either mechanically specific or rather loosely metaphorical, too particular or lacking in particularity altogether. 'Geography' is given either too narrow or too broad a definition. Hardy's writings explore where the regional begins and ends, how local and national impinge on people and their sense of themselves. His geography is highly specified and his locations identifiable, yet they lead into and are created by larger, external forces, including the literary language Hardy uses to present them. His works suggest, therefore, a way of thinking geographically about other writing – an approach to the geography of literature – and not least because they raise questions about the terms themselves.

Literary criticism, local knowledge and Tess

Hardy's presentation of Wessex, as a region and a place, can be seen then within a wider debate about particulars in literature which raises questions about the nature of the literary and the practice of criticism. Thinking about his geography leads one to think about the literary. One reason for this is Hardy's own recognition that rural places were perceived via literary models – models in which the local was elided with the pastoral. The rural became suffused with the literary and epitomized the contemplative and reflective moment which literature was thought especially to promote. Since Hardy's day, and determining how his books are read, literary criticism has frequently been committed to a form of localism. Deriving from Arnold (who in turn was developing ideas from Carlyle and Burke), literary study has tended to place the cherishing of minute particulars in opposition to an engagement with the abstractions of theory. David Simpson, for instance, has recently accused the English literary critical tradition of being wedded to 'an anti-theoretical rhetoric of exceptionalism' and as deriving 'disciplinary energy [. . .] from its efforts to impose restraints on the runaway tendencies of general ideas'.[26] Literary criticism of this kind, Simpson argues, parallels postmodernism. Both are opposed to grand narrative, replacing it with localism – with what Ernesto Laclau calls the 'attempt to show the essential contingency of all universality [and] construct the beauty of the specific, of the unrepeatable, of what transgresses the norm'; and what the geographer Doreen Massey has called 'the pastoral of the old perpetual place'.[27]

Although emphasis on literature's 'minute particulars' is characteristic of an anti-theoretical stance present in the tradition of practical criticism and close reading, something similar can be found not only in postmodernism but in Marxist readings of Hardy – ones, that is, which appear to be resisting a conservative localism. These have been influential readings and their shortcomings illustrate, I think, the elusiveness and peculiarity of Hardy's regionalism. Raymond Williams writes in *The Country and the City*:

> we miss almost all of what Hardy has to show us if we impose on the actual relationships he describes a neo-pastoral convention of the countryman as an age-old figure, or a vision of a prospering countryside being disintegrated by Corn Law repeal or the railways or agricultural machinery. [. . .] we cannot suppress [Hardy's actual society] in favour of a seamless abstracted 'country way of life'.

Images of Wessex as either a pastoral idyll or the powerless victim of change are both, according to Williams, falsifications of the novels. If so, Hardy may exemplify what Simpson commends (and what Geikie's geography aspires towards): his novels may be encouraging their readers to think outside the immediate and local and to see both as involved in the processes of the wider world. Williams's own work, however, substitutes for an idealized countryside an idealization of labour relations – a neo-pastoral convention of work. This emphasis reinstates localism by re-endowing the countryside of Hardy's novels with a redemptive power:

Feeling very acutely the long crisis of separation, and in the end coming to more tragically isolated catastrophes than any others within this tradition, [Hardy] yet created continually the strength and the warmth of people living together: in work and in love; in the physical reality of a place.[28]

Williams supports this position with a quotation from Hardy's description of Tess working in the rain-soaked fields of Flintcomb-Ash beside her friend from Talbothays, Marian. The scene, however, is tonally much more ambiguous than Williams suggests. Certainly, Tess and Marian, despite being soaked through, are protected from the cold and wet by remembering, as Hardy puts it, 'when they lived and loved together at Talbothays Dairy'. Hardy, though, presents their 'warmth' as perhaps the single fortunate consequence of a collective infatuation with Angel Clare. There is a sardonic invocation of cliché in the phrasing 'lived and loved together', as if the comfort they feel had no basis, despite being effectual – that paradoxically and pathetically they were kept warm by a fantasy. Marian is also, as Hardy mentions down the page, drinking heavily to keep out the cold.[29]

John Goode makes a similar claim to Williams's about a scene in *Far from the Madding Crowd*:

Bathsheba and Gabriel find in physical contact on the hayrick in the storm [. . .] as a physical rhythm, the fundamental expression of man's relation to the world around him.

Where Williams praises Hardy's accurate portrayal of real conditions, Goode's more positive Marxism emphasizes the transformative power of labour.[30] Nonetheless, he stresses physicality as much as Williams does. For both, Hardy celebrates labour for the insights it makes possible into fundamental truths: its escape from the deceptions of thought. Intellectual abstractions are overcome by physical realities in a version of the sublime where individuality is lost when communal personhood is affirmed. For Williams especially, work generates a local community: 'the physical reality of a place' guarantees the unalienated quality of the human warmth achieved in and through working together.[31] In both the incidents cited, however, Hardy's writing complicates the presentation of labour, showing its relative powerlessness or, in *Far from the Madding Crowd*, how the communal bonds of cooperation are easily overridden by private concerns.

John Barrell's frequently-cited and sophisticated account of Hardy's geography, published in 1982, presents another version of this Marxist–pastoral account of Hardy – though one which directs the pastoral of Wessex back at his readership. Instead of a celebratory account of rustic life, of small, remote communities or of collective labour, Hardy, according to Barrell, engages with the problematics of access, with how, if at all, pre-modern forms of experience can be rendered to a modernized readership, given that the myth of pastoral colours all modern perceptions of the pre-modern. Barrell's account employs, therefore, the dichotomy between local and general forms of knowledge which Simpson sees as endemic in English literary criticism. The reading it produces of Hardy's Tess may therefore be seen as in some respects symptomatic of how that broad tradition approaches Hardy. That is one reason why the essay has been so widely quoted. Nonetheless, it is a reading of the character and the novel which strikes me as both powerful and mistaken.

Barrell observes a gap between the narrator's understanding and Tess's:

> For the transitions [. . .] which, properly concealed [. . .] should enable the reader to step innocently over into the consciousness of the characters, seem quite impossible to conceal, and so work only to insist upon the disjunction between the two sorts of knowledge. (p.114)[32]

The novel and others by Hardy strictly divide knowledge into local and general; the local is attained only by inhabitants, the general only by visitors, tourists and readers, and they can never be joined.

> The reader can certainly grasp from *Tess* that there is such a local knowledge, in Hardy's Wessex if not in nineteenth-century Dorset; but he can grasp only the notion of its existence, not the knowledge itself. (p.113)

Local knowledge is not present in the novels because, in Barrell's view, it cannot be: 'local knowledge' is 'a myth deployed by the novel to describe us, its readers, as alienated' (p.118). Hardy's manipulation of clashing registers disrupts the complacent assumption, made by 'a smart tourist who knows about landscape-painting' (p.118), that locality can be seen and brought into harmony with a wider perspective.

So Barrell reads the novels as enacting a drama of modernity whose plot (and purpose) is to show the gradual recognition of the reader's distance from the local. The reader is being educated by the novels into a better sense of the 'absolute otherness' (p.113) of locality. This reduces the social commentary of the novels, making all the changes they describe (in agriculture, education and society) exemplify the problem of epistemology which Barrell is concerned with. The reader is seen as engaged with the possibility of seeing and knowing, regardless of which among several different available objects is currently being attended to. And, in every case, according to Barrell, the reader is brought to a sober sense of impossibility – the local can be characterized as local but local knowledge cannot be shared. Nothing is allowed to occupy a middle ground between the two poles of local and general: the reader is shown to be a violator whenever he or she attempts to acquire local knowledge; the good reader will learn from this and withdraw.

Similarly, characters are either local or foreign. When they try – or when they are forced – to move between the two, they are destroyed:

> the fact of the labourers becoming less 'local in feeling' [. . .] involves, in *Tess* particularly, not so much the exchange of one, 'local', for another, 'regional', sense of space, but the destruction of a local sense and the substitution of nothing in its place. (p.101)

Barrell says of Tess that, in her migrations, her identity vanishes, 'destroyed by her new habit of travelling without reference to a constant centre in Marlott or Talbothays' (p.110); 'Tess, in becoming less "local in feeling", has become more nothing' (p.112).[33]

There is limitless pathos to this account of the novel, but a pathos which underestimates Tess, as Hardy portrays her. Barrell's repetition of the word 'nothing' blocks out the thought that, in her migrations, Tess changes, becoming not necessarily better though certainly different. Barrell gives as an example of Tess's extinction a passage describing her walk in chapter 44 from Flintcomb-Ash to Emminster, a journey she undertakes with the aim of speaking to Angel Clare's mother and 'enlist[ing] her on her side'. Barrell does not mention Tess's purposiveness at this point – the fact that she 'took advantage of the state of the roads' under a hard frost 'to try the experiment' of visiting Angel's parents; nor that the distance is fifteen miles each way, to be completed within a day, and that her friends 'heard her footsteps tap along the hard road as she stepped out to her full pace'.[34] These exclusions make it easier for Barrell to present Tess's experience as depersonalized and empty. He quotes the following:

> Keeping the Vale on her right she steered steadily westward; passing above the Hintocks, crossing at right-angles the high road from Sherton-Abbas to Casterbridge, and skirting Dogbury Hill and High-Stoy, with the dell between them called 'The Devil's Kitchen'. Still following the elevated way she reached Cross-in-Hand ... Three miles further she cut across the straight and deserted Roman road called Long Ash Lane; leaving which as soon as she reached it she dipped down a hill by a transverse lane into the small town or village of Evershead, being now about half-way over the distance. (p.111)[35]

He then remarks:

> There seems almost nothing to notice, here, but distances and directions, the intersection of one straight road with another: none of the features, the colours, the *differences* that marked the accounts of Tess's apprehension of places earlier in the novel. And yet, what has replaced that earlier mode of cognition is not the extended, educated, inquisitive geography of the tourist or traveller. (p.111)

Barrell sees Hardy's heroine stranded between two alternative modes, neither of which is available any longer – she has lost her childhood security without gaining educated poise. The result is a kind of blank in which, again, there is 'almost nothing to notice'. Hardy, though, presents this mode of perception as a form of self-assurance not of anomie: as Tess nears Emminster, he says in the next paragraph, 'her confidence decrease[d]' with the result that 'she was sometimes in danger of losing her way'. Earlier on her journey, it appears, she was more confident and 'breakfasted a second time heartily enough' at Evershead. The distances and directions which Hardy gives here in such detail mimic Tess's careful memorizing of a route and her use of the landmarks of popular legend in conjunction with good orienteering. Tess 'steered steadily westward', with self-certainty and independence. She employs her local knowledge (of Dogbury Hill, High-Stoy, 'The Devil's Kitchen' and such like); at the same time, she conceives of her route as following a (rough) bearing; it is, for her, both a list of landmarks and a line across a map; both strategies are used in making sure she does not lose her way.[36]

Barrell is also misleading when he claims that Hardy includes nothing except 'distances and directions'; after 'Cross-in-Hand', Hardy goes on, 'where the stone pillar stands desolate and silent, to mark the site of a miracle or a murder, or both. Three miles further [. . . .]' According to what Barrell argues elsewhere, this mention of a more antiquarian interest should be read as the intrusion of an 'educated, inquisitive geography' which attempts to 'penetrate Tess's consciousness of place, and to imprint upon it his own' (p.117). Because this description of the journey does not conform to Barrell's idea of Tess's 'consciousness of place', he excludes the interruption as uninteresting. Yet the presence in the original of this off-hand and sardonic historical note ('to mark the site of a miracle or a murder, or both') complicates the oppositions Barrell wishes to sustain. It is possible, for instance, to read the history of the pillar as an image of Tess and a foreshadowing of her future destiny: she is, in some ways, desolate and alone at present; when Angel returns to her, she feels it to be a miracle ('he told me a lie – that you would not come again; and you *have* come!'), a miracle that leads to a murder.[37] Secondly, the tone in which this resonant information enters the text suggests a surprising disregard for it. That casual indifference can be read, I think, as part of Tess's consciousness; for her, other more pressing matters diminish the interest of a stone pillar. She knows but cannot remember clearly the stories attached to it and hurries on.[38] Educated knowledge does not reinforce the reader's alienation from Tess's innocence; instead, it corresponds to the novel's concern with how immediate needs overcome the power of omens, how, necessity stifles insight, how, at the moment of danger, the sense of danger blinds you to the signs of it and to the means of escape.

This aspect of the novel may be equated with the oppositions Barrell employs: necessity could be read as imprinting itself upon a subtle and differentiated apprehension of the world in the same way that landscape painting imposes its lines and structures on the local knowledge of place. Maybe, but in both areas Hardy recognizes a gain: Tess may miss the omen present in the stone but her determination to act on her own behalf and seek out Angel's parents is seen as admirable, as a coming back to life and energy confirmed when 'she stepped out to her full pace'. Likewise, Tess looks into her old home and sees it as imprisoning:

In time she reached the edge of the vast escarpment below which stretched the loamy Vale of Blackmoor, now lying misty and still in the dawn. Instead of the colourless air of the uplands the atmosphere down there was a deep blue. Instead of the great enclosures of a hundred acres in which she was now accustomed to toil there were little fields below her of less than half-a-dozen acres, so numerous that they looked from this height like the meshes of a net. Here the landscape was whitey-brown; down there, as in the Froom Valley, it was always green. Yet it was in that vale that her sorrow had taken shape, and she did not love it as formerly. Beauty to her, as to all who have felt, lay not in the thing, but in what the thing symbolized.[39]

The following paragraph is the one Barrell quotes. This preface to it rules out the idea of Tess's being deracinated into blankness. Hardy shows her instead weighing up alternatives, seeing the harshness of her present circumstances and choosing to go on in them. She lives in 'the great enclosures', not perfectly free but nonetheless self-steering and responsible. Her past life, in the Vale of Blackmoor as at Talbothays, offers the security suggested by 'always green'; it is a security, however, which is 'like the meshes of a net'.[40] Tess's awareness now is comparative, both between places and between times, so that lacking a home base, she becomes self-reliant.

The change in Tess creates tragic feeling at the novel's end, whereas Barrell's account can engender only pathos. It suggests moreover that, for Hardy, there is a regional sense of space, engendered by the greater mobility of those who were once locally fixed. Tess enters it and moves through it. Her experience of rootless mobility brings a sense of responsibility for her own affairs. Clearly, the novel at many points yearns after a paradisiac state of absorption into nature and Tess's separateness, as it gradually comes about, is blamed on successive acts of male cruelty. Separateness, though, is not nothing. In Tess's case, it brings a translation of the local into the immediate – her priorities control (to some extent self-consciously) what she attends to, so that nearby things are placed within a narrative sequence and on a mental map. Hardy's language creates a clash of registers which is sometimes internal to her and, at her few lucky moments, is resolvable by her; its multiplicity works to suggest her maturity and self-will.[41] The reader, consequently, is not simply described by the novel as alienated; more like Angel, he or she is brought to a sense of equality with Tess – an equality which is less 'the brotherhood of man' and more like what Wordsworth called 'kindred independence'.

An understanding of social life as well as of individuality and of place follow, then, from Hardy's presentation of Tess's endurance. Her 'steering steadily westward' implies too a geographical sense of one's own location – a geographical sense which (as Geikie and Huxley recommend) locates this particular place within a region and knows the region to be, in turn, a specific part of a larger whole. For Barrell, Wessex could be anywhere in Britain; the conflict between local, primal knowledge and educated pastoral is universal. For Hardy, Wessex is definitely western; the wider geography of England impinges on it as an aspect of where it is located and as part of its definition. Tess becomes aware of where she is within Wessex and senses that the world beyond bears on Wessex – on what and where it is.

Regional geography

David Simpson's discussion of localism and literary criticism is most convincing in its diagnosis of the problem. Understandably, perhaps, he finds it more difficult to give examples of the kind of reading he prefers, one whose mixture of theorization with 'openness and flexibility' would accommodate and replicate the condition of being both locally particular and subject to larger forces, personally distinctive and constituted by general ideas. Recent historically informed and yet formally attentive critical writing seeks to resolve the difficulty that Simpson identifies. Because Hardy is preoccupied so often with exactly these concerns, he seems an especially good subject for a book which similarly tries to combine formal detail with wider concern and to suggest that these two apparent opposites continually interact in our modern, deracinated, regional minds.[42]

The currency of the problem is shown by contemporary geography and spatial studies which frequently repeat the opposition Simpson discerns in literary studies. Doreen Massey's excellent work begins from the perception that 'modernism seems to have problems in really, in the end, taking seriously the autonomy of others [but] postmodernism certainly has its difficulties in doing anything more democratic than recognizing the existence of others'.[43] The local is either ignored or isolated. In response to this, Massey tries to recover and re-express the interconnection between local and general, particular and universal. The difficulties she meets in doing so centre on finding an adequate language. Massey writes with unusual alertness to the attractions and shortcomings of other possible ways of talking and adopts for herself complex, nearly contradictory, metaphorical formulations. Yet these seem to be necessary and more satisfactory than the languages other geographers use. There is a parallel here, I believe, with Hardy's jagged, ambitious and densely-textured style. Complexity, even paradoxicality, seem inherent for both writers in how local and general coexist. In both, a highly literary style does not celebrate localism, it reaches towards an understanding of regionalism – of the kind that can be found in Tess and as that term applies to persons, communities, places and countries. If this is true more widely, then criticism which valorizes literature in terms of localism not only diminishes criticism (as Simpson argues, reducing its political impact and intellectual energy), it also shrinks the literary. Imaginative literature's minute particulars are prevented from leading anywhere.

Massey's metaphors arise from a conflict very similar, as I have said, to the one Simpson finds in literary criticism. Though seemingly irrelevant to a discussion of Hardy, Massey's writing illustrates in a different context the problems and problematic solutions Hardy confronted. They and their context are worth a brief digression. Massey is wary of geographical analyses which employ solely topographical or chorographical descriptions, and so divide specifics from their context. This approach ignores socioeconomic relatedness and causes problems of epistemology. Also, like Simpson, Massey sees postmodernism repeating a traditional, conservative 'pastoral of the old perpetual place'. At the same time, she is unwilling to embrace a Marxist geography which believes local detail to have little explanatory value. On the one hand theory dominates, on the other it is excluded and, in consequence, local particulars are either disregarded or fetishised. According to Massey:

> The global is in the local in the very process of the formation of the local. [. . .] 'identities' are constructed through the specificity of their interaction with other places, rather than by counterposition to them. [. . .] The geography of social relations forces us to recognize our interconnectedness, and underscores the fact that both personal identity and the identity of those envelopes of space-time in which and between which we live and move (and have our 'Being') are constructed precisely through that interconnectedness.[44]

That stable, local identities are being washed away by rapid communications and globalization has become a familiar judgement in recent human geography. Massey argues that the local and the global are not opposed to one another; instead, they continually intersect. Massey quotes from bell hooks a more celebratory version of this idea:

> home is no longer just one place. It is locations. Home is that place which enables and promotes varied and everchanging perspectives, a place where one discovers new ways of seeing reality, frontiers of difference. One confronts and accepts dispersal and fragmentation as part of the construction of a new world order that reveals more fully where we are, who we can become.[45]

Despite the similarities in conception, the two writers are moving in opposite directions, leading to differing accounts of the relation between one place and the rest of the world. hooks takes us away from singleness towards a dispersal that makes possible a 'new world order' and *becoming*. Massey, in a language of constraint and ineluctable reality – of 'forces us to recognize' and 'underscores the fact that' – moves inward, to the need to confess that personal identity cannot be isolated from others. It is, instead, vulnerable to them and formed paradoxically through violation. Massey's language implies a sense of interdependence, of personhood retrieved from isolation and paranoia by the recognition of mutuality. bell hooks, by contrast, thinks of the self as liberated through fragmentation; liberation turns 'one' into 'we', impersonality into solidarity, the isolated and singular into the communal.

bell hooks presents a Utopian vision, fervent and exciting, and this Massey views as liable to become pastoral. The fluid, postmodern self (constantly moving between subject-positions and so no longer subjected to them) becomes hard to distinguish from the unalienated life, often communally conceived, of both Marxist and conservative nostalgia. Ideal stability and constant mobility both ignore immediate oppression – whether that oppression be the constraining limitations of each subject-position as it is successively inhabited or the determining forces of natural circumstance. Nostalgia and revolutionary Utopianism both effect a form of the sublime, freeing the self from contingency.

On the other hand, the self as Massey describes it (and as Hardy describes Tess) is in danger of being shattered by contingency. How it remains distinctive becomes the difficulty she is most concerned to portray. The geography of social relations, she says,

> underscores the fact that both personal identity and the identity of those envelopes of space-time in which and between which we live and move (and have our 'Being') are constructed precisely through that interconnectedness.

We are who we are as a result of our relations with others; the places where we are, similarly, acquire distinctiveness through being connected with other places. This account risks sounding vague and Massey adds the word 'precisely', urging interconnectedness as something to welcome rather than something to be frightened of. Still, the anxiety survives that by stressing interconnectedness you will reduce the self to a collage of fragments gathered from other 'selves'. For this reason, Massey adds in parenthesis 'and have our "Being"', using the religious term to suggest something ineffable about experience and personal identity. Neither of them can be reduced to the sum of its parts, and neither will slot readily into the received ideas we have of 'Being'.[46] Her writing is more stretched and tense than hooks's; it throws customary ideas of personal identity into question in order to suggest not that it is an encumbrance to be thrown off but, rather, to suggest that a better conception lies just out of language's reach. Likewise, Massey says later that 'What gives a place its specificity is [. . .] the fact that it is constructed out of a particular constellation of social relations, meeting and weaving together at a particular locus.' The confused metaphor (in which a constellation meets and weaves) shows Massey declaring the existence of agency within determining structures and resisting both entire stability on the one hand and free mobility on the other.[47]

What is true of language is true also, in Massey's opinion, of regional studies – the geographical discipline that describes localities. Such studies either tend to adopt a Marxist perspective in which local differences are placed second to the universal power of class or capital accumulation, or, more traditionally (following the Oxford school), they treat localities as 'internally introspective bounded unities', whose characteristics can be delineated without reference to their interconnectedness with other places (*Space, Place and Gender*, pp.135–42). The discipline has not yet, according to Massey, found a way of describing the global within the local.

Massey is resisting here the claims made by the recent geographical sub-discipline, spatial studies, to have found a way of joining theorized and particularized description. Spatial studies begins with Henri Lefebvre's *The production of space* (1974) which presents what Derek Gregory calls 'a tensely organic spatiality [. . .] rooted in the taking place of practical activity'.[48] Lefebvre focusses on the *production* of space because that shows the world being constructed practically instead of intellectually. It reveals the categories of human understanding as they exist before being distorted by intellectualism. By studying space, one can reach back to the genuinely human relation to the world. This creates the narrative structure of Lefebvre's project and it is repeated in his concept of absolute space:

> a time, long before the inauguration of either 'historical' or modern, 'abstract' spatialities, when the body's relationship to space has 'an immediacy which would subsequently degenerate and be lost'.[49]

The study of space conducted in this way will recover the immediate relation between body and space, a relation that implies mind and body in proper harmony.[50]

The similarity between Lefebvre and Raymond Williams is clear and reveals their shared indebtedness to Marxism. Lefebvre has, moreover, been adopted as a forerunner of postmodern geography. Ed Soja's influential *Postmodern Geographies: The Reassertion of Space in Critical Social Theory* (1989) cites Lefebvre repeatedly while advocating a new, spatial approach to regional studies. Soja argues in a recent essay that new theoretical inquiry into space – by geographers and others – has produced

> a fusion of the traditional distinction between objectively defined material geographies (what Lefebvre described as the realm of 'spatial practices' or perceived space) and more subjectively defined mental, cognitive, or ideational geographies (Lefebvre's 'representations of space' or conceived space).[51]

This 'fusion' is equivalent to 'the opening up of a *thirdspace*', corresponding to Lefebvre's *'lived space'*. In the new mode of spatial thinking, Soja argues, 'it is this heterotopological thirdspace, this open-ended, fragmented, limitless *lived* space [. . .] that is being explored'. Soja welcomes the new thinking because it overcomes divisions, achieving within the discipline an equivalent to bell hooks's wider liberation.

Spatial studies seem to display therefore a recoil from 'intellectualism' back into the materially definite coupled with Soja's version of the sublime, where the collapse of categories into one another makes possible limitlessness and freedom, although at the expense of material specificity. How the local is 'in the global' without becoming lost in the global remains a difficulty in analysing locality and expressing its nature. Conforming as it does to the pattern Massey sees in geography generally, spatial studies is for her unable to articulate a regional perspective, such as that of the grown-up Tess. A further example will, I hope, help suggest the dominance of this problem in geography, plus the difficulty of finding a language in which to solve it.

Brian Jarvis and Julie Kathy Gibson-Graham are geographers also attempting to recover the immediate within the theoretical. Brian Jarvis, in *Postmodern Cartographies* (1998), summarizes the position of cultural geographers such as Soja and Fredric Jameson for whom space and spatiality have become key terms in the understanding of postmodern culture. He observes in them, however, a loss of particularity:

> All places become simply a palimpsest for Capital. Like their neo-conservative counterparts producing reassuring (or, in Baudrillard's case, reassuringly apocalyptic) visions of postindustrial, post-capitalistic places, the broad brush strokes of macrogeographical models tend to obscure critical details and differences.[52]

The new macrogeographical models are as normalizing as the old ones, despite their claim to have revealed 'how relations of power are inscribed into the apparently innocent spatiality of social life'.[53] Jarvis, in phrases reminiscent of Doreen Massey, insists on locality:

> It is essential to integrate analyses of micro- and macrogeographical processes – to uncover the specificity of individual sites (streets, suburbs, nature and second nature, national and individual bodies) whilst understanding their position within larger spatial systems.[54]

According to Jarvis, regions – even those of postmodernity – provide a counter to the totalizing ambitions of theory; for him, this does not imply a rejection of the theoretical. Places show instead the presence of the larger system within the specific site and the need for 'understanding' in the process of 'uncovering'.

Jarvis's use of 'uncover', however, suggests that these sites' specificity exists independently of the larger system. It is hidden and can be found. What we need to guard against is either forgetfulness of the system or disregard for the particular object. Their separateness is not in question. When Gibson-Graham finds 'the identity of Capital confronts us at every turn', it prompts her to ask, 'Do we only ever dwell in a capitalist space? Can we ever think outside the capitalist axiomatic?' If we cannot do so, she concludes, 'We risk relegating space/life to emptiness, to rape, to non-becoming, to victimhood.' Gibson-Graham draws on Deleuze and Guattari's paradox that Capital is everywhere and yet leaves gaps: 'this mechanic enslavement abounds in undecidable propositions and movements [. . .] that provides [*sic*] so many weapons for the becoming of everybody/everything'. She uses too a comparison between Cubist space (which 'evokes a closed system of determination [. . . .] The space of modernism, of phallocentrism and capitalism') and space in Impressionism:

> a space of mists and vapours, of movement and possibility, of background that might at any moment become foreground – a 'space of excess' and indeterminacy within the modern space of fullness and closure.[55]

By attending to the fissures, to what is un-closed within the closed, we may, Gibson-Graham says, recognize things that are not determined by capitalism. The local will supply this alternative but only if it is viewed differently – viewed as the undecidable or indeterminate within the system, whose indeterminacy places it beyond the system.

Jarvis and Gibson-Graham both invoke the local as a counterweight to dominant ideology, a counterweight which, they both claim, cannot be separated from the system within which it is found. Yet Jarvis makes 'local differences' objective, placing them within the observation of empirical and material study, so reinstating traditional geography and its scientific, universalist account of space. Gibson-Graham, on the other hand, moves the local close to the undecidable, the point outside cognisance because lying outside the grasp of the system – a vaporous and vague, feminised 'other' to the system's masculine definition and closure. Despite his language of integration, then, Jarvis places the local on one side of a clash between methods, one arrogantly theoretical, the other doggedly materialist. His concepts of locality and specificity do not really allow the integration with a larger system which he aspires towards. In Gibson-Graham's essay, the local and particular remain systemic exceptions, *aporias* which the system necessarily produces. The quotidian becomes, in her presentation, the crux: an elusive and tantalizing point of transformation where system is – or will be – overturned. In both, the specific remains the 'other' of theory, either in the head-to-head conflict between empirical and theoretical geographies or as the postmodern 'thirdspace of political choice' where a 'new cultural politics of difference' is enunciated.[56]

This comparison indicates the problems in method and perception which Doreen Massey's version of locality studies is trying to address. Massey's alert, sometimes paradoxical language works to give voice to a sense of how particular and general are interconnected within locality, a sense which Jarvis and Gibson-Graham largely share but also find difficult to express. Massey's work declares that the particular is unavoidable in a full description of the whole, yet it cannot be separated from the whole, either as independent of the larger theory/system or as the exception within and beyond it. Indeed, for a particular to remain particular it needs to be neither an independent specific nor an exceptional indeterminate: both of these revert to being one side of binary oppositions (which make the specific the opposite of the general and the indeterminate the opposite of the determinate). In these arrangements, attempted isolation from the larger whole entails subjection to it. Particularity, then, requires an interaction between the specific and the general which avoids becoming a dialectic. This is sought, in Massey's work, through a language of multiple relations: the local is understood as part of the global but not as the exception to it; instead, the global is seen as consisting in innumerable factors and differing forces, allowing one to recognize a 'constellation of social relations, meeting and weaving together at a particular locus'.[57]

These at times arcane problems confronted by modern geography may seem of little relevance to a discussion of Hardy. Like their modern counterparts, however, nineteenth-century accounts of locality and region were fond of seeing them as either escapes from or instances of a larger whole. The rural was defined as country by contrast with city and rural locality was regarded either as instantiating national virtues or as escaping national vice. As I discuss at greater length in Chapter 5, Hardy like Doreen Massey used constellations as a metaphor for social experience; he also sought to represent the particularity of individuals as something inseparable from their relations with others and their relations to the structures which joined communities together. His sometimes jarring and uneasy style endeavours, again like Massey, to find a way of describing precisely this interdependence. Lastly, Hardy's sense of how individuality existed and how communities were formed brought him into conflict with the more conventional understanding of locality and nation and of individual and community – accounts, that is, which made these terms into polar opposites of one another. In this, too, his project is analogous to Massey's and it finds comparable solutions.

2
The Imaginative Geography of the West Country

By choosing to set his novels in 'Wessex', Hardy selects 'the south-west counties', an identifiable as well as imaginary part of England.[1] One motive for the choice was Hardy's familiarity with the area, his native-born local knowledge. Yet his local knowledge is nationally situated. Hardy's map of 'The Wessex of the Novels' (first published in the 1895 collected edition) shows Casterbridge, Melchester, Port Bredy and all the other named places of Wessex located in the British Isles. These imaginary places have an obvious connection of some kind with Dorchester, Salisbury and Bridport; similarly, 'South Wessex' is evidently some sort of equivalent to Dorset. Hardy's home ground, therefore, is set within the country as a whole. The private experience of home, which one might expect to offer a retreat from the noisy, social world outside, is presented here as lying within range of the communal knowledge that establishes maps and puts places on them. The presence of the map, confirming the correspondence between fictional and real places, prevents one from reading the novels solely within a dichotomy between country and city; the particular part of the country involved is pushed to the fore. The novels are set in Wessex and this is visibly part of England, 'South Wessex' exactly corresponding to the county of Dorset.

The same feature of the novels problematizes the relationship between the communal and the personal, between Casterbridge and Dorchester, between the authority of cartography and the authority of private experience. By presenting the two perspectives via the same map, Hardy suggests the question which Doreen Massey and David Simpson address more directly: how can we coordinate the concrete and the conceptual, the local and the universal?

The following three chapters describe the associations of the West Country in the nineteenth century and by doing so situate Hardy's

Wessex within its period's imaginative geographies. In general, this context helps clarify how Hardy understands centre and periphery, nationalism, provincialism and locality; more particularly in this chapter, *The Mayor of Casterbridge* is read in the light of the changing transport system and the impact it had on ideas of local independence. The chapters are arranged to some extent chronologically, giving first the eighteenth-century geography of the West Country and second its nineteenth-century version. The chapters also move from an emphasis on the empirical and economic aspects of imaginative geography towards an account of the cultural ones. These two aspects continually overlap in the conceptual and affective framework people bring to a particular area, district or region and, as is the case in Tess's journeys through Wessex, both cultural associations and empirical fact contribute to local knowledge. In the same way that Hardy's places are positioned on a recognizable map of England, his novels acknowledge and respond to the existence of established pictures of the 'south-west counties' – images and mappings which, according to the novels, can neither be ignored nor accepted.[2]

In each chapter, too, other writers exemplify the assumptions being made about the West Country and the West of England. Hardy's self-definition as a novelist and as a regionalist takes place through his encounter both with particular writers and with a wider culture. Distinguishing between the influential writer and the merely indicative one is not always easy and sometimes cannot be done. In the chapter that follows, Henry Fielding and William Wordsworth are discussed in relation to the West Country and Hardy's understanding of it. Hardy, who was notoriously secretive and disingenuous about his literary mentors, evidently modelled his early poetry on Wordsworth; he also expressed an unusual degree of admiration for Fielding, given the taste of his day.[3] Whatever the degree of literary influence, Fielding and Wordsworth are important here because they express convictions about the value of local freedoms. In both cases and in different ways, these convictions are linked to the transport system going out of use in Hardy's day. *The Mayor of Casterbridge*, I argue, tracks the replacement of coaches by railways – a change that had particular consequences for Dorchester and Dorset. Their loss of importance is mirrored in Henchard's decline and both reflect the danger that rail travel posed to local, indigenous forms of governance. The novel, therefore, can be seen as addressing particular conditions in southwest England – the region's traditions, economics and transport system – which Hardy presents not only as examples of modernity and its problems, nor simply as local variants of universal problems. The novel remains *'of Casterbridge'*, resistant to extrapolation or generalization, even while it prompts recognition of general laws at work. To establish this reading of *The Mayor of Caster-bridge* will require, however, a fair amount of background information.

The country-party, King Alfred and the western parts of England

In the eighteenth century, the western parts of England, as they were usually called, were often represented as backward and remote, inaccessible and primitive. The accent was especially strong, the roads particularly bad. The same region could be defended, however, as a bastion of national virtue. It was the original England, founded by King Alfred, and via King Alfred it embodied the tradition of 'patriotic monarchy' which he began. In other words, the western parts of England were associated with a particular view of how centre and periphery should relate to one another within the state – the view of the 'country-party'. These opponents of Walpole advocated government by the king in parliament, whereas according to them Walpole's regime encroached on the freedoms of the balanced constitution by bringing parliament under the sway of a ministerial oligarchy. This upset a constitution seen by the country-party as 'founded upon a principle of balance between independent parts' – parts whose independence was guaranteed by the ownership of land.[4]

  The country-party's alignment with King Alfred and with western England is evident at Stourhead in Wiltshire, where 'King Alfred's Tower' was erected with an inscription in the king's honour. He

> Established a Militia;
> Created and exerted
> A Naval Force;
> A Philosopher and Christian;
> The Father of his People;
> The Founder
> Of the English Monarchy,
> And of Liberty[.][5]

Just as Great Britain's naval power originated in Alfred so did the nation's constitutional monarchy, whose institution was regarded by the country-party as the great achievement of the Glorious Revolution in 1688. Stourhead, a great country house (belonging to the family of

Lord Stourton until the eighteenth century, when it passed to the Hoare family) expressed the independence of the landowner, whose impartiality was necessary for the health of the nation as a whole. Alfred could be invoked as an ideal king – devoted to his people and the protector of their freedoms – representing a form of rule which Walpole's regime was undermining. His name claimed that those in opposition to the government of the day were more profoundly loyal to their nation than were the time-servers and placemen supported by the regime.

King Alfred suggests, therefore, the original English virtues and forms of governance espoused by the country-party; at the same time, because of Alfred's wars against the Danes, places connected with him can be associated with the Saxon nation as it resisted the Danes advancing from the east. Consequently, the self-proclaimed loyalty of the country-party to the ancient liberties of the nation, first established by Alfred and seen as restored by William III, could change from a political claim to a more broadly nationalist one. Alfred's war against the Danes ended, moreover, in a victory which involved compromise. He made a treaty with his opponents instead of banishing or massacring them. This meant that Alfred could epitomize a form of kingship which harmonized diversity instead of imposing homogeneity.

The most famous episode in Alfred's career was his retreat to Athelney in Somerset to escape the victorious Danes and gather his forces against them once more. This incident becomes the focus of nearly all the Alfred literature of the eighteenth and early nineteenth centuries. In these texts, however, Athelney's location remains rather vague. Athelney, where Alfred's disappointment, despair, recovery and renewed hope were frequently dramatized in eighteenth-century accounts of his life, remained a generic location with few Somersetshire features. It is important as the historical instance of a 'robber's cave' – a place of rural, Horatian retreat in which Alfred learns wisdom and (like King David of the Bible) gathers a band of outlaws against a cruel overlord. Its rurality provides access to purity of vision and serenity, both of which are the prerequisites of successful reconquest and Alfred's subsequent government. It seems an accident that the rural scene happens to be placed in Somerset. On the other hand, King Alfred's Tower at Stourhead lays claim to his heritage as an aspect not only of the country landowning class but on behalf of Wiltshire and the surrounding counties in particular. Gilpin on his tour of the '*Western Parts of England*' comes across other reminders of Alfred and repeats the whole story of Alfred's life in Athelney. This is usual; the West of England is habitually connected with Alfred and the form of liberty he is taken to represent, yet that liberty is a quality of country living and landownership which will be found wherever these take place.[6]

King Alfred is of interest to a study of Hardy because of this traditional connection and the conflict it presents. Alfred himself is strikingly absent from Hardy's work, given his adoption in 'Wessex' of the kingdom Alfred ruled.[7] There are a few hints of him: Stourhead is marked on the 1912 map of 'The Wessex of the Novels and Poems' where it occupies almost the exact midpoint; Francis Troy in *Far from the Madding Crowd* was originally named Alfred; 'Alfredston' in *Jude the Obscure* is the equivalent of Wantage, Alfred's birthplace. These distant reminders keep Alfred faintly visible in the background of Hardy's Wessex, as the original ruler and establisher of the kingdom. He is one point of possible reference for someone seeking to establish the unity of Wessex or the unity of Hardy's works, even for someone looking to find in the novels a late nineteenth-century version of country-party politics. Hardy offers the possibility without granting it authority; as a result, Alfred contributes only one of the many historical and cultural layers which make up Wessex.[8]

Although Hardy keeps his distance from Alfred, separating his Wessex from the Saxon king's ancient kingdom, the issues which the figure of Alfred raises are central to his novels. Firstly, because of their prominence in country-party writing, Alfred and Athelney were the focus for disputes over the relations between liberty and national unity, particularly during the 1790s. These disputes foreshadow Hardy's preoccupations eighty or more years later. Secondly, the country-party position on nationhood and the independence of parts creates two different understandings of geographically remote places in England; Hardy (perhaps following Wordsworth's example) adapted these for Wessex.

The most successful and famous of the eighteenth-century Alfred texts was the masque, *Alfred* (1740–41), written by James Thomson and David Mallet, with music by Thomas Arne. It was first performed in the presence of Frederick, Prince of Wales and revived several times later in the century. Its popularity is indicated by the fame of its final number, 'Rule Britannia'. In the masque, Athelney – '*a place then rough with woods and of difficult access*' – is presented as England in miniature. It is an 'island' between two rivers and is, therefore:

> of strength. Nature's own hand
> Hath planted round a deep defence of woods,
> The sounding ash, the mighty oak; each tree
> A sheltering grove[.]

As is most often the case in Alfred literature, locality vanishes here beneath the meanings given to the scene; likewise, the peasants are independent freeholders, whose 'Patience of toil' leads to manners which are 'sincere, / Plain, hospitable [and] kind'.[9] They speak standard English without any sign of the West Country accent so frequently made fun of in other literature of the period.[10] Alfred's Queen wakes to find herself in Athelney and exclaims: 'Oh!——where am I?——heaven? [. . .] Blest be the tempest that has driven me hither, / Into this safe, this sacred harbor!'[11] The masque was first performed at Cliveden House, near Maidenhead, Buckinghamshire, and the country house of its performance is elided with the Athelney of its setting.

The thoroughly refined speech of the peasants and the masque's other erasures of locality are characteristic of the universalizing tendency in country-party writing. Prospect landscapes, offering an 'equal, wide, survey' of the surrounding countryside, are employed to reflect the responsive and responsible behaviour of the good landlord; such behaviour is made, in turn, into a synecdoche of good government. It is tempting to connect prospect landscapes of eighteenth-century loco-descriptive writing with the erasure of particularity and to regard 'the disenchantment of the world' brought about by Newtonian mechanics as something appropriated by a centralizing regime in order to disem-power localized and popular forms of authority.[12] In the case of Athelney, erasure is easier to find because the place had literally gone off the map. In the guidebooks which began to be published in the late eighteenth century (such as *CARY'S New Itinerary* and *Paterson's Roads*), Athelney is not marked.[13] It remained the mythical site of Alfred's retreat in *Alfred, An Historical Tragedy* (1789) and *Science Revived, or The Vision of Alfred* (1802) but, to Gilpin, travelling through the area in the 1770s, it is an obscure, forgotten place.[14] The invisibility and virtuality of Athelney makes it attractive to those, like James Thomson, for whom all retreats are the same, each representing and making possible a social order that applies everywhere; one which, when put into practice, will unite the nation.[15]

Not all country-party writing is the same, however, and not all eighteenth-century opponents of Walpole regard the local and rustic as no more than an emblem of English freedoms and English virtues. There are alternatives to the 'equal, wide survey' and, consequently, other relations possible between educated and authentic, national and local. Henry Fielding, for instance, who locates *Tom Jones* in 'the western division of this kingdom [. . .] called Somersetshire' differently conceives the presence of metropolitan authority within particular communities.

His novel's hostility to London is mixed with ridicule for those in the country (such as Sophia's aunt, Mrs Western) who endlessly refer to the city as the centre of both fashion and wisdom.[16] Within the novel's argument, therefore, the good magistrate needs to be independent of London in the same way that the good teacher needs to be wary of universal truths. It may be important to this aspect of the novel that Ralph Allen, the principal model for Fielding's Squire Allworthy, made his fortune by instituting a system of 'cross-posts' – that is, a postal service which ran between local centres, where beforehand the post had gone into London and back out again.[17] Similarly, Tom Jones turns out to have been fathered by a man named 'Summer' and is linked by that name not only to plenitude and vitality but to the indigenous and local as well – to the 'somer' in Somerset.

In Fielding, then, local loyalty exists in balance with the acceptance of national rule: the 1745 rebellion engenders a sturdy nationalism which resists the Stuart dynasty, whose foreign allegiances are made worse by their taint of Roman Catholicism and its universal claims. For Fielding, a proper nationalism is defined by a love of local independence. Every Justice of the Peace needs to respond to their particular circumstances and these are seen as altering with geography. Likewise, prospect views occur in the novel and they may be extremely pleasing; they do not, however, lead the viewer to apprehend the whole of which the prospect is a miniature.[18] Fielding encourages his readers to see the pleasure as intrinsic to the view rather than a consequence of what the view can mean. This preference implies a politics which is subtly different from Thomson's; it draws attention, too, to the peculiarity of Somerset.

Squire Allworthy's house looks out over 'a river, that for several miles, was seen to meander through an amazing variety of meadows and woods, till it emptied itself into the sea; with a large arm of which, and an island beyond it, the prospect was closed'. This valley is enclosed by the hills where the house stands and, on the further side, beyond the park, by 'a ridge of wild mountains, the tops of which were above the clouds.'[19] Editors identify this prospect with the Somerset levels south and west of Glastonbury, the 'wild mountains' being the Quantock Hills. This was a remote area, difficult to reach or cross because frequently waterlogged. Celia Fiennes, the eighteenth-century traveller, wrote that on leaving Taunton you enter 'a large common or bottom of deep black land which is bad for the rider but good for the abider, as the proverb is'.[20] Inaccessibility is joined in Fielding's mind with an oppressed loyalty.

The Man of the Hill, whose story Tom and Partridge listen to obediently in book 8, joined the Duke of Monmouth's rebellion against James II's Roman Catholicism, a rebellion defeated at the Battle of Sedgemoor (1685). Sedgemoor is just east of Bridgwater, situated in full view of Squire Allworthy's house though hidden, it seems, amidst the 'amazing variety of meadows and woods'. The Man of the Hill's loyal opposition to James II has the same reasons and motives as Tom's joining up to fight against the Jacobite rebels of 1745. Each has 'resolved to take arms in defence of my country, of my religion, and my liberty' (*Tom Jones*, book 8, chapter 14, p.427). After the Battle of Sedgemoor, Judge Jefferies travelled through the West Country punishing the defeated rebels with notorious severity. Athelney and the region nearby are presented in the novel, therefore, as the specific place, within living memory, where ancient liberties declared themselves against a disloyal regime and endured the oppression inflicted by the centre's agents. Not only propertied independence (as is the case with other country-party writing) but Somerset itself provide a bastion against tyranny – something which Tom (along with the reader) discovers during the journey to London.[21]

Wordsworth and local independence

Later in the eighteenth century, both Wordsworth and Coleridge celebrated Somerset as a remote centre of ancient freedoms in terms reminiscent of Fielding. In Coleridge's 'Lines Written Upon Leaving a Place of Retirement', 'Fears in Solitude' and 'France: An Ode', the district around Nether Stowey is conceived as being a peculiarly secluded site of independence, somehow separate from the mainstream of English politics and metropolitan self-understanding, offering an alternative to conceptions of the whole nation which have been established at and by the centre.[22] Similarly, Wordsworth in the first of his Salisbury Plain poems, shows a traveller moving through the impenetrable darkness of the deserted plain and looking, as the sun sets, into the 'troubled west'. Later the female vagrant of the poem is carried away to the American War of Independence and a connection is made between the 'troubled' western sky and the war abroad – a war which was seen as a version, writ large, of the dispute between country-party and corrupt government.[23] The look into the west also suggests a further connection: that between the American rebellion and the one attempted earlier by the Duke of Monmouth in Somerset. Both have produced strife revealing the ruthless will to power of London government.

Wordsworth's unease and political radicalism emerge more clearly from his geography when one compares his look west with William Crowe's prospect views in his poem *Lewesdon Hill* (1788). The comparison reproduces in many respects the differences between Thomson and Fielding. Wordsworth read Crowe's poem in 1795 and was influenced by its simple diction and its cautious but deliberate use of provincialisms. In it, the speaker ascends Lewesdon Hill, in the west of Dorset, inland from Bridport, and looks successively in all directions, though predominantly southwards. The American colonies are seen to lie beyond the English Channel, in a south-westerly direction (rather than Wordsworth's geographically less accurate due west). Trading links and ideas of the extension of England into America inform Crowe's geography, as does his reading of the American Revolution. Crowe celebrates the 'patriot Conqueror':

> who in the western world,
> Thine own deliver'd country, for thyself
> Hast planted an immortal grove, and there
> [. . .] sit'st beneath the palmy shade[.][24]

The leaders of the colonies now possess the independence of free-born, property-owning Englishman; indeed, their victory is a victory for England in the sense that they now replicate 'in the western world' the politics of the country-party.

Wordsworth's Salisbury Plain poem hints at the blandness of these assumptions and his discomfort with the too confident imposition of universal laws on particular circumstances. Somerset and the West Country in general suggest local forms of independence from the centre. Wordsworth developed this idea much further, however, when he returned to the Lake District in 1799, finding in Grasmere another area within Great Britain which was both an epitome of national virtues and one which kept its distance from centralizing government.[25] In *Home at Grasmere* particularly, Wordsworth presents his belief that a place or community may epitomize nationally or universally admirable qualities despite or, indeed, by virtue of its distinctiveness. The poem was started early in 1800 and probably completed in the course of the year. It describes Wordsworth's journey back to the Lakes, his arrival in Grasmere and his settlement in its enclosed retreat. There are reasons for believing that Wordsworth was comparing Grasmere with Athelney, his feelings about locality with those espoused by the country-party, and that this running comparison led him to think further about the universality or otherwise of rural virtues.

When Wordsworth returned to the Lakes, he travelled with Coleridge, re-establishing their partnership with all its pathos, excitement and complication. This fact has tended to obscure the other person who travelled with them in autumn 1799; that is, Joseph Cottle, the publisher of the *Lyrical Ballads* and a generous patron to Robert Southey as well. Cottle left Bristol with Coleridge on 22 October 1799, accompanied him as far as the Lake District and then returned home, turning back on October 30th.[26] Coleridge mentions Cottle's presence and departure in a letter to Dorothy Wordsworth:

> It was most lucky for us that poor dear Cottle returned. His timidity is indeed not greater than is easily explicable from his lameness & sedentary STATIONERY occupations; but it is extreme & poor dear fellow! his self-involution (for Alfred is *his* Self) *O me that Alfred!* William & I have atchieved one good Thing – he has solemnly promised not to publish on his own account.[27]

If Cottle ever made such a promise, he soon broke it and published *Alfred, an Epic Poem* the following year. Coleridge is, of course, condescending here and snobbish: Cottle was not well-born or university educated; his work as a stationer (hence Coleridge's pun) was of low status; it brought with it, apparently, such physical weakness and cowardice that he could not keep up with the hearty poets. Coleridge presents him as unsuited by education, class and physique for the grand project of writing an epic. It is clear, nonetheless, that *Alfred* was being mentioned pretty frequently as the three companions walked along and, although there is no evidence that Wordsworth read the poem, he seems to have shared Coleridge's irritation at Cottle's self-identification with the patriot-king. 'Alfred is *his* Self,' Coleridge writes, emphasizing with the original underlining Cottle's exclusive claim and, with the capital letter, Cottle's (inappropriate) self-aggrandizement.

Cottle's poem repeats the main elements of the Alfred story – defeat by the Danes, withdrawal to Athelney, the gathering of forces there and final victory. In talking about it, evidently, Cottle identified with his hero and this may have been easier because, unlike Coleridge and Wordsworth, Cottle was a native of Bristol. Moreover, the poem enthusiastically aligns itself with Alfred, as if his virtues can straightforwardly be emulated. *Home at Grasmere* includes some verbal recollections of country-party language and of King Alfred, as if Grasmere might be an equivalent of Athelney. Yet, for Wordsworth, the appropriateness and the appropriation of past heroic models is an area of difficulty and uncertainty, both morally necessary and morally questionable, even delusional. Thus, for instance, the Vale of Grasmere is called a 'legislative Hall' and, Wordsworth claims:

> In this enclosure many of the old
> Substantial virtues have a firmer tone
> Than in the base and ordinary world.[28]

Here, like Alfred, Wordsworth will gather strength and grow able to impart wisdom to a corrupt world outside.[29] Where Cottle's unselfconscious moral earnestness allowed him to think of Alfred and himself inhabiting the same moral universe and the same physical world, Wordsworth's poem highlights the act which underlies that alignment: that is, the act of possession. '[A]nd now 'tis mine for life,' Wordsworth declares, 'This solitude is mine', 'The unappropriated bliss hath found / An owner, and that owner I am he' (MS B, ll, 52, 83, 85–6, *Home at Grasmere*, pp.40, 42). Grasmere is Wordsworth's home territory as Somerset is Cottle's, but Wordsworth, unlike Cottle, highlights both his right to claim it and the act of doing so.[30]

Analogously, poetic models are revived and remodelled in *Home at Grasmere*: it is not '*an Epic poem*' although it has epic features and bardic pretensions. Elements of a received country-party vocabulary are adopted and then redeployed; in the same way, a narrative of retreat into the world of restorative pastoral is taken up in order to be reclaimed as local feeling. These features of the poem have political implications: Wordsworth's argument with Cottle is conducted amidst his dissent from the interested universalism of Thomson as well as from the national and international prospect landscapes of *Lewesdon Hill*. They also have a consequence for Wordsworth's sense of history: Cottle's work makes past and present continuous with one another, the duty of the present being simply to repeat the lesson visible in the past. (This may be to do with Cottle's Calvinism.) For Wordsworth, by contrast, the past cannot be passively relied upon, it needs instead to be continually remade, by freemen 'sound and unenslaved' (MS B, l, 443, *Home at Grasmere*, p.66). Wordsworth's sense of his own agency as an invader and possessor is repeated in his engagement with (as well as his absorption of) literary tradition and in his alertness to the agency of particular individuals within historical processes.

Agency also affects the geography of the poem. *Home at Grasmere* narrates a journey westwards, from Yorkshire, over the Pennines and into the Lake District. Wordsworth links it to the journey of Moses through the desert to the Promised Land, to that of the Wise Men 'from the East' to find the new-born Messiah and to the contemporary radicals (Coleridge among them) who planned or had planned to establish utopian communities in the new world across the Atlantic. These figurative associations are in accord with those of Alfred's journey into Somerset.[31] *Home at Grasmere*, however, denaturalizes the imaginative geography it works with, so that geographical awareness is seen as actively created as well as something adopted and inherited. Geographical perceptions come to seem a part of the made environment, of the environment we build around ourselves as we travel through a landscape and inhabit it:

> 'What would ye?' said the shower,
> 'Wild Wanderers, whither through my dark domain?'
> The Sunbeam said, 'Be happy.' They were moved,
> All things were moved; they round us as we went,
> We in the midst of them.
> (MS B, ll, 232–6, *Home at Grasmere*, p.50)

This embrace of the travellers by their native valley seems like a dance of joy (as all objects move around the couple walking and 'are moved' emotionally); in this way, it confirms their welcome. The whimsy which colours the elements' questions and exhortations – 'The Sunbeam said, "Be happy"' – is accounted for as the result of Wordsworth's being himself equally moved. His place within the midst is established even by the exclamations which sound, initially, fanciful and picturesque. However, the joy of that reception – in which the place accepts Wordsworth and equally his fancy-forming mind – is made by Wordsworth's phrasing to seem nearly an optical illusion. It is the impression you naturally get when walking along that objects ahead move closer, separate into right and left and then close again behind you, the whole movement being a kind of circling. The really astonishing thing for Wordsworth is his perception that this constant and inevitable centring of the world around oneself is tolerated by and participated in by the natural objects in Grasmere. The imaginative geography Wordsworth brings with him (one which makes a retreat of Grasmere and reads a journey westward as a journey into real pastoral and true community) is both confirmed by this and actively reperceived. In the same way, the politics which it implies is made into a duty and a motivating power. Grasmere may become another Athelney insofar as we make it one. *Home at Grasmere*'s tense energies derive, then, from its struggle with the necessity of creating something natural.[32]

Lucille Herbert intelligently discusses Hardy's employment of landscape descriptions deriving from eighteenth-century poetry, 'the moralized landscapes [which] seem to have become part of the language in the form of topographical metaphors that imply attitudes to social and intellectual history.'[33] She contrasts Hazlitt's cosmopolitanism with Wordsworth's localism and argues that Hardy is divided between the two, his philosophy of 'long views' and abstract reason sitting uncomfortably with a nostalgia for small communities and a conservative sociology. This general position produces a reading of *Tess* in which Tess is portrayed as lacking 'egoistic drive', as dependent upon 'traditional wisdom' and 'at a crisis, [she] yields to every kind of compulsion from within and without'. Analogously, the novel's clashing viewpoints produce in the end an overview in which Hardy 'makes vivid to the modern imagination, the real differences among alternative views of life'. The book is seen as adopting in its concluding movements a stoic cosmopolitanism and giving up its attachment to Tess. Long views must eventually come apart from local attachments so that Tess is left behind as the epitome of a departing localism.

Herbert's reading ignores Tess's evident ability to adapt and assimilate, leaving out her power of combining particular and universal forms of knowledge. Her account of the novel suggests that localism can survive in Hardy only in the form of elegy – the decline of rural community equates with the disappearance of unquestioning love and both are mourned as irretrievably lost. If, however, Hardy challenges this mourning with his sense of Tess's adaptiveness and her resolve then local attachment does not disappear when it is conjoined with a wider perspective. The division which Herbert rightly identifies becomes more unstable, more subject to a person's power to combine cosmopolitan and local.[34] *The Mayor of Casterbridge*, in its geography and in the fate of its central character, Michael Henchard, expresses and personalizes the clash between cosmopolitan and local which Herbert describes. It shows, as a result, how Hardy's thinking draws on Wordsworth's sense of agency's importance in the creation of locality and independence.

Roads, railways and Hardy's Dorset

Fielding's Somerset can be linked with Wordsworth's Lake District; both suggest forms of regional loyalty that are different from those implied by the celebration of rusticity in Thomson, William Crowe and Gilpin. In the eighteenth century, Somerset is attractive as a model of local independence within the nation because of its recent history and physical inaccessibility. By the mid-nineteenth century, because of changes in transport, Somerset had become less remote and, by comparison, Dorset was more so. The new turnpike roads of the mid- to late-eighteenth century and, more importantly, the railways built in the 1830s and 1840s, allowed Somerset to be crossed and Dorset to be bypassed. As a result, Dorset lost its place within the network of relations that made up the kingdom. This greater isolation is registered by Hardy and its possible consequences are addressed: Wordsworthian celebration of an autonomous yet permeable region is checked by the danger that remoteness means marginalization and provincialism, the authority of the centre being confirmed in the districts it first ignores and later sentimentalizes. In some respects, then, his novels reconsider the divergence between Wordsworth and William Crowe, between Thomson and Fielding, in a setting which had become the nineteenth-century version of eighteenth-century Somerset.

The different lines of communication in Hardy's novels – turnpikes, by-ways, railways, Roman roads – are used to show not only the various layers of history or the encroachment of modernity. They show, too, that there are simultaneously different, competing ways in which (using Doreen Massey's terms) the global is in the local and vice versa. Changes in transport brought about empirical changes in the national geography, shortening journey times to and from Somerset while making those to and from Dorset comparatively longer. The new developments (railways and turnpike roads) also presented, visibly within the landscape, a new conception of how province and capital were related – or, one might say, a different understanding of national space. This altered not only Dorset's place in the nation but its status as a region.

The turnpikes came rather late to the south-west; the road from Salisbury to Dorchester was turnpiked in 1756 and from Dorchester to Weymouth in 1761. This is twenty or so years after the hey-day of the turnpike trusts. The most frequent route into the western parts of England from London during the eighteenth century was, nonetheless, via Dorset. Celia Fiennes, Defoe and Gilpin all travel via Salisbury, Dorchester, Bridport, Lyme Regis and on to Exeter before returning via Somerset, through Taunton, Bridgwater, Wells, Bristol and/or Bath. This is the established touring route and the one followed by the judges on the Western Circuit. Pigot & Co.'s *British Atlas* (1840) gives this route in its Distance Table for the journey from London to Falmouth.[35] It competes with two others: the first via Salisbury, Shaftesbury, Sherborne, Yeovil, Chard and Honiton (the present A30), turnpiked in 1753, and the second heading due west from London to Bath and then south through Somerset (roughly, the present M4/M5 route). Defoe speaks of turning off the first of these routes and heading southwards, in order to explore Dorset and the south coast. He thinks of this region as something of a backwater. Its soil is less fertile than that of Devon and its ports of less strategic or commercial importance than those further east or west (than Portsmouth, Southampton, Exeter and Plymouth). Of Dorchester, he comments: 'a man that coveted a retreat in this world might as agreeably spend his time, and as well in Dorchester, as in any town I know in England'.[36] Its seclusion, though, is easily exaggerated: Weymouth was a watering-place patronized by royalty. Ships embarked from there to the Channel Islands and to France. Dorchester was *en route* to fashion, foreign parts and the outer reaches of England.[37]

Railways too developed late in Dorset. A line linked London and Southampton in 1834 and Brunel's Great Western connected London and Bristol in 1835, Bristol and Exeter the following year. No railways were built anywhere in Dorset until 1847, ten years later, when the line was opened between Southampton and Dorchester. For a further ten years, nothing else was built. These delays were the result of the war of the gauges combined with a conflict between two possible routes into the southwest. The Great Western was broad gauge; the line via Southampton narrow gauge. The narrow gauge companies wanted to build a line linking London and the southwest to rival Brunel's and this, naturally, was opposed by the Great Western. Among the narrow gauge companies there was a further dispute over routes during the railway mania of the mid-1840s: the 'coastal route' (Southampton, Dorchester, Lyme Regis, Exeter) and the 'central route' (Salisbury, Yeovil, Honiton, Exeter). The coastal route was abandoned in 1856 and the central route built in 1860. In the same period, a broad gauge line was built, finally, running north–south from Yeovil to Weymouth; the Dorchester to Weymouth section was built using a mixed gauge, so that trains from Southampton could use it too. 'The South Western trains commenced to run through to Weymouth on the same day as the Great Western.'[38] Choosing the 'central route' made Dorchester a dead-end, as far as railway travel was concerned, diverting the commerce to and from the southwest towards towns on the 'central route' – Yeovil, in particular, which became an important railway junction. This change coincided, more locally, with the completion of lines to Weymouth: visitors could travel there direct without changing at Dorchester onto horse-drawn carriages. Even the branchline to Bridport (built in 1857) joined the mainline at Maiden Newton, north of Dorchester, confirming the sense that what had once been a hub of the area's transport network was now a less important halt.[39]

One of the observable consequences of the railways was the decline in wealth of places they bypassed. Dorchester was on the network and could even boast of being served by two different routes into the capital. Yet it was no longer a staging-post on the route west, as had been the case when it stood on the turnpike road from London to Exeter. It was the last stop on the 'coastal route' which naturally became of secondary important as soon as the 'central route' was completed; it was also a stop on the route joining Weymouth to the ports on the north Somerset coast.[40] Though the railway links prevented Dorchester from suffering radical decline (and places left outside the network certainly suffered, especially, it appears, in Dorset), nonetheless the form the connections took diminished its status within the national transport network.[41] This change is the more marked by comparison with Weymouth.

Weymouth's hey-day was during the Napoleonic wars when it enjoyed great military importance and profited from George III's regular visits. Little mention is made of this period, however, in the 1863 edition of the county history, which Hardy used; instead, its decline before the Georgian period is contrasted with its more recent revival. The first edition of 1774 is quoted, describing Weymouth as 'formerly a considerable seaport [. . .] till the increase of Poole, and the late wars with France, &c. caused its decay'. This decline stands in contrast with modern elegance. 'Of late years,' the county history states,

> Weymouth – more particularly on the Melcombe Regis side – has been much improved. The Esplanade is a feature which greatly enhances the attractions of the latter as a place of sea-side resort and residence. It follows the margin of Weymouth Bay, is nearly semi-circular, and upwards of a mile in length, and for the greater part of this distance forms a spacious promenade, faced towards the sea by a substantial wall of masonry, and separated on the opposite side by a wide roadway from the houses, which now line its whole extent.
>
> (Hutchins, *Dorset*, II, p.443)[42]

The description emphasizes safety and elegance, a spaciousness and width that are healthy rather than congested, and an Esplanade possessing the smooth, open lines of a Regency crescent. These improvements counter any lingering suspicions of decline and earlier decay is halted by improvement. It was railway links which helped Weymouth re-establish itself as a tourist attraction ('a place of sea-side resort and residence'): connections north made it a frequent holiday destination for workers from Swindon; later connections east gradually drew it into the chain of south coast resorts.[43] Improvements to the local architecture ensured that it appeared healthy, orderly and able to cope with this expansion.

The railways elevated Weymouth while they contributed to Dorchester's decline. Pigot and Co.'s *British Atlas* marked all railways 'completed and in progress', giving details of their development in its notes to each county. The only entry under this heading for Dorset (other counties have many more) reads: 'The line of the projected WEYMOUTH and BATH RAILWAY will pass from the former town through or near to Dorchester, Stalbridge, Gillingham and Frome, and thence [. . .][44] Secondly, Weymouth changed from being a far-flung resort, dependent on eccentric royal patronage, and entered into competition with the other seaside towns accessible by rail: Bournemouth closest at hand, Worthing and Brighton further east. The failure of the 'coastal route' to be built had the effect of separating Devon and Cornwall from the counties making up 'the south coast': Kent, Sussex, Hampshire and, most remotely, Dorset. Imaginatively and culturally, Weymouth no longer lay to one side of the main route from London westwards to Exeter and beyond; instead, it stood at the far end of a route south out of London, rather like Margate, Brighton or Bournemouth.[45]

The Mayor of Casterbridge, Weydon-Priors and Budmouth

These changes in the transport system of Dorset and their economic and cultural consequences form one of the subjects of *The Mayor of Casterbridge*. Henchard and his wife appear in the first chapter approaching 'Weydon-Priors'. From 1895 on, Hardy's map made clear that this is his Wessex equivalent of the actual place, Weyhill, just outside Andover. On its first publication, the novel would have left the reader more doubtful – the road Henchard and Susan walk along 'might have been matched at almost any spot in any county in England at this time of the year'. Similarly, after Henchard has sold his wife, then tried unsuccessfully to trace her, he hears that she has probably left the country with her new 'husband', Newson.

at a western seaport [. . .] he derived intelligence that persons answering somewhat to his description had emigrated a little time before.

Then he said he would search no longer, and that he would go and
settle in the district which he had had for some time in his mind.
Next day he started, journeying southward, and did not pause till he
reached the town of Casterbridge, more than a hundred miles off.

(Hardy, *Mayor*, chapters 1 and 2, pp.4, 19)

Although it is no more than seventy miles or so from Bristol to Dorchester, the only major 'western seaport' to the north of Dorset is Bristol.
It seems in this edition, then, that Henchard arrives in Casterbridge
from the north; in 1895, however, Hardy altered the direction, cutting
'western' from 'a western seaport' and revising the last sentence to read:
'journeying south-westward, and did not pause, except for nights'
lodging, till he reached the town of Casterbridge, in a far distant part
of Wessex'.[46]

This alteration establishes from the beginning a connection between
Henchard and the route out of Casterbridge to the east and northeast
– a connection which the novel increasingly emphasizes. On the night
of the skimmity-ride, he tries to find Farfrae (in order to bring him back
to save Lucetta) by following the road east, towards Weatherbury. Again,
when he leaves Casterbridge for the last time, Henchard 'pursued his
solitary way eastward' back towards Weydon-Priors; his attempts at
reparation draw him always in that direction whereas what threatens to
overwhelm him comes up the road from the south, from Budmouth,
the Wessex equivalent of Weymouth. Elizabeth-Jane meets her lover,
Farfrae, on the 'Budmouth Road' and Henchard watching through a
telescope sees Newson, her real father, coming to meet her on the same
road. 'Henchard lived a lifetime the moment he saw it.'[47] Henchard had,
he believed, successfully deceived Newson into thinking his daughter
dead. Now, the road south proves him wrong by showing him the 'new'
man re-entering to claim his child.

Movement east connects Henchard with Cain: the rivalrous elder
brother, a marked man, driven out of Eden to the east. The opposing
directions so emphasized at the end of the novel also realize a scheme
suggested from the beginning, connected with the novel's interest in
questions of modernity. Directions of travel and geographical relation-
ships focus questions and feelings about modernity's invasiveness.
When for instance Farfrae, Henchard's opponent, first arrives in Casterbridge it is odd he should be there. He is a Scot and he tells Henchard,
'I am on my way to Bristol, from there to the other side of the warrld.'
Casterbridge (Dorchester) should not be on his route. Has he got lost?
Is he spending some free time before his ship embarks by roaming these

little-known, west country districts, rather as Angel does in *Tess of the D'Urbervilles*? The reader is entitled to wonder, if only for a moment and, to confirm a feeling of uncertainty, Hardy has one of his rustics comment that Farfrae is 'a sort of traveller': what sort nobody knows.

It is characteristic of the novel's clipped intensity of focus that this anomaly is never explained: where Farfrae is going to or coming from remain unknown; we gather only that he is 'far frae' home. Later, in chapter 18, Lucetta writes to Henchard saying she will be coming through Casterbridge on her way back from Bristol to Budmouth. That route links Lucetta to Farfrae (who was on his way to Bristol) and retrospectively suggests that Farfrae may have been coming up from Budmouth himself when we first met him. Consequently, two routes seem to cross at Casterbridge: one runs southwest and northeast, from London out into the distant reaches of the kingdom – to Dorchester itself and beyond to Falmouth (where Susan lives with Newson).[48] The other route runs south–north, linking a fashionable seaside resort with a centre of commerce and money.[49] The first route follows the old coach road to and from London; the second follows that of the 'WEYMOUTH and BATH RAILWAY'. Each route, furthermore, is associated in the novel with characters who gradually emerge as representatives of competing world-views, with Henchard (northeast/southwest) and Farfrae (north/south). Until the end of the novel, Henchard's family and associates, though separated from him, remain on his, rather than Farfrae's route. When it emerges that Newson has moved with his family from Falmouth to Budmouth, it feels as if he has shifted himself and Elizabeth-Jane from Henchard's world to Farfrae's; it seems to follow inevitably that Farfrae will marry Elizabeth-Jane and that Henchard will die. Newson, now known to be Elizabeth-Jane's real father, moves from one route and one world to the other, giving his blessing now to the young couple and becoming established as their progenitor.

By the book's end, in addition, Budmouth and Casterbridge seem more closely connected. Characters move between the two of them more freely and frequently now whereas, at the beginning, Casterbridge is seen alone within the landscape, 'set in the midst of miles of rotund down and concave field'. Its compactness and lack of suburbs, with a 'stockade of gnarled tress which framed [it] in' give the impression of fortified independence. Gradually, that early Casterbridge is replaced by a more fluid one, drawn into an exchange with Budmouth (from where Casterbridge can now be referred to as 'the other town') and, equally, drawn away from the routes northeast and east which have become the retreat for the outdated, the failed and the unnecessary. Accordingly, the fair at Weydon-Priors is in constant decline through the novel: its gaiety and wealth in the opening chapter is fading by chapter three, eighteen years later; by the end of the book it is deserted: 'now bare of human beings, and almost of aught besides. A few sheep grazed thereabout, but these ran off when Henchard halted upon the summit.'[50] As Henchard loses power, Falmouth is replaced by Budmouth, and, at the other end of the road, Weydon-Priors decays.

This correspondence between the journeys of Hardy's characters and the changing transport network of nineteenth-century Dorset may be thought coincidental. Or Henchard's connection with old ways and Farfrae's with the new can be regarded as merely confirmed by the topography of the novel. Coincidence seems unlikely given Hardy's interest elsewhere in the impact of the railways and the care he takes when choosing directions, revising them in many places between editions.[51] Noticing, moreover, how Hardy gives geographical expression to the process of modernization shows what is involved for him in the change from traditional to commercial, antiquated to mechanized. Local independence, comparable to what Fielding celebrated, is being lost in favour of homogeneous prosperity. Farfrae's dominance over trade seems to produce a dominance over geography, bringing Casterbridge nearer to and into association with Budmouth. Casterbridge's distinctiveness – partly quaint and laughable, partly of valued peculiarity – is diminished as the two more cosmopolitan figures, Farfrae and Newson, jointly divide the spoils. At Farfrae's wedding to Elizabeth-Jane:

> the town band had been hired, and lest their convivial instincts should get the better of their skill, the further step had been taken of engaging the string band from Budmouth, so that there would be a reserve to fall back upon in case of need.[52]

As in *Under the Greenwood Tree*, the local and unreliable is in the process of being supplanted by something more dependable and elegant, strings replacing serpents as an organ replaces the musicians in the gallery. This is progress: Farfrae comes across as a decent man, Newson's broadmindedness arises out of kindness and generosity more than indifference.[53] Its mixtures and compromises cannot be condemned even though they seem to emphasize the pragmatic and worldly-wise ('a reserve to fall back upon') at the expense of the uninhibited ('convivial instincts [getting] the better of [. . .] skill'). Neither can one decry the modern as deracinated where the antique was rooted: Henchard is scarcely more indigenous to Casterbridge than Farfrae; indeed, all the protagonists are recent settlers, conquering and being conquered in successive waves.

One impulse, then, in the novel is to contrast Farfrae and Henchard within a long view of history in which their struggle becomes archetypal, with parallels down the ages and a general validity which renders historical particulars insignificant. Henchard goes back into the untouched earth of Egdon like the earliest inhabitants defeated by the Belgae or the Belgae defeated by the Romans or the Romans replaced by the Saxons. Through being made archetypal, the conflict between Henchard and Farfrae can stand for a war between parts of the self or stages of life. When he wakes up, after the drinking bout during which he sold his wife, Henchard sees the morning sun 'streaming through the crevices of the canvas' in the tent. Similarly, in his autobiography, Hardy recalls an incident when, as a boy, he lay with his straw hat over his eyes watching the sunlight peeping through the gaps and wished never to grow up.[54] In the novel, Henchard's integrity opposes Farfrae's adaptability like youth and age, though the older man, Henchard, is the more childlike. As in *Tess*, Hardy is considering the price of maturity yet, as his geography suggests, maturity is not considered in isolation from sociality nor socialization viewed independently of the form of society to which the self adapts. Although the novel pushes towards a universal perspective on its protagonists (a cosmopolitan, wide survey of its characters and their actions), it includes a counter-movement which stresses particular historical conditions. Henchard is asked to adapt himself to a world of tacit but intense conformism, of obligatory superficiality and forgetfulness. Hardy connects his inability to make this adaptation with a universal quality – the incongruity between human self-consciousness and natural life – and with a particular event: the relegation of Dorchester from regional centre to provincial backwater.

The collocation of these two perspectives prevents his death from becoming the subject of either elegy or protest. Likewise, instead of the book concluding with either a geography of local knowledge or of cosmopolitan mapping (to use John Barrell's terms) or in an opposition between invasive turnpikes or railways and organically constituted byways and footpaths, it ends with Henchard constructing a world of his own which remains tied to the real one because it is centred in another person:

He intended to go on from this place [Weydon-Priors] – visited as an act of penance – into another part of the country altogether. But he could not help thinking of Elizabeth, and the quarter of the horizon in which she lived. Out of this it happened that the centrifugal tendency imparted by weariness of the world was counteracted by the centripetal influence of his love for his step-daughter. As a consequence, instead of following a straight course yet further away from Casterbridge, Henchard gradually, almost unconsciously, deflected from that right line of his first intention; till, by degrees, his path, like that of the Canadian woodsman, became part of a circle, of which Casterbridge formed the centre. In ascending any particular hill, he ascertained the bearings as nearly as he could by means of the sun, moon, or stars, and settled in his mind the exact direction in which Casterbridge and Elizabeth-Jane lay.[55]

There are many of Hardy's poems which resemble Wordsworth's *Home at Grasmere* in having the natural world speak to the incomer. Hardy hears more quizzical voices and more rueful ones, implicitly or explicitly querying the assumption on which their speech is based: that man and nature fit somehow harmoniously together.[56] Wordsworth, though, does not simply represent, for Hardy, the naïve optimist his post-Darwinian disillusionment yearns after and regrets. Instead, Henchard's circling of Casterbridge is a modified version of Wordsworth's landscape circling him as he walks into Grasmere. It is as if Henchard's loving attention to Elizabeth repeats the landscape's relation to Wordsworth, so that Hardy is displacing nature's benevolence onto lovingkindness between people. Henchard's move from centre to circumference reflects his newly-found capacity for disinterested affection, his love for his 'step-daughter', who is now acknowledged to be beyond his power. It could be read as a rebuke not only to Henchard's egotism but to Wordsworth's as well, who orients Grasmere around himself and, in *The Excursion*, locates the different homes that make up the valley's community by indicating their bearings from a common centre, the Churchyard, where the poem's dialogue is conducted. Yet, in the same way that Wordsworth highlights his own desire to possess (instead of suggesting his possession is passive or natural) and hints that he cannot help this will to command his surroundings (that it is inevitable given the self-centring quality of his perceptions), so Hardy shows in Henchard a geography that is centred, if not on the man himself, then on his desires.

Henchard's retreat to the periphery, then, does not imply a return to nature or a superhuman act of self-sacrifice. He follows his instincts more readily, Hardy suggests ('he could not help thinking of Elizabeth'), and he renounces any claim he might have on her. These changes produce a peculiar kind of invisibility in him and a different way of travelling. One might expect that, when he stops 'following a straight course yet further away from Casterbridge', he will leave the highway or turnpike road in favour of byways and side-roads, which offer seclusion and retreat. In the final chapter, when Farfrae and Elizabeth go looking for him, they find he has 'turned back from the Casterbridge coach-road by a forking highway which crossed Egdon Heath' and, though they can follow his 'track' for a time, 'the ramifications which [. . .] began to reveal themselves in the route made further progress in the right direction a matter of pure guess-work'. Hardy's brusqueness here voices Farfrae's anxious impatience to get home and suggests the businessman's sensible reluctance to explore each and every possibility.[57] Henchard seems, by this, to have been dispersed into the landscape, yet the marked change in tone between this chapter and the previous one raises the idea that such a view of him may be a 'modern' mistake. To Farfrae, to outsiders generally, Henchard's movements appear to be simply self-obscuring and, in consequence, his fate can be linked with the withdrawal of old English values into the least accessible parts of an otherwise briskly efficient country. Without denying those associations, Hardy declares as well that Henchard is orbiting his step-daughter, that the move away from a 'straight course' means a 'path' of another kind, internally if invisibly coherent.

Accordingly, the 'centrifugal tendency' and the 'centripetal influence' governing Henchard's movement are introduced with an arch incongruity the reader should not fall for. Their over-elaborateness creates the possibility of feeling a disproportion between object and description, between an old man's poignant, sentimental attachment to the daughter he has treated badly and terms which suggest scientific curiosity accompanied by the pleasure of discovering a neat equipoise. Henchard may seem undeserving of such attention or deserving of better, because, against the formality of his scientific terms, Hardy places the neutral 'Out of this it happened that' and the unadorned phrase, 'his love for his step-daughter'. The sentence's diction shows the 'counteracting' of various possible attitudes towards Henchard with two related consequences: his heroism or worthlessness check each other and different sorts of dispassionateness collide. These work to convey a regard for Henchard that is neutral without becoming condescending. In the same way, in the final chapter, the idea that Henchard has sunk back into the earth confronts 'MICHAEL HENCHARD'S WILL' – the obstinately self-assertive and memorable expression of his wish to be forgotten and allowed to disappear.[58] The narrative confirms that, when Henchard starts to create (or admits his need of) a personal geography, Hardy's portrayal of him seeks a language in which his personhood can emerge. Similarly, prospect landscape turns from an overview into an act of devotion:

> In ascending any particular hill, he ascertained the bearings as nearly as he could by means of the sun, moon, or stars, and settled in his mind the exact direction in which Casterbridge and Elizabeth-Jane lay.

The eighteenth-century tradition of loco-descriptive writing is invoked here (as often elsewhere in Hardy's work) but instead of providing either a melancholy or a celebratory account of changes in the landscape, a hill-top elevation allows a brief survey of the heavens which enables the one, important spot to be picked out or, failing that, its direction 'settled'. In Joseph Warton's poem, *The Enthusiast* and constantly in Mrs Radcliffe's novels, the elements in a prospect landscape gather together and rise at the horizon into an image of the heavenly; in Thomson's *The Seasons* a similar trajectory leads to a vision of the whole nation within which the particular landscape finds its place and completion.[59] The movement into larger and larger frames of reference is precisely reversed by Henchard's look first to the stars and then, with their help, down to the little spot of earth.

The reversal implies a Wordsworthian recognition that spaces are distinctive because they are loved by particular individuals and that to subsume places in the larger whole (of nation or a heavenly realm) is to endanger their distinctiveness. Hardy, however, by putting Henchard on the circumference, suggests the presence of others like him, whose geographies are quite as personal as his and incommensurate with one another. Casterbridge happens to be his centre; it could have been elsewhere and for others it certainly would be. Likewise, in the novel, the symbolic associations of Casterbridge are always subjective – the place varies according to who sees it and, secondly, its centrality is a result of the decision to tell this story and not another. Wordsworth makes a greater claim for the universal virtues of Grasmere and the Lake District, for their representative value within the whole of England. This claim exists in tension with his desire to keep the Lake District uninvaded; if its virtues apply elsewhere, then elsewhere is present within it. Yet, as John Barrell points out, place cannot be intelligibly described except in a language which is readable elsewhere; Wordsworth cannot speak of the Lake District without beginning to make its places representative and so opening it to the elsewhere he wishes to keep at bay.

For Hardy, a place becomes representative if you choose to make it so. Your creation of representativeness, with respect to one place and one 'exact direction', happens while others are doing something similar with respect to other places and, sometimes, the same ones. As far as Hardy is concerned, this competition between differing perspectives on 'the same landscape' is less problematic than its opposite: the obstruction of individual perspectives by the cultural dominance of a single, central one. Under modern conditions, Wessex may come to stand for particular qualities and the coexistence of different, personal perspectives be prevented by the imposition of a normative point of view. He is more eager than Wordsworth to deny that this region has identifiable qualities and he frequently parodies the attempt to impose them. Wordsworth's internal conflict (with the urge to raise the Lake District towards universality) is matched in Hardy by his opposition to the same threat seen now as external and modernizing. Wordsworth risks becoming a Burkean patriot; Hardy may become (and has been read as) a nostalgic ruralist. He perceives modernity, however, as bringing with it into Wessex a nostalgia for rurality. His novels are concerned, therefore, with how to resist modernity without succumbing to it or, in other words, with the status and possibility of personhood in mass society.

3
Ruralism and Provincialism in the Victorian Novel: North and South

Changes in nineteenth-century transport lessened internal distance times, drawing the country closer together. At the same time, para-doxically, they made Dorset comparatively more remote. London and Southampton were brought nearer to Dorchester while Dorset became more of a backwater. Or, perhaps it should be said, a different kind of backwater. A revolution in communications brought with it shifts in power, both economic and executive. It reduced the importance of regional centres while bringing them within easier reach and generated new centres within the regions – the railway towns like Swindon or Crewe, the tourist resorts such as Torquay or Bournemouth which expanded with the railways. As is apparent from the preceding chapter's discussion of *The Mayor of Casterbridge*, Hardy's novels register and reflect on these changes in their mappings and their sense of geography.

Material developments brought with them cultural reconfigurations: the West Country was changed physically and economically by the nineteenth century; it was also differently placed and differently under-stood as Victorian culture restructured the imaginative geography of the British Isles. This and the following chapter attempt to sketch two major aspects of this reconfiguration, ones which had a particularly important bearing on Hardy. The first concerns how the perception of outlying dis-tricts altered. Provinces and provinciality acquired different meanings and were put to new uses in a culture that was urbanizing rapidly.[1] This is evident in the changing practice of the provincial novel. The second of these two chapters principally concerns the way westerliness and the West of England were seen in mid-century. It identifies several versions of the west and, of particular significance to Hardy, a semi-rural, sub-urban west, situated in or near the Thames Valley, which embodies stability and projects districts further west as barren wilderness, as feudal or neo-feudal.

Connecting these two – the changing idea of province and the differing senses of 'west' – is a tradition of ruralism, which begins in the early
part of the century in travel-writing, painting and anecdotal depictions
of country life. Ruralism's emphases bear on the provincial novel as it
developed in the course of the nineteenth century, prompting hostility
and allegiance in different places and at different times. Its landscapes
and ideals are taken up in order to be celebrated, challenged or reformed.
These reactions reveal how the term 'provincial' was actively contested
both when it was used to define a social category and when applied to a
novel. By using ruralism as a starting-point, the following discussion aims
to illuminate the arguments going on within the genre of the provincial
novel, shedding light on how provincialism was perceived and, equally,
on the various possibilities the genre offered to Hardy.

Hardy's work develops out of the sensation novel as well as the provincial novel. Ruralist scenes are ubiquitous in the sensation novel, their
frequency enhancing the sense that they, like so much else, are clichés,
open to question, parody or psychological interpretation. Moreover,
ruralism's picture of the rural carried within it a geographical model,
focussed on the south of England, Hampshire especially, and connected
to the sense that the Thames Valley was a route leading back from
corrupted modernity to pristine England (an England often connected
with King Arthur, variously linked with the west of the country).

Hardy's sense of Dorset is complicatedly related to these three aspects
of his period's conception of places outside London: firstly, he works
both with and against an inherited tradition of ruralism; secondly, he
absorbs and modifies both the rural provinciality of Victorian provincial novelists and the half-playful, half-profound allegories built into
the locations of sensation fiction. Thirdly, Hardy's sense of westernness
is a response to the prevailing conception of southern England, centred
on Hampshire, and to the relations between east and west that go along
with this version of the rural. Portraying provincial communities which
are located in the West Country, Hardy's novels draw on and reconsider
his contemporaries' feelings for and understanding of the provincial
and the western; they can be read too as an assessment of and counter
to Victorian ruralism.

Ruralism

In her 1992 study, *Scheherazade in the Marketplace: Elizabeth Gaskell and
the Victorian Novel*, Hilary Schor shows Elizabeth Gaskell in 1838 entering the literary marketplace by writing 'audition letters' to William and

Mary Howitt. These describe 'a childhood visit to Stratford-upon-Avon' and 'the customs of the country where she grew up'.[2] The Howitts were highly successful writers who published a series of books about rural life. In the same year, 1838, they had published (under William Howitt's name) *The Rural Life of England*.[3] Elizabeth Helsinger, in her study of how ruralism contributed to British nationalism after Waterloo, places the Howitts' work alongside Mary Russell Mitford's *Our Village* (1824–32); Mitford and the Howitts, she says, 'organized a national audience around personal and collective memories of rural English origins' and did so in conjunction with 'the rural landscapes that illustrate the lives and editions of English authors in the 1830s'.[4] Elizabeth Gaskell starts her career by aligning herself with ruralism of this kind – an alignment which influenced her subsequent fiction while the genre of ruralist writing bears more generally on the rural fiction of Gaskell's contemporaries and successors, including Hardy. How far it did so and in what ways are questions that can be answered only when this tradition of describing and valorizing rural landscapes has been looked at more closely.

William Howitt's *Rural Life in England* is constantly enthusiastic about the countryside:

> There is nothing which strikes foreigners so much as the beauty of our country abodes, and the peculiarity of our country life. The elegances, the arts, and refinements of the city, are carried out and blended, from end to end of the island, so beautifully with the peaceful simplicity of the country, that nothing excites more the admiration of strangers than those rural paradises, the halls, castles, abbeys, lodges and cottages, in which our nobility and gentry spend more or less of every year.
>
> (*Rural Life*, pp.3–4)

He urges his readership to take pride particularly in the dispersal of refinement from the city into the country. In earlier generations and still now in some of the remotest 'nooks' of the kingdom, country life is one of isolation, ignorance and 'the rust of whole ages'. Modernity, however, brings travel and commerce, linking town and country and able 'to diffuse education'. It brings newspapers to the country gentleman and, consequently, he

> sits in the midst of his woods and groves, in the quietness of the country a hundred miles from the capital, and is as well acquainted

with the movements and incidents of society as a reigning prince could have been some years ago.

(*Rural Life*, pp.12, 197, 219)

A similar marriage of progress and stability works to support the established social order in Edward Bulwer-Lytton, *England and the English*:

> What an enviable station is that of a great country gentleman in this beautiful garden of England [. . . .] In London, and in public life, we may improve the world [. . .] but we never *see* the effects we produce [. . .] in the country, if you exert equal industry and skill, you cannot walk out of your hall but what you see the evidence of your labours: Nature smiles in your face and thanks you. [. . .] above all, as you ride through your village, what satisfaction creeps around your heart.

Bulwer-Lytton's attachment to a ruralist image of England appears also in his *Eugene Aram* (1832); this begins in a 'sequestered hamlet' situated in 'a landscape [. . .] entirely lovely and picturesque' and made up of 'scattered cottages'; flowers, bees, blue smoke rising from chimneys all figure, making up collectively 'an English scene'; here attractiveness is joined to thrift: each cottage possesses 'at its rear its plot of ground apportioned to the more useful and nutritious product of nature; while the greater part of them fenced also from the unfrequented road a little spot for the lupin, the sweet pea, or the many tribes of the English rose'.[5]

In both Bulwer-Lytton and Howitt, the ruralist picture of England is at once progressive and nostalgic: Howitt is alarmed and saddened by the avarice and ignorance of remote districts untouched by commercial development. In such places, crimes are easily committed and with difficulty detected; solitary houses are full of dangers and terrors. On the other hand, Howitt condemns the capitalization of agriculture because it leads to larger farms ('a dozen of moderate farms are swallowed up in one overgrown one') and, in place of independent peasant farmers, produces an anonymous crowd of wage labourers. Factory methods leave 'almost all our working population cooped up in large towns in shops and factories'; similar methods applied to country life would be ruinous:

> what an England would it then be! The poetry and the picturesque of rural life would be annihilated; the delicious cottages and gardens, the open common, and the shouting of children would vanish; the scores of sweet old-fashioned hamlets, where an humble sociality and

primitive simplicity yet remain, would no more be found; all those
charms and amenities of country life, which have inspired poets and
patriots with strains and with deeds that have crowned England with
half her glory, would have perished[.]

(*Rural Life*, pp.101, 131)

Country life possesses the advantages of commercial development and
none of its drawbacks. It is both a retreat from industrialization and an
example to the industrialist of the society they ought to create. The
nationalism of the account is also very marked; it is concentrated, as in
Howitt's title, on England. Scotland and Wales appear in the book
almost exclusively as tourist locations.[6] The England of delicious
cottages and gardens is, moreover, distinctively southern:

There, on the edges of the forests, in quiet hamlets and sweet woody
valleys, the little grey-thatched cottages, with their gardens and old
orchards, their rows of beehives, and their porches clustered with
jasmines and roses, stand [. . . .] In many of the southern counties,
but I think nowhere more than in Hampshire, do the cottages realize,
in my view, every conception that our poets have given us of them[.]

(*Rural Life*, p.411)[7]

Cottages are not the only form of country life which Howitt praises but
they are pre-eminent, especially 'the sweetest paradises in the world –
the cottages of the wealthy and the tasteful'; these include 'the cottage,
formerly that of Mrs. Southey, at Buckland, on the border of the New
Forest; of Miss Mitford, at Three-Mile-Cross [*sic*]; or that of Wordsworth
at Rydal' (*Rural Life*, pp.412, 413).[8]

George Levine remarked of this landscape of 'country villages, gently
sloping hills, fertile lands' that it 'figures forth the life of moderate
expectations'; it is 'characteristically low and domesticated'. This landscape, he says: 'at once denies and imitates more absolute and frightening realities, and accommodates itself to the more subtle shades, the
less checkered pattern of the novelist's reality'.[9] The Victorian countryside of southern England is contrasted here with the Alps of Romanticism. It conforms to what Levine sees as the dominant intent of realism
– to counter the dangerous extremism of Romantic art. Howitt's text
suggests other motives: the more patriotic one that Helsinger noted and
a more progressive one. Howitt makes the near-contradictory claim that
the blended rural scene expresses modernity and, at the same time,
realizes the old ideal to which the modern, destructive world should be

redirected. The landscape represents moderation only in the limited sense that it embodies enlightened progress, by contrast with the wildness and backwardness of remote areas. Lancashire, according to Howitt, has been corrupted by industrialization; Yorkshire by contrast possesses a bulwark against corruption in its remote dales – these are 'perhaps the most perfect nook of the world that England holds' where, Howitt claims, in language recalling Wordsworth, 'the social sympathies are strongly called forth' and 'a sort of kinship seems to pervade the whole neighbourhood' (*Rural Life*, pp.226, 243). For Howitt, remoteness can either imply 'primitive simplicity' as here or eccentric narrowness; it depends to some extent on the point of contrast. Hampshire cottages provide, all the same, a third alternative, uniting simplicity and taste and, analogously, combining the benefits of commerce with the virtues of a country life.[10]

A tension remains in Howitt, nonetheless: for him, the country must be commercially in touch with cities and factories but still preserve its 'primitive simplicity'. His argument recalls the good landowner, as portrayed by Maria Edgeworth or Susan Ferrier, who improves as he preserves. Nevertheless, Howitt buries the novelists' recognition that improvement and preservation are in some respects at odds. Hampshire's cottages are idyll and ideal simultaneously. Their idyllic quality risks turning them into no more than a wishful alternative to industrialism – a more tender and comfortable version of the Yorkshire that Howitt opposed to Lancashire. At the same time, Howitt's praise of progress attempts perhaps too superficially to lessen that danger. The emphasis on cottages becomes greater as Howitt focusses more closely on Hampshire; earlier, he discussed halls, castles and farms as well with their economic foundations in agriculture and their role in local government. Through his praise of 'Cottage Life', however, Howitt turns the whole county into a kind of tasteful, well-appointed cottage; its landscape epitomizes the same retirement from and claim to be up-to-date with the modern, urban world.

Howitt's ruralism emphasizes 'the southern counties' and these become the location for 'the South' in Elizabeth Gaskell and others. Neither of these is quite the same conception as 'the south country', which developed gradually in the last quarter of the century. This later geography – linking up the southern counties along the ancient chalk-down ridgeways to recreate an old, intact kingdom, sometimes centred on Avebury – is closer to 'Englishness' in its nostalgia, antiquarianism and desire to escape to London. It develops in part from the late nineteenth-century celebration of the Thames Valley and has an important bearing on Kipling's Sussex. Hardy's Wessex lies just outside both versions of the south and responds over his career to the inflections of both.

Mary Russell Mitford's portrayal of ruralism appears broadly similar to Howitt's. Elizabeth Helsinger stresses Mitford's concern in sketching her village, Three Mile Cross, just south of Reading, with 'the rural scene as a socially organized space of exceptional stability and harmony'; people know each other there and they know their place within 'a hierarchical social structure'; moreover, Helsinger argues, Mitford's descriptions and stories 'translate public social problems into personal histories that can be more easily concluded, with fewer consequences for the stability of the larger society'.[11] Rural changelessness again contrasts with urban and industrial instability; simplicity and freedom in the country compare well with the crush, duplicity and exhaustion of city life. The rural as Mitford portrays it offers relief and security.

Helsinger is subtle in her account of how Mitford is disconcerted by the awareness that she is placing her rustics within pictures and so reducing them to picturesque types. The main focus of her discussion, however, is the contrast between Mitford and William Cobbett, whose *Rural Rides* were published in the same period. Cobbett, in Helsinger's view, encourages 'an active and critical understanding of the relations of power that tie local, rural places to national politics, economics and culture'; Mitford does the reverse: 'England for her is embodied in an idea of the local that obscures relations between rural locality and the larger nation.'[12] Howitt is implicated by Helsinger in the same disguise of the real – the attempt to substitute the rural for the national and, analogously, to solve 'public social problems' through 'personal histories'.

Paintings of rural scenes produced during the 1830s can be seen as committed to a similar programme; Helsinger stresses the importance of Constable to it and the disruptive power by contrast of Turner's *Picturesque Views in England and Wales*. Christiana Payne, discussing cottage scenes in particular, shows that their idealized portrayal was ideological:

> these paintings were perceived as having an influence lower down the social scale. Not only could they reassure their upper and middle class viewers, they could also act as models for the urban working class, who were regarded as lacking in those virtues which still survived in the countryside.

In an environment of urban chaos and agricultural unrest, cottage scenes employed the 'stability' of rural life to improve the morals of the deracinated urban poor and calm the fears of the wealthy. Payne reads the paintings in a context of moral instruction, giving less attention to political or nationalistic aims, but the interface between the two remains clear: 'The emphasis on virtue was, of course, an important component in the efforts [. . .] to combat poverty and revolution.'[13] Though with some qualifications, Howitt's *Rural Life of England* gives support to this overall view – that ruralist art worked to establish an idealized impression of country living, for the edification and encouragement of city-dwellers. The rural was represented as a lost world whose characteristic virtues of simplicity, mutual help and stability should and could be retrieved in the present.

Hardy's response to this well-established view of the countryside forty or fifty years afterwards is many-sided and complex. It is, in some respects, the subject of this book as a whole. Helsinger argues that the tradition founded by Constable and Tennyson survived until 1870 despite being contested by Cobbett, Turner and others; after 1870, she says, with the onset of agricultural depression, 'a nostalgic reappropriation of the rural scene as a cherished cultural memory' precipitated 'Englishness' from Constable's images and Tennyson's poetry.[14] In the process, it normalized Cobbett and simplified Mitford. If Hardy is read as a spokesman for ruralist nostalgia, then his works fit neatly into this historical thesis, confirming the gradual emergence of 'Englishness' from the 1870s on. Alternatively, within the same model, Hardy can be seen, like Cobbett, as remodelled by the sensibilities of Englishness so that he is perceived retrospectively as conforming more closely to its demands. This congruence with 'Englishness' can be seen as imposed on him or internalized by him.[15]

Hardy's novels, though, do not fit very neatly into this English tradition of 'nostalgic reappropriation of the rural scene'; instead of repeating the language and feeling characteristic of ruralist writing, they engage with it and the perceptions it implies. This is clearest perhaps from the opening of *The Woodlanders* where, in what has become a familiar passage, William Howitt's manner and vocabulary are evoked and obliquely challenged:

Thus they rode on, and High-Stoy Hill grew larger ahead. At length could be discerned in the dusk about half a mile to one side, gardens and orchards sunk in a concave, and as it were snipped out of the woodland. From this self-contained place rose in stealthy silence tall stems of smoke, which the eye of imagination could trace downward to their root on quiet hearthstones festooned overhead with hams and flitches.[16]

This, Hardy goes on to say, is 'one of those sequestered spots outside the gates of the world where may usually be found more meditation than action, and more listlessness than meditation'; here, 'dramas [. . .] truly Sophoclean are enacted in the real'. The importance to the novel (and to Hardy's work more generally) of the claims in this second sentence has thrown into the shade Hardy's preceding ones about Little Hintock's position within the landscape. Consider them, though, alongside these from Howitt's *Rural Life of England*:

> Often when I see those healthy, hardy, full-grown sons of the soil going out of town, I envy them the freshness and the repose of the spots to which they are going. Ample old-fashioned kitchens, with their chimney-corners of the true, projecting, beamed and seated construction, still remaining; blazing fires in winter, shining on suspended hams and flitches, guns supported on hooks above, dogs basking on the hearth below.
>
> (*Rural Life of England*, p.89)

Howitt's good cheer composes a setting out of components presented as familiar: chimney-corner, blazing fire, meat hanging from the ceiling, guns on the wall, dogs on the hearth. The listing of these items makes the old-fashioned into the well-known, the universally well-remembered. Howitt's interjection of more particular detail about the chimney-corners ('of the true, projecting, beamed and seated construction') makes his syntax awkward, leaving 'still remaining' a long way distant from its subject, 'kitchens'. Yet, again, the detail invites his reader to remember and discriminate. The specificity of his description caters to his audience's love of the already known and, simultaneously, demands that love. Readers are expected to know what he is referring to; part of enjoying the text consists in bringing to it the common, expert knowledge which it presupposes.

It is plain that Hardy's writing is more complex in its emotions and in how it plays on a reader's expectations. His diction repeatedly jars in small ways: '*sunk* in a concave' is a transparent idiom until it is placed alongside '*snipped* out of the woodland'. Similarly, '*quiet* hearthstones' is a conventional description which passes hardly noticed before Hardy adds 'festooned overhead with hams and flitches'. 'Festooned' has a grotesque quality, too boisterous for the quiet hearth and too flowery for meat. It sounds as if there may be a spectacular amount of ham. Howitt's imagining of plenty – '*Ample* old-fashioned kitchens' and '*blazing* fires' (my emphases) – is repeated here as a misplaced fantasy.

The 'eye of imagination' supposes the familiar conjunction of peace and prosperity; Hardy turns it into the outlandish mixture of 'quiet' and 'festooned' with the consequence that the clichéd image takes a kind of revenge. The 'stealthy silence' emerges retrospectively as at once reticent and threatening.

These dictional surprises are all the more prominent because they occur within such a conventional structure. Hardy seems to be following a traditional pattern of ruralist feeling and imagining, comparable to Howitt's, in order to disrupt its assumptions and point out its complacencies. That pattern, however, is still present and available: as the carriage travelled on, these things 'could be discerned' and, whether deceptively or not, the 'eye of imagination could trace' the smoke downward to hearth and fire. The modal 'could' – not 'should' or 'would' or 'might' – suggests narratorial neutrality while its repetition and the move from passive ('could be discerned') to active ('could trace') draw attention to the existence for the spectator of choice within possibility. Interpreting these phenomena and giving them a value are seen as subjective processes and yet treated like phenomena themselves. This tracing can happen; people habitually decide to read the countryside in this way. Not only, therefore, does Hardy acknowledge and resist the image of the country presented by Howitt and others like him, he also registers its assumption that everyone shares in this image and in the feelings that attach to it. His impassive recognition of 'the eye of imagination', with its falsities and power, has the effect of revealing the more clearly that Howitt's manner is coercive, tugging the reader into acceptance by raising in him or her the fear of ignorance and marginality. The presence of these stylistic surprises within a passage of apparently conventional sentiment corresponds to Hardy's accommodation and disturbance of an accepted picturing of rural England.

As Elizabeth Gaskell's affiliation with the Howitts makes likely, her novels of provincial life are frequently coloured by the ruralist tradition. The same can be said of George Eliot. Hardy's semi-parodic adoption of a ruralist vocabulary carries within it, therefore, not only a response to Howitt but a response to writers for whom Mitford and the Howitts were a point of reference and refuge. Clearly, however, neither Gaskell nor Eliot simply adopt Howitt or his and Mitford's 'idyllic realism'; both are at points sceptical about its claims and wary of its pattern of feeling. Other provincial novelists, notably Emily Brontë, ferociously attack the assumptions of the ruralist tradition. These assumptions appear to Brontë as characteristic of 'the provincial novel' – a genre she sees as innately patronizing. Partly as a consequence of the link between ruralism and provincial novels, Hardy's opening to *The Woodlanders* addresses not only ruralism but, through that style, the difficulties and paradoxes of writing provincial fiction.

Ruralism and the provincial novel

Literary historians usually date the beginning of provincial and/or regional fiction from the beginning of the nineteenth century, in the work of Maria Edgeworth and Walter Scott.[17] The genre as it first appears is usually said to be characterized by its portrayal of a particular locality, distant from the metropolitan centre. Where eighteenth-century picaresque novels tended to stereotype provincial characters (the stage Irishman, the gruff and tightfisted Scotsman), provincial/regional fiction is identified by its effort to offer a more precise and detailed depiction of people and communities outside the centre. Accordingly, the novels represented non-standard English as exactly as possible, gave instances of local customs without automatically deriding them as primitive and registered as significant the highly localized differences which habits of stereotyping ignored.[18]

It is arguable whether there is in fact a single, identifiable genre, appearing around 1800 and lasting until the present day, and called the provincial or the regional novel. Most recent work has assumed and sought to trace such a continuous thread, including within the same genre Edgeworth and Scott, George Eliot, early twentieth-century ruralists such as Constance Holme, and post-war writers as various as Alan Sillitoe, Pat Barker and Catherine Cookson. Doing so requires a loose definition of the genre but tends to impose a single definition nonetheless. K.D.M. Snell and W.J. Keith present such a set of characteristics for the genre; their chosen writers are judged according to how far they conform to the standard.[19] A vaguely defined but single account of the regional novel determines the merits of each example considered.

To my mind, the genre is less free-standing than such a history suggests: many novels with regional/provincial elements are not striving (or failing) to become fully-fledged regional/provincial novels. In the same way, the regional novel is not defined in theory beforehand and then the ideal realized more and more perfectly by the efforts of novelists over time. Such a model is unlikely to apply to the emergence of any genre and, in the case of regional/provincial novels, it obscures the disputes conducted within the novels over time.[20] Hardy writes at a particular moment within a historical sequence. The sequence starts in the localism of Edgeworth, Scott and others – a localism that was nationalist in its interests and cosmopolitan in its origins. This work contributes to the emergence of writing which is, in important respects, opposed to it: that is, both the provincial and anti-provincial novels written in England around mid-century (the Brontës, Gaskell, George Eliot); these in turn are followed by novels, like those of Trollope and Oliphant, which assimilate the provincial to the suburban, moving the rural from the distant provinces closer to the fringes of London and later, through a kind of counter-move, by 'the rural tradition' of the late nineteenth and early twentieth century – novels in which remoteness becomes the sign of authenticity.[21] Features used to characterize the regional/provincial novel – dialect; local, topographical detail; rurality – are to be found in each of these different types but they work to delineate quite different understandings of province, region and nation, centre and periphery. These understandings are reached, in part, through reflection on and dispute with earlier novels' presentation of the same phenomena, though the development is never the result solely of a dialogue within the genre. Other literature and historical change are involved as well. Hardy, who fits uncomfortably into the genre definitions made by Snell and Keith, makes better sense when placed within this chronology of novels and novelists.[22]

In the first kind of regional novel, the accurate delineation of topography, dialectal accent and local custom is achieved by means of annotations to the narrative text. In Edgeworth and Scott, glossaries are included for dialect words while footnotes or endnotes explain the curious local customs met with in the course of the story. Susan Ferrier's novels (*Marriage* (1818), *The Inheritance* (1824)) and those of Sydney Owenson, Lady Morgan (in particular, *The Wild Irish Girl* (1806) and *The O'Briens and the O'Flahertys. A national tale* (1827)) share this feature, though to a lesser degree.[23] These visible features (of style, presentation and proportion of description to narrative) can be correlated with these novels' wider purposes. Annotation and the difficulties surrounding its use reveal problems in the way these novels address their material – problems which later writers noticed and responded to. They provide a way into the tradition of writing about regions and provinces that Hardy inherited.

Katie Trumpener's recent work on the development of the Irish national tale and the Scottish historical novel makes the connection between how these novels address their subject and how extensively they employ annotation – footnotes, endnotes and glosses. Trumpener sees both the Irish and Scottish forms of regional/provincial writing as at once nationalist and cosmopolitan, romantic and enlightened:

> [they] continue to be centrally concerned with the claims of a bardic nationalism, and with the new sense of time and place it engenders, even while their plots of national survey continually invoke, revise, and revile the Enlightenment tours of inspection undertaken by figures such as Young and Johnson.[24]

Trumpener goes on to argue that this division between an Enlightenment disregard for cultural difference and a nationalist celebration of it becomes in Edgeworth a divided loyalty. Edgeworth is seen by her as, principally, a successor to Arthur Young, whose survey of Ireland catalogued its condition in order to ascertain how and where it might be most successfully 'improved'. Edgeworth's *Castle Rackrent* manifests this division in its use of both glossary and notes:

> Like Young, Edgeworth advocates the economic and political reconstitution of Ireland, and she is critical of antiquarian traditionalism as an impediment to this process. The regressive character of such traditionalism seems visible in the very conventions of antiquarian scholarship, as *Castle Rackrent*'s pseudo-antiquarian footnotes make clear. There the 'editorial' addition of layer after layer of glossing antiquarian footnotes weighs down the narrative action and slows the progress of the reading eye across the page.

Trumpener suggests that, for Edgeworth, this textual delay parallels antiquarianism's relation to modernization and shows cultural nationalism to be a regressive force. Yet, simultaneously, Edgeworth glosses the dialect of *Castle Rackrent*, showing greater sympathy for cultural nationalists because (again according to Trumpener) the glossary reveals the illegibility of Irish idioms, the difficulty of translating them, and therefore 'demonstrates continually how capaciously, how complicatedly cultural history and cultural practices are preserved – and rendered visible – within language itself'.[25]

This account of how annotation works in *Castle Rackrent* and of Edgeworth generally is open to question. The antiquarianism of the explanatory notes is not unequivocally 'pseudo-' nor clearly ironized; the glossary likewise may reveal the illegibility of Irish idioms without suggesting Edgeworth's sympathy for their preservation; glossing in itself implies a desire to translate the specific and local forms of language into terms which all may understand, whether or not that translation is seen as preserving the culture or erasing it in the interests of interchangeability. Edgeworth has been seen as complicit in the naturalization of Ireland and hence in its conquest by England; she has been seen too as actively supporting Irish customs and language and thus as part of the resistance to English hegemony.[26] Either way, and most importantly, she cannot help but occupy a mediating position. However one reads the impact of Edgeworth's various forms of annotation, they derive from an impulse to present local, exotic Ireland to an English-speaking and mostly distant readership unfamiliar with its distinctive features. Despite the differences in political position and cultural situation between Edgeworth and Scott, Scott's annotated texts similarly help the reader from outside to become familiar with a strange world.[27]

In both cases, annotation separates understanding from encounter; that is to say, unusual features, customs or idioms whose meaning remains doubtful to an outsider are explained in a footnote, rather than becoming gradually meaningful over the course of a story. In novels like *Waverley* or *Ennui*, a narrative of entry into an unfamiliar environment leads to the hero discovering the coherence of a backward community; that coherence will not save such communities from the forces of historical change, nor does it make them ideal and beyond improvement. Instead, it reveals the hero's tendency to a falsifying idealization of the remote.[28] Explanatory notes may express the respectful and clear-headed approach to strange cultures which is being sought by the narrative and manifested by the detail of its descriptive passages; both notes and precise description may jolt the reader out of the idealizing reverie enjoyed by the hero. They do so, however, by interrupting the hero's process of experiencing and coming to terms with a new world. In preventing fancifulness, they risk destroying a reader's openness to the unforeseen.

Annotation aims at explaining the true nature of things which it is easy to exoticise or to ignore. Usually in these texts, it accompanies precise observation and clear, detailed portrayal of places, costumes, customs and so on. Annotating a narrative of encounter risks foreclosing the reader's experience of encounter; likewise, an ideal of accurate representation endangers its objects of attention. Marilyn Butler has remarked about Edgeworth's portrayal of Irish types that

> many of the eloquent talkers briefly encountered in the Irish tales [. . .] benefit from the discontinuities of tone Edgeworth habitually uses, her practice of isolating a speech or an anecdote as a single event, unique to its place and time, which asks us to consider it just

as it is. [. . .] the shoeblack and his kind never become 'characters' [. . . .] They are more like passers-by snapped by a photographer, autonomous, resilient, and somewhat mysterious.[29]

This is well-put and perceptive. Edgeworth is, moreover, sensitive to the difficulties of accuracy: her writing recognizes the paradox that making people into 'characters' may be patronizing and yet denying them characterfulness may be to continue an isolation which the person described would rather overcome. Edgeworth does succeed (as Marilyn Butler says) in granting her eloquent talkers an autonomy that is denied to the 'stage-Irishman'. She gives them her unprejudiced and undivided attention. But honouring people with your undivided attention may be to grant them a special status which keeps them outside the world inhabited by the observer. Accuracy and stereotyping may equally prove to be methods of exclusion.

The special status of the observed object always presents a problem for science and an especially difficult one in the scientific study of human culture. It is hard for a scientist, particularly an anthropologist, to ensure that people are not adjusting their behaviour in response to the special conditions of being observed; secondly, the practice of 'isolating a speech or an anecdote', in order to observe it 'just as it is', may remove it from the context in which it has meaning, one possible element in that context being the observer. Accordingly, observations and notes which claim to present a provincial culture with objective accuracy may falsify it, even if unconsciously. Part of the falsity in the representation arises from the unusual relations set up between the observer and the observed.

Consider this example from Susan Ferrier's *Marriage*:

It was now Miss Nicky's turn.

'I'm afraid your Ladyship will frighten our stirks and stots with your finery. I assure you they are not accustomed to see such fine figures; and,' putting her hand out at the window, 'I think it's spitting already.'*

The authorial footnote at the asterisk reads: 'A common expression in Scotland to signify slight rain.'[30] This explanation clears up any possible confusion about 'spitting', so that a reader is not misled into thinking that the old Scots servant had odd ideas about the weather. At the same time, her seeming vulgarity is excused on the grounds that the expression is 'common' and so does not carry the coarse associations which it would in the mouth of an English character. Providing this information seems harmless enough and even rather helpful. It means, however, that the Scottish expression remains quaint; it becomes in fact all the more quaint for being explained. Including the phrase substantiates Ferrier's accuracy in her depictions of Scotland; the footnote claims authority for her in that respect while it also intends to forestall southern prejudice. These gains are achieved at the expense of reinforcing the idea that Scottish people are objects of curiosity.

At the same time, the dialect words 'stirks' and 'stots' are left unexplained. The Oxford editor glosses them as a phrase, 'bullocks and bulls', although they are probably more likely to mean 'bullocks and heifers', both words also being applied to foolish or clumsy people.[31] Publishing in Edinburgh may have meant that Ferrier was reluctant to explain terms which a large part of her audience already understood and added notes only where the Scottish expression could appear disreputable to strangers. The English reader would probably be left guessing about 'stirks and stots' (although both were used in northern and midland English dialects) but if so it would not matter much. The gist of Miss Nicky's speech comes through clearly enough; to an outsider, the unexplained words are meaningless rather than misleading. They create local colour and may safely do so as long as they remain inessential to the story.

This tiny moment in Ferrier's text serves to exemplify dangers which afflict the genre as a whole. These novels, whether called national tales, provincial fiction or regional novels, mediate a distant, usually rural community to an urban readership or to several differently distanced urban readerships. Striving for accuracy – within the prose as well as by annotating it – may obscure strangeness and so work against a narrative of maturation through experience; the same aim tends to objectify the observed, substituting a detached curiosity for previous disregard. Furthermore, the project of explaining a culture clashes with that culture's internal coherence and autonomy because the universal terms employed in explanation threaten to erode distinctiveness even when aiming to preserve it. Explanation competes too with aestheticization: 'stirks and stots' could be glossed but if the words remain obscure they gain an air of mystery and charm. Writers must choose on each occasion between clarity and glamour, judging their various audiences' willingness to tolerate or even to enjoy uncertainty and, on the other hand, their patience with explanations.[32]

Wuthering Heights demands that its audience learns to put up with uncertainty – a process which lies on a continuum with their beginning to accept mystery. At the beginning of the novel, Lockwood visits the remote, moorland farmhouse and construes it in the light of writing like Howitt's. The 'apartment' he enters, would he says 'have been nothing extraordinary as belonging to a homely, northern farmer, with a stubborn countenance [. . .] his mug of ale frothing on the round table before him'. Lockwood identifies the stereotype via an excited anti-quarianism, noting the occurrence of the expected elements:

> One end, indeed, [of the huge fire-place] reflected splendidly both light and heat from ranks of immense pewter dishes, interspersed with silver jugs and tankards, towering row after row, in a vast oak dresser, to the very roof. The latter had never been underdrawn: its entire anatomy lay bare to an inquiring eye, except where a frame of wood laden with oatcakes, and clusters of legs of beef, mutton and ham, concealed it. Above the chimney were sundry villainous old guns, and a couple of horse-pistols, and, by way of ornament, three gaudily painted canisters disposed along its ledge. [. . .] In an arch under the dresser, reposed a huge, liver-coloured bitch pointer, sur-rounded by a swarm of squealing puppies, and other dogs haunted other recesses.[33]

This description is at once visually precise – sometimes fussily techni-cal – and eagerly condescending. On the dresser, the 'pewter dishes' are '*interspersed* with silver jugs and tankards' while above the chimney are 'sundry *villainous* old guns' (my emphases). 'Interspersed', like 'dis-posed' a little later, would be appropriate in an exhibition catalogue. Lockwood deploys an aesthetic vocabulary firstly to indicate his high standard of cultivation while making these observations and equally his urban superiority to these essentially vulgar, though curious materials. 'Villainous' confirms his sense of superiority by being amused; the guns conform splendidly to Lockwood's expectations of roughness – a rough-ness he assumes can do him no harm. Amusement can modulate into sarcasm as when 'by way of ornament' refers to 'gaudily painted canis-ters' – these are, to Lockwood's eye, ugly and tasteless.

Overall, the furnishings of 'Wuthering Heights', like its location, prove it to be an instance of the rustic. If, in Howitt's writing, a univer-sal familiarity with rural life is presupposed (in order that his particular version of it can be made normative), then in Brontë's Lockwood inquiry replaces advocacy. The rural is standardized in the same way but Lockwood presents himself as having little more than an antiquarian interest in it. Howitt assumes the existence in himself and his reader-

ship of a harmlessly envious desire for the rural world's 'primitive simplicity'. Lockwood moves absurdly between brash detachment and over-
confident identification, seeing the place as engagingly backward and as
suiting him down to the ground. 'A perfect misanthropist's Heaven,' he
declares, 'and Mr Heathcliff and I are such a suitable pair to divide the
desolation between us. A capital fellow! He little imagined how my heart
warmed towards him.'[34] Through Lockwood, Brontë seems to be exposing the contradictory impulses unconsciously present in Howitt; the
drive, that is, at once to control the rural and to be imbedded in it.

Lockwood and Howitt both assume they know what they are talking
about – Howitt that his image and valorization of the country life is
accepted as true; Lockwood that the 'entire anatomy of the place lay
bare' to his 'inquiring eye'. Similarly, in the passage from *The Woodlanders*, the 'eye of imagination' generates its own image of the country,
amplifying and modifying what is actually 'discerned' according to
expectations and traditions from outside. Hardy is alert to (and resigned
to) the subjectivity of such perceptions, even though they have objective consequences. Brontë brings out how the arrogant visitor is wedded
to an objective understanding of his or her perceptions. 'Anatomy' and
'inquiring' both derive from a scientific vocabulary and Lockwood
believes himself to be equally a connoisseur and a scientist. Science,
though, has reductive effects. Because there is no ceiling, Lockwood
says, you can see the roofbeams, except where they are hidden by a
'frame of wood laden with oatcakes' and meat. He lacks the precise
terms to describe this object and, likewise, not having heard perhaps of
'flitches', he describes the hanging meat awkwardly as 'clusters of legs
of beef, mutton and ham'. 'Clusters' produces an incongruous effect
comparable to 'festooned' in Hardy's sentence, although for different
reasons; 'festooned overhead with hams and flitches' sounds like a
parody of Lockwood's aesthetic vocabulary (his use of 'interspersed' and
'disposed'); 'clusters of legs of beef' seems, by contrast, a consequence
of Lockwood's anatomizing pretensions. It aims at a neutral tone of
simple information-giving, rendering the unfamiliar via minutely
specific descriptions; the speaker assumes you will ignore moments
when this approach leads to jarrings of register or accidental oddness,
like 'clusters of legs'.[35]

In Lockwood's descriptions of the house and its inhabitants that open
the novel, Emily Brontë reveals his ruralist assumptions and, equally,
his pretensions to accurate description – his adoption, in other words,
of the postures of enlightened visitor and provincial novelist, capable
of portraying the unusual and accounting for its unusualness. His sub-

sequent discomfiture is paralleled by the novel's reluctance to explain and be explained. Heathcliff's servant, Joseph, speaks as follows in the second chapter:

> 'Aw woonder hagh yah can faishion tuh stand thear i' idleness un' war, when all on 'em's goan aght! Bud yah're a nowt, and it's noa use talking – yah'll niver mend uh yer ill ways; bud goa raight tuh t' divil, like yer mother afore ye!'

Brontë's exact transliteration of Yorkshire speech obstructs a reader's understanding. There is little here that deserves glossing – most of the speech is close to standard English, despite the accent – and certainly Brontë provides none.[36] Accuracy in this case seems restricted to presentation, a phonetic transcription that refuses to accept the duty of representation. Making sense and discovering significance remain the reader's task. This is emphasized by Lockwood's blunders in the same chapter: he mistakes dead rabbits for kittens and repeatedly misconstrues the family relations of the household. He even takes this speech to be directed at himself although Joseph is actually speaking to the younger Catherine. In these respects the chapter epitomizes the novel as a whole. In *Wuthering Heights*, local characteristics can be recorded while the world they occupy cannot be defined. Brontë's multiple narrators offer a series of accounts which judge very differently Heathcliff and Catherine; cumulatively, they move the reader towards acknowledging elusiveness. Uncertainty about the nature and worth of the relationship between the novel's leading characters corresponds to the reader's discovered inability to judge provincial life. For Emily Brontë, genuine accuracy prevents understanding by continually revealing the limiting effect of an observer's presuppositions. The genuine remains beyond reach, in the case of both the love between Heathcliff and Catherine and the life of provincial folk.[37]

Emily Brontë, then, resists the presumptions of provincial novels and the quaintness of ruralist perceptions. Both, according to *Wuthering Heights*, conspire to mask the provincial, forcing it under their gaze into a parody of itself or a version that suits the perceiver's expectations. Accurate depiction becomes inaccurate as soon as it seeks either to justify local distinctiveness or to make it an object of comparison. Her novel, in other words, seeks to dictate absolutely the terms of the mediation between province and centre which it cannot help but perform. Though less forthright and less uncompromising than Emily Brontë, Hardy's work similarly recognizes the invasive force of quaintness and presumption. The different form of his opposition to the same enemies (ruralist and provincialist assumptions) does not derive simply from temperamental differences, even though personally Hardy was more compromising and secretive than Emily Brontë. Hardy's work appears soon after the great achievements of the English provincial novel made by George Eliot and Elizabeth Gaskell, whereas Emily Brontë's come before. His writing has to negotiate with their culturally authoritative and complex accounts of provincial life, its relation to the centre and the blessings of rurality.

George Eliot and Elizabeth Gaskell: provincial novelists

George Eliot was seen by reviewers of Hardy's early novels as possibly their author or, if not, then their dominant influence. This identification bears witness to Eliot's high reputation at the time (Margaret Oliphant's Carlingford novels were also thought to be written by George Eliot, even though they now seem much nearer to Trollope); nonetheless, Hardy's early fiction, *Under the Greenwood Tree* (1872) and *Far from the Madding Crowd* (1874) in particular, echo and rival Eliot's novels written ten or fifteen years before, especially *Adam Bede* (1859). George Eliot's novels evidently contain ruralist elements; they admire the beauty of a country landscape dotted with nestling cottages and peaceful villages. At the same time, they presented particular localities and communities so accurately that readers claimed to identify the real people represented by her characters. Her realism extended also into plots which could focus on alcoholism and domestic violence, on infanticide as well as seduction. Eliot's willingness to approach subject-matter which disturbs the rural idyll is coupled with the momentum in her narratives towards repentance and reform. Hetty cannot be saved but Adam can and does learn through his (and her) suffering; Janet, the abused wife in 'Janet's Repentance', is redeemed by her love for the Christ-like curate, Edward Tryan; most plainly of all, *Silas Marner* recounts a fable of sin and redemption, centred on Silas and with corollaries in the experience of Godfrey, Eppie's father who disowns her, and his wife, Nancy. Consequently, where Maria Edgeworth's writing risks turning the local into an object, George Eliot's may make it into an instance. The tensions and contradictions which characterize anthropology are less important here than the difficulty of reconciling a mimetic ideal with a moral one.

The later sections of *Adam Bede* and *Silas Marner* are repeatedly concerned with the impossibility of undoing the past – sometimes it is, George Eliot insists, really too late to mend. 'No – O God, no,' Adam groaned out, '[. . .] *it can never be undone*. My poor Hetty' and later, speaking to Arthur, 'I don't see how the thing's to be made other than hard. There's a sort of damage, sir, that can't be made up for.' Godfrey says to Nancy in *Silas Marner*, at the end of chapter 20, 'perhaps it isn't too late to mend a bit there. Though it *is* too late to mend some things, say what they will.'[38] The novel's weight of fact aims to obstruct a pat morality, which would underestimate the cost of misery by seeing it as purgatorial. Similarly, in 'Janet's Repentance', Eliot is concerned to show that the divine of orthodox religious belief appears in the human – that it is, in fact, only human.[39] The text's realistic detail corresponds to its human-centred idea of divine love. The archetypal quality of Eliot's narratives means, then, that their local detail serves as a clothing around these examples of universal laws and conditions; at the same time, her humanism lends a moral purpose to detailed representations – they can hold back judgement and encourage true understanding of others, of oneself and of the holy.[40] From the first perspective, Eliot's localities are dispensable – their worlds are scenes for allegories, possessing a fairy-tale minuteness and exemplarity. From the second perspective, the details and the detailing are both symbolic; they express the capacity to attend sympathetically.

Consequently, geography matters less in her work than one might expect. It is possible, from external evidence, to work out where her novels are set; just from reading them, however, one cannot tell. Henry Auster remarks of these early works:

> although their locale is recognizably that of the Midlands, there is nothing insistent or inevitable about that identification, as there is, say, with Hardy's Wessex. Phyllis Bentley, in defining George Eliot's regionalism, finds that her 'fictitious topography is extensive and corresponds fairly closely to reality, but it does not draw the reader's attention as does that of Trollope'.[41]

Characteristically, a setting is given near the beginning of her novels and then its geographical position is allowed to slip into the background as events unfold within a single community, whose structure, tensions and changes epitomize those beyond.[42] The local becomes the world in miniature, recognizably within the pastoral tradition and released from the recognitions which a more specific geography would bring in its train. The local setting possesses stability, despite being surrounded by and on the brink of change, and thus figures the universality of the conflicts portrayed.[43] Secondly, however, the stable, rural world is responsive to careful attention. The landscapes of ruralism – with hedgerows, hidden flowers, secret recesses, nestling cottages – stand in contrast to those of industrial modernity and symbolize the compassionate regard which the novels aim to encourage.[44]

Elizabeth Gaskell's provincialism appears to be more concerned than Eliot's with the qualities of particular places. As we have seen, one of her affiliations is to the rural nostalgia of the Howitts and her work as a whole has frequently been read as radically divided between country and city – between fondly imagined rural idylls and meticulously realistic portrayals of contemporary urban life.[45] In the second of these roles, Gaskell was seen by some of her contemporaries as 'bent on doing for Lancashire and the Lancashire dialect what Miss Edgeworth did for Ireland and Scott for the land across the border'.[46] Her first novel, *Mary Barton: A Tale of Manchester Life* (1848) includes dialect words, glossed in footnotes, and in the fifth edition (1854) she added *Two Lectures on the Lancashire Dialect* written by her husband. It may seem, therefore, all the odder to argue, as I do, that her work runs against Scott and Edgeworth when in addition to these features it characteristically argues for reconciliation between warring factions: North and South, master and man, Anglican and Dissenter, ancient and modern are repeatedly differentiated by her novels and set against one another. Conflict teaches characters in her narratives to desire 'that a perfect understanding, and complete confidence and love, might exist between masters and men; that the truth might be recognized that the interests of one were the interests of all'. Gaskell's writing consistently seeks to resolve conflicts by instilling in her readership an awareness of mutual dependency. Her aim of helping to harmonize a divided nation resembles Scott's argument, presented most explicitly in *Waverley* itself, in favour of a marriage between Lowland and Highland Scottish cultures. Likewise Gaskell's ideal factory owner is akin to Edgeworth's ideal landowner; both see the need for 'educated workers, capable of judging, not mere machines of ignorant men', and both aim to substitute mutually respectful relations for tyranny and enslavement, whether that of colonial rule or of *laissez-faire* capitalism.[47]

Nonetheless, there are differences. John Lucas, comparing Gaskell with George Eliot, sees a disagreement over progress:

Mrs Gaskell was very conscious of George Eliot's approach to history and of her positivistically derived belief in social evolution. But though such an approach can sometimes be detected in *Sylvia's Lovers* it isn't at all part of Mrs Gaskell's historical imagination.

From this standpoint, Lucas has to derogate the assertions Gaskell does make about the superiority of the present day over the past; these come, he says, from 'the primly complacent official Mrs Gaskell', discernible when 'a brisk no-nonsense air [. . .] comes over the prose'.[48] All these epithets sound off-beam but the fundamental insight is convincing, the more so by contrast with Joseph Kestner's emphasis on 'assimilation':

> Gaskell's focus in *North and South* (1855) is on transition and assimilation. [. . .] Assimilation is the concept uniting the stories of Margaret Hale and the manufacturer John Thornton, as well as most of the remaining characters in the novel. [. . .]
> If Margaret Hale's growth in self-awareness leads to assimilation, Gaskell is equally concerned with the corresponding process in her factory owner John Thornton.[49]

In the novel, however, Margaret does not exactly assimilate to the new environment and culture of Milton Northern. At its close, when she is united with John Thornton, he draws out 'his pocket-book, in which were treasured up some dead flowers'. These prove to be roses picked at Helstone, the place where Margaret grew up and John explains: 'I wanted to see the place where Margaret grew to what she is, even at the worst time of all, when I had no hope of ever calling her mine.' His words imply an apology for trying to change her from 'what she is' and affirm that their marriage will be based upon mutual acceptance amidst difference. If this is assimilation, it does not involve acculturation or adaptation; tolerance of and respect for difference are the key factors and 'growth in self-awareness' brings with it a greater awareness of the distinctiveness enjoyed by other people.[50]

Evidently, however, Gaskell places this discovery in a novel depicting both personal growth and improvement over the generations. Margaret's parents fare less well than she does; John's mother remains prejudiced against her future daughter-in-law. Progress of a kind occurs in the novel but, all the same, Lucas's judgement seems right: Margaret's development is presented in moral more than historical terms, as if she would need to learn her lesson at any time and place; moreover, the novel represents a form of progress in which paradoxically nothing is changed: north and south remain what they were, if anything more finely discriminated at the end of the novel than at the beginning. Analogously, Gaskell's novels tend towards stasis. *North and South*, as is well-known, hurries to its end, cramming incidents into the final chapters. This happens because earlier events have been dwelt on so long. In

Sylvia's Lovers a similar pattern of long delay followed by sudden, rapid eventfulness is used to convey the experience of enforced passivity, especially among women. Gaskell focusses on this condition, more interested in its nature than in protesting against it or seeking a remedy. And, characteristically, her work delineates situations, especially group situations, identifying the various, equally valid perspectives that are brought to bear at and on a particular moment.

Likewise, Gaskell's sense of science differs from that of Edgeworth or Scott. Her lack of deep investment in ideas of progress means that her novels move towards coexistence rather than unity. That is reflected by her writing's continually articulating the unspoken feelings of reticent, secondary characters, paying heed to their separate autonomy in a crowded room and an unthinkingly oppressive world. Likewise, science in her novels appears as a study of a specific object or creature. She places little emphasis on its power to classify, its creation of a system which turns particular things into instances of or variants upon a larger class. Roger Hamley in *Wives and Daughters* is her most developed portrait of a scientist and is presented as first and foremost a collector of specimens. He finds Molly in tears, early on in the story, and is able to help her, because he is such a good naturalist:

> He did not see Molly as he crossed the terrace-walk on his way homewards. He had gone about twenty yards on the small wood-path at right angles to the terrace, when, looking among the grass and wild plants under the trees, he spied out one which was rare, one which he had been long wishing to find in flower, and saw it at last, with those bright keen eyes of his. Down went his net, skilfully twisted so as to retain its contents, while it lay amid the herbage, and he himself went with light and well-planted footsteps in search of the treasure. He was so great a lover of nature that, without any thought, but habitually, he always avoided treading unnecessarily on any plant; who knew what long-sought growth or insect might develop itself in what now appeared but insignificant?[51]

Roger's actions as a scientist are scrupulously unintrusive because he is so deeply attached to what he studies. The same could be said of Gaskell's novels; author and character are equally protective of the odd things – 'growth' and 'insect' both carry unpalatable connotations – which 'might develop' themselves within the apparently insignificant. In Gaskell's mind, even a collector (perhaps a collector most of all) cherishes the autonomy of the thing collected.[52]

Gaskell's science, like the structure of her plots and her pleas for coexistence based on tolerance and mutual respect, all work against the more assimilating tendencies of regional fiction from the Romantic period. Emily Brontë's violent hostility to observation is matched in Elizabeth Gaskell by the search for forms of observation and depiction which leave the object able to develop itself and allow the person, like Margaret, to remain 'what she is'. Her ideal of attentive scrutiny resists the unifying pretensions of scientific objectivity accepted to differing degrees by Scott, Edgeworth and their contemporaries. Instead, for Gaskell, proper attention reveals the distinctive and autonomous forms present in an infinitely varied world. Yet distinctiveness and autonomy occur, predominantly, in the rural world: Gaskell's scientist is a naturalist, treasuring wild flowers, insects and the 'treasures of nastiness' dredged from ponds and ditches. In this incident, that endeavour leads him to find Molly, privately distraught about her father's remarriage, on 'the hidden seat under the ash-tree' where she breaks out 'with a suppressed passion of grief'. The rare plant in flower and Molly in distress are drawn together so that her hidden life promises to be understood and cherished by Roger in the same way that he treasures natural things. The foundation of their later marriage is hinted at here. At the same time, Gaskell locates Molly's inner life within the woodland, as if her true feelings and essential nature were present here as nowhere else. Similarly, John Thornton carries in his wallet flowers from Helstone which represent Margaret's inner being.[53]

Gaskell's continued similarity to the Howitts emerges, then, not so much through a celebration of the rural world – in fact, in *North and South*, she is unusually critical of such sentimental delusions; instead, Gaskell portrays the inner life via rural images so that, even in the city and even when showing the merits of industrial life, as in *North and South*, truth and genuineness still seem part of a rural world.[54] This alignment continually qualifies the objectivity of Gaskell's gaze, turning her science into a pastoral, but at the same time it helps her to join autonomy to harmony. That is to say, properly discerning the personal and distinctive reveals the inner life which becomes, in Gaskell's lexicon, something like a flower. Such flowers conjure up a world of mutual regard – in Howitt's words, one 'of primitive simplicity and humble sociality' – and they bring such a world to life in the actions of Roger Hamley and John Thornton. Both men behave respectfully, humbly and affectionately towards the women whom they see most clearly via flowers.[55] Consequently, Gaskell can seem to be doing two things at once: claiming to respect the absolute individuality of different people and places and, simultaneously, finding a language in which they prove to be parts of one another, implicitly harmonized by the rural heritage they share. Her provincial worlds enjoy, therefore, an ambiguous self-sufficiency; their exact depiction will not, ideally, reduce or violate them yet in its ideal form such depiction will uncover naturally occurring sources of unity between different places. For Gaskell, human brotherhood will overcome all barriers erected by national or religious allegiance even though it is represented in and through a distinctively English rurality. The dividedness of Gaskell originates in the contradiction that all provinces are different and equally valuable yet, at the same time, to truly appreciate the provincial, you must see it as the rural. The southern English landscape celebrated by Mitford and the Howitts becomes in Gaskell an emblem of both the inner life and the form of attention which values the inner life of others. Because that attention is seen as scientific and is practised by the forward-thinking, modernity is made (as in the Howitts) into the means of restoring social harmony. Science discloses what it practises, a mutuality that is natural.[56]

As is made most clear in *The Woodlanders*, perhaps, for Hardy science has disclosed a world of mutual predation, where trees growing close together 'rub each other into wounds'. Scientific inquiry is viewed with equal suspicion: when pursued wholeheartedly, as in *Two on a Tower*, it engenders an innocent ignorance of sexual feeling and a disillusioning, inhuman perspective on the ordinary scale of life to which we are confined. It can have the same impact on an amateur, like Henry Knight in *A Pair of Blue Eyes*, whose sensitivity towards Elfride is not enhanced by his knowledge of fossils or his aquarium full of zoophytes and shells.[57] Though Fitzpiers in *The Woodlanders* is at times 'a real inquirer', his science principally has the effect of making him more than ever fascinating to the local people. Mutuality is not achieved so much as the social structure reinforced.

These examples show not only Hardy's Darwinian perspective on nature but the overlap between science and questions of community and rurality. Fitzpiers enters *The Woodlanders* carrying an association with the progressive possibilities of a scientific future and, by living in a rural world, he could be used to show the emergence of a beneficial harmony between old and new.[58] Consequently, his character and behaviour, as they gradually emerge through the novel, work against the ideal which Elizabeth Gaskell presents in Roger Hamley. Hardy's presentation of science and scientists through Fitzpiers corresponds to the rest of the novel's engagement with a ruralist ideal, an engagement which informs other novels as well and their subsequent organization within Wessex.

Hampshire, ruralism and *Tess*

As well as presenting a view of rural life in general which Hardy throws into doubt, the ruralist tradition within the Victorian provincial novel also celebrated in particular the rural life of Hampshire. Hardy's work is influenced by this choice; his Wessex includes 'Upper Wessex', corresponding to Hampshire, though comparatively little use is made of it as a location. The novels and stories are concentrated on 'South Wessex' (Dorset) but move beyond it quite frequently to places in the other counties of Wessex. It is notable, however, that Wintonchester (Winchester, Hampshire) occurs much less frequently than Melchester (Salisbury, Wiltshire). A tendency to avoid Hampshire is coupled with the particular associations Hardy gives to Hampshire locations when he chooses them; both his use and avoidance of Hampshire are coloured by the period's established cultural geography.

Hampshire's prominence in novels more easily aligned with ruralism can be illustrated from *North and South*. Margaret Thornton's childhood home, Helstone, is located both vaguely and recognizably: it lies quite close to, though not on, a railway route to London and Margaret dislikes the close proximity of 'shoppy people' who have made their money in Southampton. It is surrounded by forest – trees broken up by commons and a few fields. This New Forest setting is reached from Oxford by a cross-country train journey in which Margaret sees

> the old south country-towns and hamlets sleeping in the warm light of the pure sun [. . . .] Broods of pigeons hovered around these peaked, quaint gables, slowly settling here and there, and ruffling their soft, shiny feathers, as if exposing every fibre to the delicious warmth.

This passage opens the chapter describing Margaret's visit home during which she is troubled by changes and improvements wherever she turns. These make up her first experience of the world's instability, as Gaskell remarks through Mr Bell, and they lead to a despondency which is relieved only when she accepts her own changeability. Margaret decides, at the chapter's end, not to visit Helstone again even though she realizes she is still attached to it and will always be so: 'Oh, Helstone! I shall never love any place like you.' 'Helstone' seems to be named after Caroline Helstone, the heroine of Charlotte Brontë's *Shirley*;

in Brontë's novel, Caroline's experience takes her from repression and misery to a marriage of reconciliation. Margaret's path is similar. Consequently, Helstone is praised unequivocally only as it is left behind; early in the novel it is damp, confined and 'relaxing' (in the sense of enervating); later, Mr Bell discovers that its primitiveness is violent. Gaskell seems close to the Howitts in arguing that rurality needs to be joined to modernity before it will reveal its supportive strength.[59]

There was a railway line running from Oxford to Southampton direct, via Didcot, Newbury and Winchester; the halts between the last two are evocatively rural: Woodhay, Highclere, Burghclere, Litchfield, Whitchurch and Sutton Scotney. Gaskell evokes this rural world as rather like 'the warm south' of Keats's odes with resident, brooding pigeons occupying the place of Keats's departing swallows. Their luxurious restfulness confirms the lack of any danger here. Instead, tranquillity and peace provide solace which, in turn, leads to insight. In a similar sequence in *Sylvia's Lovers*, Philip Hepburn, Sylvia's estranged husband, returns to England wounded and scarred from fighting in the Napoleonic wars; he lands at Portsmouth and sets off on foot north towards his home in Monkshaven (Whitby, North Yorkshire). On the way, he finds himself 'drawing near a stately city, with a great old cathedral in the centre keeping solemn guard'. Here he finds welcome and shelter in the medieval almshouses of St Sepulchre, modelled on those of St Cross near Winchester, that city lying on the route Philip would have taken. Philip is fortunate enough to be granted permission to remain permanently at St Cross if he wishes as one of its bedesman. Staying there over the winter, he recovers his health but soon after decides he must go home. He is 'restless and uneasy in the midst of all this peace and comfort'; however, he only resolves finally to go after reading the tale of Sir Guy and Lady Phillis from the *Seven Champions of Christendom* – a book which he finds by accident in his room. The lives of the medieval lovers mirror Philip's situation very closely, and Gaskell adds:

> The old room, the quiet moonlit quadrangle into which the cross-barred casement looked, the quaint aspect of everything that he had seen for weeks and weeks; all this predisposed Philip to dwell upon the story he had just been reading as a faithful legend of two lovers whose bones were long since dust.

Thinking about the story as a faithful legend impels Philip to travel on and by doing so he brings about a reconciliation with his wife, albeit a brief and in many ways painful one. The place he leaves has created the stillness in which he can discover the right way forward. Both story and medieval almshouse appear 'quaint', antique structures misplaced in a modern world. Indeed, Gaskell draws attention to the likely fancifulness of the story and the peculiar customs of the almshouses. Yet these outdated things prove necessary, offering an example of ideal behaviour and a place in which it can be absorbed. The incident makes a subtle and discreet defence of imaginative writing, Gaskell's included. Secondly, though, it repeats the pattern of *North and South* in arguing that out-of-the-way, quiet places provide sustenance for those who live in bustle and busyness. A traditional rural world may be 'quaint' but it offers nonetheless access to truth – in Margaret's case, a person's truest and best nature; for Philip, the course of action that is right for him.

Gaskell, then, is employing a well-established geography to aid the recognition of 'south' in *North and South*, centring rural England on Hampshire. Moreover, her writing supports the link between this part of the country and quintessential England – the England within us all and image of our mutual life. By comparison, Hardy's writings conspicuously avoid Hampshire, entering it rather infrequently, and what references do occur are increasingly uneasy. The county becomes, as Hardy's career continues, a place of endings and failed escapes. Southampton figures in *Desperate Remedies* and, more fleetingly, in *A Pair of Blue Eyes*, *The Hand of Ethelberta* and *Two on a Tower*. In each case, the town remains a comparatively anonymous transit point, where people change trains or catch boats; similarly, in *The Trumpet-Major*, Portsmouth is referred to several times as the naval base where Bob Loveday embarks and lands. Winchester, Ringwood, the New Forest and other places in Hampshire are barely mentioned in the *œuvre* until the 1890s.[60]

At the close of *Tess*, Angel Clare and Tess take flight from her murder of Alec by travelling north, believing that the south coast ports will be guarded; from Sandbourne (Bournemouth), their journey takes them 'into the depths of the New Forest' where they hide for some days in the empty mansion, 'Bramshurst Court' (based on 'Moyles Court, three miles north-north-east of Ringwood').[61] There they are safe, until the weather changes, lifting a dense fog and prompting the caretaker's return – to 'air [the] house thoroughly on such a day'. The mansion provides an idyllic retreat for the lovers yet the wooded landscape and the foggy weather connect it with 'The Chase' from earlier in the novel. On the night when he violates Tess, Alec calls 'The Chase', 'the oldest wood in England', takes Tess there and gets conveniently lost, again in fog. '[O]wing to this fog which so disguises everything,' Alec says, 'I don't quite know where we are myself.'[62] These reminders mean that, although Tess does find peace in the New Forest, it depends upon her 'absolute seclusion' and on their making 'fire without smoke'. This hiddenness can last, it is felt, only so long, given that other people are present within the forest as much as outside it. The New Forest is peopled by intruders on Tess's privacy; in that respect, it is no different from anywhere else.

Secondly, Hardy mentions that Bramshurst Court is for rent: this 'desirable Mansion to be Let Furnished'; its availability is another reminder of Alec, whose house 'The Slopes' is also separated from the surrounding land which it seems to command. It is a 'country-house built for enjoyment pure and simple', rather than 'a manorial home in the ordinary sense'; and although it stands within sight of 'The Chase', 'a truly venerable tract of forest land', Hardy adds that, 'All this sylvan antiquity [. . .] was outside the immediate boundaries of the estate' (Hardy, *Tess*, ch.5, p.41). Bramshurst Court is less garish than The Slopes, but Hardy creates these hints of similarity both to suggest that the threat from Alec has not disappeared despite his death and to rob Tess's retreat of the security which she desires and the audience would associate with the New Forest.[63] The detail that Bramshurst Court is for rent implies that the England's most venerable forest participates in a national economy.[64]

Hampshire's resonance for Hardy emerges too in *A Group of Noble Dames* (1890, 1891), written as he revised *Tess* for serial publication. Several stories in the collection have Hampshire connections: 'Lady Mottisfont' opens in Wintonchester (Winchester) and the action takes place at Deansleigh Park (Broadlands, west of Romsey); Lady Icenway, in the story of that name, marries twice, the second time to Lord Icenway and moves to his seat 'beyond Wintonchester' (probably Herriard House, south of Basingstoke); the ninth of the ten stories, 'The Duchess of Hamptonshire', is set 'in the neighbourhood of Batton', though exactly where Hardy intends by this remains uncertain (perhaps Tottenham House, Wiltshire, southeast of Marlborough). This story is older: it was first published in 1878 and again, revised, in 1884; the version in *A Group of Noble Dames* is the only one to refer to 'Hamptonshire' (Pinion, *Hardy Companion*, pp.61–2, 93–4, 238, 294, 373). The Duke of Hamptonshire is an abusive husband; Lord Icenway grows 'crustier and crustier' as he grows older; Lady Mottisfont brings up her husband's illegitimate daughter but abandons her as soon as she has children of her own and the daughter later marries a road-contractor: 'in the heart of this worthy man of business the poor girl found the nest which had been denied her by her own flesh and blood of higher degree'.[65] In the collection, homeliness is linked to happiness and aristocracy to violence and oppression; this opposition is frequently gendered – where women are in the ascendancy ordinary, unpretentious pleasures survive – and it is often mapped onto counties: within Dorset, the stories are more likely to end on a note of muddle and success; outside, and especially in Hampshire, they end in rigid misery.

Likewise, 'Master John Horsleigh, Knight', first published in 1893 and collected in *A Changed Man* (1913), is set in the New Forest in the sixteenth century. Horsleigh hides his legal wife at 'Oozewood' (Ringwood), and appears publicly as still married to someone else. The public marriage is invalid because the woman, although believing herself a widow, has a husband living. Horsleigh's secrecy is tactful and accepted by his legal wife; the arrangement is practical and their marriage loving. It comes to grief when the wife's brother discovers the arrangement, misreads it, feels dishonoured and murders Horsleigh. As early as the sixteenth century, therefore, the New Forest offered only a fragile retreat from the world's invading oppressions. Hardy seems to be suggesting that the site of remoteness and seclusion has never offered the security connected with it and claimed for it. Not only do tyrants from abroad, like William Rufus, die there but so do innocent, decent men.[66]

Hardy chooses the New Forest for Tess's last attempt at escape partly in order to suggest that a circle is being closed. What happened on 'The Chase' led to Tess's wandering around 'South Wessex', as far west as Emminster and south as far as Wellbridge and Sandbourne; at the moment when she has tried definitively to free herself – by murdering Alec and running away with Angel – the choice of route returns her to the beginning of her social exclusion and imprisonment, 'The Chase' lying just a few miles to the west of the route she follows through the forest. At the same time, however, the New Forest is a choice dictated by Hardy's decision to locate Alec's murder in Sandbourne (Bournemouth). Since 1974, Bournemouth has been part of Dorset but before that time it lay in Hampshire, the county boundary running between Poole, the older settlement, and the new resort rapidly growing a few miles to the east. Hardy shows this on his own map of Wessex, marking with a dotted line the boundary that separates Bournemouth and Poole, Sandbourne and Havenpool.

The opening of chapter 55 of *Tess* gives a description of Sandbourne which connects it to Alec d'Urberville's home 'The Slopes' – the town is another 'glittering novelty' on 'the very verge of that tawny piece of antiquity', Egdon Heath. His other 1890s novels present the same image: in *The Well-Beloved*, the youngest Avice settles down in Sandbourne with her husband Henri, leaving Pierston to embark on unromantic if practical improvements to the 'Street of Wells' (Fortune's Well, Portland). In the earlier version, *The Pursuit of the Well-Beloved*, although Avice's final destination is not given, the action is concentrated on Budmouth instead of Sandbourne. In *Jude the Obscure*, Sue's undergraduate friend and would-be lover 'came home merely to die' and Sue 'went down to Sandbourne to his funeral'. The place seems to epitomize for Hardy a soulless modernity; Angel Clare sees it, in phrases reminiscent of Dickens, as 'a fairy palace suddenly created by the stroke of a wand, and allowed to get a little dusty'.[67]

Hardy makes few references to Sandbourne's county; as far as I know, it is only in *Tess* that he mentions it at all (a little later on as 'the boundary between Upper and Mid-Wessex' (Wiltshire and Hampshire) which the lovers cross after leaving Bramshurst).[68] He prided himself on being generally less concerned with counties, county identities and county loyalties than other writers. On this subject, he could clearly differentiate himself from William Barnes to whom in other respects he owed so much.[69] If its county location is forgotten or deliberately set aside, then Sandbourne possesses a force within Wessex. It is seen as bringing modern, foreign ways right into Tess's country and this implies that county boundaries have become irrelevant to locality, given the new economic and social conditions of the late nineteenth century. Counties have become, from this perspective, inherently nostalgic. When Angel Clare travels to Sandbourne, he finds it hard to imagine Tess in this new and exotic environment, dislocated from her rural life; yet there Tess is. Her 'country' extends beyond the limits he would place around it in the same way that her personality contains more variety and possibility than he would perhaps like. Confining Tess within rurality would find an equivalent in insisting on counties as separate, distinctive territories and of making county boundaries less permeable than they actually are.

What importance counties had or should have was disputed during the nineteenth century with, generally speaking, progressive opinion arguing against and reactionary opinion arguing in their favour. In Hardy's lifetime, the balance between central and local government oscillated – centralization was forwarded by the Public Health Act of 1848, local authority by the Local Government Act of 1858.[70] The resurgence of local power was matched by a widespread preoccupation with localism and decentralization among mid-century historians, who as

John Burrow establishes saw these as English qualities by contrast, first and foremost, with the centralizing French. The 1850s and 1860s saw the highpoint of 'Respect for local initiative and community' and was followed by their gradual weakening during the last quarter of the century. That decline coincided, ironically, with the establishment of county councils in 1888 and more broadly with the rise of county archaeological and antiquarian societies, culminating in the *Victorian County History* whose multi-volume histories of the counties began to appear in the 1890s.[71]

Hardy's depiction of Wessex responds to the ambiguous status of counties in the period. His maps of Wessex show the county boundaries of Hardy's day and each sub-division of Wessex corresponds in his maps and his writing to the actual counties. However outdated by modernity and however 'open', these borders are residually present, as if the territories they mark out have only been subordinated to a larger picture, overridden but not erased. They enjoy an uncertain status as both potentially authentic traces of a more ancient division of the kingdom and, equally, as symptoms of a quaint, factitious and yet powerful modern insistence on sticking to and reviving county loyalties. In the case of the border between Dorset and Hampshire, the county boundary is also a boundary between two dioceses, that of Salisbury, which covers Wiltshire and Dorset, and that of Winchester.

If it is felt, even to a small degree, that Sandbourne lies in Hampshire, then this alters several things. Where in *The Mayor of Casterbridge*, a partial accommodation is reached between old and new, between Casterbridge and Budmouth, it seems as if in the 1890s Hardy no longer regards this as likely or even possible. As changes to *The Well-Beloved* indicate, Hardy was becoming more insistent about the pressure of the new on the old and as he did so he moved the site of the new to Sandbourne. Sandbourne and the Isle of Slingers (Portland) represent two different historical worlds; if county boundaries matter, then the same happens to 'South Wessex' (Dorset) and 'Upper Wessex' (Hampshire). Characters in Hardy's later novels are becoming paradoxically more mobile – able to move to houses further afield and travel further in search of work – yet at the same time less able to assimilate because the new place has become drastically foreign.[72]

Secondly, though, and more specific to *Tess*, a Sandbourne which lies in Hampshire leads to and forms part of the same world as Wintonchester (Winchester), where Tess is hanged. The execution can occur nowhere else because the murder was committed in Hampshire and Winchester is the county town. The result is a final chapter which questions the validity of ruralist thinking by insisting on the juxtaposition within Winchester of 'Wintonchester – that fine old city, aforetime capital of Wessex' – and the modern world, last seen in the glitter of Sandbourne and the letting of country houses, now more brutally present in the processes and architecture of state revenge.[73]

Wintonchester is seen lying 'amidst its concave and convex downlands in all the brightness and warmth of a July morning'; within, 'that leisurely dusting and sweeping was in progress which usually ushers in an old-fashioned market-day'. Likewise, from the hill outside the town, Angel and Liza-Lu see:

> the city they had just left, its more prominent buildings showing as in an isometric drawing – among them the broad Cathedral tower, with its Norman windows, and immense length of aisle and nave, the spire of St. Thomas's, the pinnacled tower of the College, and, more to the right, the tower and gables of the ancient hospice where to this day the pilgrim may receive his dole of bread and ale. Behind the city swept the rotund upland of St. Catherine's Hill, further off, landscape beyond landscape, till the horizon was lost in the radiance of the sun hanging above it.

J.B. Bullen has brilliantly shown how the sun in *Tess* is connected with Druidic religion and made into a 'harsh, indifferent and judgemental power'.[74] As important is Hardy's semi-parodic adoption of guidebook phrases, more pronounced as the list of buildings goes on and culminating in the clichés of nostalgic sentiment, 'where to this day the pilgrim may receive his dole of bread and ale'.[75] Hardy is referring in this ancient hospice to Winchester's St Cross, accepted as an ideal by Elizabeth Gaskell and used by Trollope in *The Warden* to epitomize an old order whose passing should be mourned. Characteristically, Hardy accepts its presence and meaning without endorsing their value. In the same way the city does appear 'amidst' its landscape, conforming to an ideal of harmony between town and country and that harmony can be seen spreading wider and wider into a landscape radiant with light, as if beatified. Subtleties of diction warn against this reading – 'an isometric drawing' suggests a modelled, excessive perfection; 'the rotund upland' sounds primly plump – and a reader alert to the novel as a whole would be wary of the sun, especially when it is 'hanging' over the scene.[76] Nonetheless, these are muted objections; primarily, Hardy allows Wintonchester to represent what it is usually taken to represent, a 'fine old city', leisurely in its ways and beautiful to behold.

The above quotation ends one paragraph and the next begins:

> Against these far stretches of country rose, in front of the other city edifices, a large red-brick building, with level grey roofs, and rows of short barred windows bespeaking captivity – the whole contrasting greatly by its formalism with the quaint irregularities of the Gothic erections. It was somewhat disguised from the road in passing it by yews and evergreen oaks, but it was visible enough up here.

An 'ugly flat-topped octagonal tower' rises from this building and seems 'the one blot on the city's beauty'. Hardy has drawn such architectural contrasts before, the nearest to this one being the depiction of Casterbridge jail at the end of 'The Withered Arm'.[77] Here, the city's pretensions to an idyllic serenity collapse. Hardy sets, against the previous paragraph's familiar bland style, two different alternative ways of talking: the plain descriptions of 'level grey roofs' and 'short barred windows', modulating into a sardonic taciturnity, 'it was visible enough up here'; and, secondly, the exaggerated euphemisms of 'the whole contrasting greatly by its formalism with the quaint irregularities of the Gothic erections'. The unnamed building is embarrassing and all too plainly out of place. It contests the city's received image, transforming 'the more prominent buildings' into quaintness and irregularity. The euphemistic turn of phrase indicates most clearly an embarrassed attempt to disguise the building's actual cruelty and also reveals its most dangerous power. By standing where it does, the building transforms an ideal into a fantasy, reducing the Cathedral and surrounding churches to 'edifices' and 'Gothic erections'.

Hardy could have achieved a similar effect had he set Tess's death in Salisbury or Dorchester. By choosing Winchester, he invokes a place which had come to epitomize a traditional account of rural life, whose social harmony and happy blending of old and new were seen as lacking in the contemporary world and necessary for its improvement. Such harmony, Hardy implies, is no more than an image and one which is used to disguise violence and oppression. And, although Tess is harried in 'South Wessex', that part of the region does offer her various boltholes; in 'Upper Wessex', the Hampshire especially praised by this ruralism, she is afflicted beyond endurance and then made to pay the penalty. It does not offer the retreat which Hardy's first readers would have expected. That depends on an 'absolute seclusion'. The peace at the heart of England will not survive for more than a blissful moment or two, being instantly disrupted by even the smallest disturbance from the outside world, such as a caretaker peeping through the door and going away. Neither does the rural world of Hampshire actually exhibit the social harmony claimed for it. Order is preserved through retribution and the exertion of force, the image of rurality serving to hide oppressive brutality behind serenity and naturalness, so lending it greater power.

4
Ruralism and Provincialism in the Victorian Novel: East and West

Angel and Liza-Lu leave Wintonchester by 'the West Gateway'. Hardy adds a moment later that, 'From the western gate aforesaid', they follow the highway to the 'top of the great West Hill'. It is from here that they look back on the city. Their leaving by this route allows Hardy to make the tower and its black flag appear as blots against the rising sun and his wish to create such a visual and symbolic effect may account for the choice of direction. Hardy, however, writes often about travelling, moving or looking westwards.[1] Particularly when he is thinking of his first wife, whom he courted in Cornwall, westernness carries a peculiarly intense emotional charge for him. A second personal reason can be found in Hardy's sense of himself as coming from the West of England. Looking westward suggests formative, unalterable moments in his past and, at the same time, the regional identity he has in part created, in part discovered himself to possess and in part been saddled with by others. The 'westward' naturally has cultural meanings as well as personal ones and the two overlap, interacting together so that a personal resonance has cultural components and the cultural meaning can be modified by personal association.

Naturally, too, these meanings are multiple and even contradictory. For instance, in Hardy's day, going westward leads, generically as well as actually, to both Devon and Cornwall, places with different and in some ways conflicting connotations. Devon is the perfection of England – a little England beyond Dorset, as Pembrokeshire is a little England beyond Wales; Cornwall, on the other hand, evokes wildness, barrenness and isolation. It presents an image of the savage and uncivilized while Devon makes civilization incarnate. Devon's rural landscapes share, from Gilpin's day, similar features to those of Hampshire; it is the perfection of a particular idea of England.[2] One can travel westwards, therefore, to discover either the epitome of 'England' or its opposite. The west can be situated at both centre and periphery; a journey westwards leads to the rediscovery of either the ancient foreign (Cornwall) or the original native (Devon). Such a journey either aligns the traveller with the recognized centre and its values or it does the opposite, making the traveller a figure of alienation from the capital who journeys in the hope of finding a new centre, one which may, of course, be old.

These either or choices, which appear stark when explicated, are not always manifest, however, nor strongly felt because of their common denominator: travelling westwards implies a less clearly defined desire to find origins and recover sources of value. Whether these are found in Devon or Cornwall depends to a large extent upon what one is looking for and the west is attractive because it accommodates both points of view. Hardy has feelings in common with those of his period about looking and stepping westward but his work also voices suspicions about his contemporaries' construction of the west; that is, their finding in the west the location for whatever they especially cherished – their making it pristine and giving it the meanings they desired. Hardy confronts, in other words, an idea of the west which has an impact similar to the idea of rurality, at once idealizing places and invading them.

To show Hardy's reactions and intentions here, one must look first at his contemporaries and predecessors, to discover what significance attached to west and east and to journeys westward at different times in the century and in different sub-genres of the novel.[3] Doing this will show in addition how sophisticated Victorian novelists frequently were in their deployment of geographical locations and trajectories, complicating the picture which modern critics have tended to draw. A pattern emerges, from Dickens on, in which journeys westward from London lead into a semi-rural suburbia, representative of advancing modernity and driving further before it the real west, which becomes an endangered ideal or an unwanted vestige of the past. Trollope's Barset and Margaret Oliphant's Carlingford both occupy the west that borders London, conducting through that location a debate about how stability can survive amidst progress. Their solution to the problem is broadly similar and ruralist: the two can be harmonized through the local provincialism of old-fashioned, genteel and undeveloped cities and country towns. Ruralism's comparison of north and south is, however, coupled with one between east and west. The 'Northern Metaphor' and the 'Southern Metaphor' are combined with a set of associations following the line of roughly the Thames Valley eastward and westward.[4]

Ruralism's ideal defines itself now in opposition to London, to the east, and to a primitive, romance wilderness further west. Similarly, the resonances of going east and of England east of London depend largely on how the west is seen; east connotes confinement or containment, the prevention of quest or the end of the need for quest. In sensation novels especially, eastern places and eastward trajectories reveal the rigidity that hides within the apparently stable and orderly harmony of Trollope's and Oliphant's west.

The westward look

In eighteenth-century literature, as was shown in Chapter 2, the west of England was associated with King Alfred and the aspirations to local autonomy embraced by the country-party. In nineteenth-century literature, the more powerful association is with King Arthur and looking or travelling westward acquires an almost mystic significance, connected at some level with King Arthur. Arthur and Alfred are similar in symbolising the origin of the nation and a source of national unity. Arthur, though, is less historical; the stories surrounding him were open to allegorical readings so that, for instance, he was understood with reference to prehistoric solar myth from the 1840s onwards. Simultaneously, nineteenth-century historians attempted to identify Arthur more precisely – as a warrior king, fighting for the Celts against the Saxons – and as the ruler of an identifiable kingdom: Cornwall and Brittany, both banks of the lower Severn Valley and the Scottish borders, including Westmorland, were all claimed as Arthur's true locality.[5] Glastonbury, Arthur's legendary burial site, figured in both Cornish and Welsh accounts of his topography and its dominance gave particular Arthurian resonance to Somerset. Western locations, within or bordering on the Celtic fringe, became associated with the ideal, quintessential, mythic England and journeys in that direction, especially those along the Thames valley westward, turned potentially into quests.[6]

William Morris's *News from Nowhere* (1890–1) protests against the suburbanization of the Thames valley in a gaze westwards that yearns after lost youth and a lost medieval England, chilvarous and Arthurian. Richard Jefferies's *After London; or, Wild England* (1885) similarly invests the Thames Valley with Arthurian qualities. In a fantasy of the future in which industrial society has collapsed, London been abandoned and the Thames valley been flooded, creating a lake with little towns along its shoreline, Jefferies's hero gradually re-establishes the English nation as a federation of city-states. The Arthurian connections are even closer here and figure Jefferies's hostility to Victorian England's London-centred centralization. Twenty-five years earlier, George Meredith's *The Ordeal of Richard Feverel* (1859) employs an Arthurian feeling about westwardness and the Thames Valley, combining these with the geography of southern England more widely. The relation between the novel's concerns and this geographical structure implies a sophisticated engagement with ruralist assumptions, one which reveals the currency of those assumptions and their attendant geography as well as perhaps influencing Hardy, who had friendly dealings with Meredith and respected him.[7]

The novel's interest in westerliness emerges, as often in nineteenth-century novels, through a mystification of sunset:[8]

> Golden lie the meadows: golden run the streams: red gold is on the pine-stems. The Sun is coming down to Earth, and walks the fields and the waters.
>
> The Sun is coming down to Earth, and the fields and the waters shout to him golden shouts. He comes, and his heralds run before him, and touch the leaves of oaks, and planes, and beeches, lucid green, and the pine-stems redder gold [. . . .]
>
> Peeps of the revelling splendour above, and around, enliven the conscious full heart within. The flaming West, the crimson heights, shower their glories through voluminous leafage.[9]

The novel, however, also develops a geography of west and east which corresponds to this ecstatic pursuit of 'the flaming West'. Richard grows up at Raynham Abbey, his father's country house 'in a certain Western County folding Thames'. His youth is spent exploring the countryside around and, particularly, visiting Farmer Blaize at Lobourne, which is a few miles west. There Richard meets Lucy Desborough, Miranda to his Ferdinand, and a few years later falls in love with her when they meet by chance on an island in the Thames. Richard has been rowing upriver when he finds her, making a journey that is ardently Arthurian in its inspiration:

> Somewhere at the founts of the world lay the land he was rowing towards: [. . .] Oh, why could not one in these days do some high knightly deed which should draw down ladies' eyes from heaven, as in the days of Arthur! (pp.124–5)[10]

Lucy and her family come from further west, Dorset in fact, as Meredith makes a point of specifying. While the couple are falling in love, Richard's father is trying to arrange a suitable marriage for him and he does so, unsurprisingly, in London. Meredith intercuts the two stories, emphasizing not only the vulnerability of youthful freedom to the schemes of age but, in addition, the alignment of his story's opponents on a geographical axis – not only country versus city, but London versus Dorset, east versus west.

Richard's ordeal is produced by the clash between his father's educational system and Richard's natural impulse towards self-fulfilment; the novel investigates the patriarchal oppression of individual will. Meredith conducts this through an opposition of east and west – the contrast of a secluded island on the upper reaches of the Thames and, in the east, an engrossing and guilt-inducing social world. Raynham Abbey, accessible by train from London and yet still in the country, occupies a situation comparable to Richard's, caught between the world demanded of him and the world he naturally desires. It pretends, in the person of Richard's father, to achieve a compromise between the two, a retreat from which the world's system can be better managed. Meredith's novel, however, sees such a compromise, such a landscape, as at best delusory. For Richard and Lucy it proves destructive.

Dickens and Gissing: Twickenham and Wattleborough

Raynham Abbey's location corresponds with its owner's attempt to compromise between two worlds, east and west, new and old. This aspect of Meredith's geography imitates that of ruralism in order to question its agenda. For Hardy, the Arthurian associations of the west have great resonance, as shown by *A Pair of Blue Eyes* (1873) and many of his poems; likewise, the numinous, heavenly west, lit by the setting sun, appears in his novels from *Desperate Remedies* to *Tess*, though nowhere is its promise unequivocally endorsed.[11] I would say, however, that Hardy's Wessex and his sense of what westwardness can signify are also deeply affected by the two kinds of western landscape present in Meredith's novel and occurring elsewhere in the period's fiction – one far to the west which represents purity, naturalness and freedom; one, nearer London, which promises to balance social demands and private feeling. Meredith's novel participates in a debate about whether the promise of a harmonious society can be fulfilled, a debate that recurs among the novelists of the 1850s and 1860s, the period when east and west became important.

Not only George Meredith's *The Ordeal of Richard Feverel* (1859) but his *Evan Harrington: or, He Would Be a Gentleman* (1861) and *Rhoda*

Fleming (1865) concentrate on west versus east and on counties to the west and south of London. Trollope's Barsetshire novels, published between 1855 and 1867, and Margaret Oliphant's Carlingford series, which appeared in 1861–6 and 1876, occupy the same setting. All three represent a trend in regional/provincial writing of largely avoiding the north and industrial settings. They may have influenced Elizabeth Gaskell (whose last novel, *Wives and Daughters* (1866) no longer opposes town and country, industry and rurality, but concentrates on the life of a country town) and George Eliot's, whose career follows a similar pattern, beginning with the opposition of industrial and rural – in, for instance, the Stonyshire and Loamshire of *Adam Bede* (1859) – and ending with *Daniel Deronda* (1876) which delineates London's Jewish community and has a heroine from 'Wessex'. The same trend is reflected in poetry of the period: Tennyson's *The Princess* (1847) is structured around differences between north and south, whereas the *Idylls of the King* (1859–84) valorize the west.

While this new east/west geography overlaps with and develops the ruralist associations of southern England, it also extends into the south of England the imaginative geography of London's East and West Ends, the extension of the geographical pattern coinciding with London's extraordinary expansion in the period. The 'stockbroker belt first started to appear in Berkshire and Surrey' in the 1860s, the 'critical decade of the residential exodus', as John Summerson has called it.[12] Although the expansion took place in all directions, it was particularly marked on the western side of London; in 1830, William Cobbett protested bitterly about the poor land on London's western side (the whole area between Egham and Reading) being enclosed and cultivated at the expense of better land further away. This was the beginning of a process which led to the expansion of suburbia into Berkshire in the second half of the century. That county's changing position within the geographical imagination of the period is indicated by its and Buckinghamshire's inclusion in the Home Counties by the end of the century. Earlier, the Home Counties had referred to Middlesex, Essex, Kent and Surrey – those counties on the Home Circuit, 'the assize circuit which has London at its centre'. It would be odd now to think of Essex as one of the Home Counties, whereas Berkshire seems quintessentially one of them.[13]

Dickens's work recognizes these changes in the geography of the southeast of England and reflects upon them. Arguably, he responded to the fashion for more rurally-based novels by locating his final book, *The Mystery of Edwin Drood* (1870) in a cathedral city rather than London. The novel reads at times like a sardonic parody of Trollope.

More importantly, he develops a subtle and profound account of east and west, one which contributes to (as well as illustrating) the cultural geography/geographies which Hardy inherited. The geography of Dickens's writing has usually been read more simply. Franco Moretti's *Atlas of the European Novel* (1998) contains a map showing 'A geography of Dickens' endings' in which 'London is the elective abode of most villains'. For Dickens, he claims, 'the urban experience has been so devastating that London cannot provide a plausible setting for the happy ending' and the good characters have to escape – to Kent in *Great Expectations*, to the north in *Bleak House*. In fact, Dickens's geography is much more complicated than this, just as his feelings about London are more ambiguous.[14] Esther in *Bleak House* does follow this pattern by moving to the new 'Bleak House' in Yorkshire and discovering there a rural paradise comparable to those of Howitt and Elizabeth Gaskell.[15] But this is exceptional. Joe and Biddy have always lived in Kent, apart from Joe's one disastrous visit to London and his unnarrated rescue of Pip. Pip himself at the end of *Great Expectations* departs for the Far East. Furthermore, in other novels, London does becomes the setting for the happy ending: in *David Copperfield*, David and Agnes choose to settle there; in *Little Dorrit*, so do Arthur Clennam and Amy. Although part of Dickens, certainly, was terrified by London, seeing it as a city of death, and was drawn to imagining the countryside as its life-giving opposite, that opposition is qualified by his dislike of a stagnant complacency, especially visible in the country and sustained by its economics.

Consequently, in Dickens, the landscapes characteristic of ruralism become suspect and corrupt. These are most often to be found in the western suburbs of London, such as for example Twickenham in *Little Dorrit*. It is here that Clennam visits Mr and Mrs Meagles and their daughter, Pet, with whom he is falling in love. On his way to the house, Clennam meets up with Daniel Doyce, a self-educated inventor from the north of England, and grows to like him as they walk along together. While in Twickenham itself, Clennam finds himself competing with Gowan, the well-connected and mediocre painter who is courting Pet. In these two characters, Dickens opposes an innovative, energetic industrialism to a serenely complacent, southern Establishment, based on bureaucracy, financial services and the tentacles of 'family connections'. Clennam finds the Meagles disappointingly close to the second. As Clennam struggles to choose between the two, the familiar north/south opposition of ruralism is re-evaluated: the north is strikingly vigorous, the tranquil south hampered and deceitful.

Twickenham represents a pretence of the stability associated with the southern English rural landscape. The 'charming place [. . .] on the road by the river [. . .] defended by a goodly show of handsome trees and spreading evergreens' is shadowed by Mr Meagles's weakness for genealogy and family privilege – his 'striving for something that did not belong to him' – and Pet's weakness for a worthless man, the painter Gowan.[16] Furthermore, by the end of the visit, the 'show' is collapsing: 'The rain fell heavily on the roof, and pattered on the ground, and dripped among the evergreens and the leafless branches of the trees. The rain fell heavily, drearily.' The 'handsome trees and spreading evergreens', seen so happily before are now more wearying. Retrospectively, this lends a more suspect intonation to 'spreading', as if the evergreens (they may be rhododendrons) are encroaching on a natural scene, rather as the suburbs are expanding across Middlesex. Evergreen, exotic trees are a frequent indicator of the invasive and the *nouveau riche* from Jane Austen onwards; Dickens uses them here to suggest that Twickenham is not the real country, despite Clennam's powerful desire to find it so. Dickens's polemic against 'the south', with its inward-looking self-importance by contrast with the energy and truly cosmopolitan life of the north, finds its target in a western suburb of London. Clennam goes there, in a conventional dream of blissful marriage to Pet; he returns, chastened and more practical, sets up in business with Doyce and later marries Little Dorrit. London proper and its western suburbs occupy opposite poles in the novel as much as north and south. Similarly, in *Great Expectations*, Herbert Pocket's parents live in Hammersmith – upriver from London – and like the Meagles nourish social pretensions there. Their position contrasts with Wemmick's eccentric but sturdy suburban house in Walworth (due south of the City) and, more distantly, with the innocent semi-rural retreat Mr Pickwick enjoys in Dulwich at the close of *Pickwick Papers*.[17]

Country, then, as far as Dickens is concerned, cannot be found very easily to the west just as for Meredith social harmony cannot be found there. Both writers are contesting an established, ruralist pattern. London, though, for Dickens is not the only opposite to west. He has also pronounced and precise feelings about east and counties lying east of London, feelings which contribute to the geography of the sensation novel and that of the darker moments in Trollope. In *Great Expectations*, Dickens places Joe's forge in north Kent, specifically the marshes that form the southern edge of the Thames estuary. Similarly, David Copperfield runs away into Kent, to find refuge with his aunt at Dover. These choices of location can and have been read autobiographically but they carry wider and national symbolic meanings as well. In *David*

Copperfield, the Dover Road leads with David's own boyish self-certainty directly to its destination.[18] On David's arrival, Dover seems at once to epitomize a fortified border and the place where a nation faces its ancient enemy: David's aunt rushes towards him out of the house, seeing off intruders with her peremptory yells: 'Go away! [. . .] Go along! No boys here!'[19] Her behaviour echoes other moments when David is attacked or robbed on the road, heightening the fear that his may prove to have been a wasted journey. It turns out better than this and Aunt Betsy's fierceness helps in her later dealings with David's relations; they evoke too a national self-image (of fearless self-defence) in a setting particularly linked with that self-image. These qualities are the more marked because Dover is contrasted in the opening sections of the novel with Blunderstone in Suffolk, where David was born.[20] 'Blunderstone' sounds like a symbolic name, connecting the place with the cruel Murdstones, whom David blunders against, and suggesting too the burden of stupidity. Yet there is a real place, Blundeston, situated as in the novel, roughly half-way between Lowestoft and Yarmouth. This is the very northernmost corner of Suffolk, almost surrounded and cut off from the rest of the county by Norfolk and the sea.[21]

Dickens's use of Blundeston gives a sense of enclosure, isolation and of geographical uncertainty – David is not sure whether he was born there 'or "thereby" '. The location reflects his unclear sense of himself as a little boy before he is given support and oriented by his aunt in Dover. The provincial isolation of Blunderstone leads to petty tyranny and an almost disabling melancholia. Later, when David travels from Blunderstone to Yarmouth on Barkis's cart, it is seen as producing vulnerability to glamour: for David this results in the mistaken hero-worship of Steerforth and for Emily it leads to prostitution. (The name 'Steerforth' implies the attraction to someone like David, marooned on the social margins, of a person who appears to be making their way in the world.) Because of all this, David's later journey leads to Dover in particular: to Dover understood with reference to its customary, national associations and Dover set in contrast to another eastern seaport, Yarmouth, which is reached not by a refreshingly straight highway but via 'many deviations up and down lanes' (*David Copperfield*, ch.3). David's story is mapped onto a symbolic geography, in which his 'personal history' has social implications. The Dover road, as opposed to the winding lanes of Suffolk, offers David the exciting possibility of entering the nation as well as of making his personal fortune.

Joe's forge, lost in the 'meshes', more nearly resembles the Suffolk world of *David Copperfield* than that novel's Dover. *David Copperfield* concludes in a confident engagement with the world via David's writing and through the mature fulfilment achieved in his second marriage. *Great Expectations*, by contrast, ends in several versions of exile: Pip's to the East; Joe back to his remote obscurity; Estella to a loveless marriage. London in this novel cannot be conquered; one is faced instead with a choice between hardening oneself against it (as Jaggers and Wemmick do in different ways) or of withdrawing from it. Joe's forge suggests that obscurity need not necessarily mean defeat and losing faith in a national project need not lead to personal despair. The byways and lanes leading off the high-road towards Joe's forge lead also to a more mature and disillusioned understanding of one's place in the nation and of what expectations it is sensible to have of the world outside. *Great Expectations'* Kentish marshes offer an alternative to London, certainly; they also suggest a way of escape from the narrative of successful assimilation (success via assimilation) which the earlier novel presents through the contrast between Dover and Yarmouth.

In Dickens, then, some parts of rural England are tainted by the self-serving complacency of the Barnacles; other parts exemplify the narrowness and insecurity of provincial life; others again show how vigorous self-assertion and stoutly defended autonomy create the social conscience which grounds a national community. Moreover, these examples indicate that Dickens divided up the world, as much between west and east as between country and city. The country around London as well as London itself is valued differently according to where it lies. Although everywhere is symbolically potent and notably particularized in Dickens, country to the east of London feels different from country to the west: Yarmouth, Dover, Joe's forge are all easterly; the Meagles at Twickenham, the Pockets at Hammersmith and Estella, residing at Richmond, are all in the west. The easterly is older and more rigidly oppressive but offers examples of defiance and integrity; the westerly has more glamour and it lies closer to the mainstream of modern society, with its compromises and subtly captivating fictions. It is a cosier world and one harder to resist.[22]

Also, beyond the factitious, suburban west, there are glimpses in Dickens of the true country which suburbia attempts both to imitate and replace: as *Great Expectations* ended, in its first version, Esther had married after Drummle's death a doctor from Shropshire – a doctor who 'had once very manfully interposed' when Drummle was being particularly cruel to her. Esther lives in modest retirement in Shropshire and has learnt compassion.[23] Shropshire's out-of-the-way, western remoteness possesses the strength and integrity ('manfully interposed') which

Drummle's violence envies. Pip too in the novel is charmed at a distance by Herbert's cousins, up in London from Devon, their sweet wholesomeness seemingly confirmed by their home in the far west. In *Bleak House*, Shropshire is mentioned again, in the figure of the other 'ruined suitor, who periodically appears from Shropshire, and breaks out into efforts to address the Chancellor' (ch.1, pp.51–2). Last spasms of hopeless resistance to Jarndyce and Jarndyce linger in that distant county, and this dismally proves how Chancery is gradually infecting the whole of the country. The novel's panoramic sweep is indicated by using 'Shropshire'; consequently, at its end, the retreat of 'Bleak House' must offer an alternative to the whole of England, an escape from geography into ruralism.[24] Esther yearns for this escape and 'Bleak House' provides it in an idealized Yorkshire.

Dickens's conviction in this novel that Chancery gets everywhere helps produce the country versus city geography which Moretti observes. Even so, Dickens suggests in it the two kinds of westernness which his later work develops more fully; that is to say, the man from Shropshire creates a fleeting image of integrity located in the far west and this image contrasts with Esther's ideas of an idyllic countryside, lying nearer at hand. The comparison is more telling because of the way in which Esther describes her journey to 'Bleak House':

> The day had brightened very much, and still brightened as we went westward. We went our way through the sunshine and the fresh air, wondering more and more at the extent of the streets, the brilliancy of the shops, the great traffic, and the crowds of people whom the pleasanter weather seemed to have brought out like many-coloured flowers. By and by we began to leave the wonderful city, and to proceed through suburbs which, of themselves, would have made a pretty large town, in my eyes; and at last we got into a real country road again, with windmills, rickyards, milestones, farmers' waggons, scents of old hay, swinging signs and horse troughs: trees, fields, and hedgerows. It was delightful to see the green landscape before us and the immense metropolis behind.
>
> (*Bleak House*, ch.6, pp.109–10)

Esther's pleasure apparently conforms to Moretti's idea of Dickens's world: the day brightening as the city is left behind; the fullest joy being reserved for the 'real country road' where Esther can lose uneasiness and self-consciousness through compiling a list of traditional, rural things: 'windmills, rickyards, milestones, farmers' waggons' and so on. This paragraph opens chapter six, which is entitled 'Quite at Home', and Esther seems far more at ease in the country. She no longer interrupts herself with professions of inadequacy as she moves beyond the scenes of societal anxiety into a real country road 'at last'. There, it seems, she can straightforwardly enjoy a whole world of delights and the list she compiles gives the impression of an ever-expanding realm – the 'wind-mills, rickyards' and other specific objects are joined to something more explicitly evocative, the 'scents of old hay', which colour what follows, the 'swinging signs and horse troughs', before everything is summed up and included in 'trees, fields and hedgerows'. The placing of these more general terms implies Esther's sense of entering and herself forming part of a larger whole – one in which she is quite at home.

Similarly, greater self-assurance characterizes her next remark: 'It was delightful to see the green landscape before us and the immense metro-polis behind.' Esther feels qualified to pronounce the conventional sen-timent: her ruralist delight lies in feeling, on the one hand, free of the city and, on the other, poised between the country ahead and the city behind, at a point where they are balanced and in harmony. Both are pleasurable now, while one is glad at the same time to be in the country, moving out into the freedoms and possibilities of 'the green landscape'. The phrasing sounds suspiciously neat, however, in the same way that the list of idyllic components in Esther's 'real country road' makes it sound an image more than a reality. The scene she describes conforms exactly to her expectations of such scenes, expectations that the reader-ship would recognize and largely share. This country road is a 'real' one because it fits the pattern and not because it is distinctive or odd.

Part of the effect here depends upon the context: only a few chapters earlier, in Esther's account of her childhood, Dickens mentions two earlier journeys: one following the death of Esther's godmother when she travelled from Windsor to Reading, the second her journey back to London six years later. In Reading, she lived with the two Miss Donny's at a house named 'Greenleaf' (*Bleak House*, ch.3); the journey had been miserable and frightening but the destination turned out to be an affec-tionate home. It is as if Esther is focussing on the prospect of another welcome and putting out of her mind her memories of travelling as a young girl through a wintry and hostile landscape. Because the 'real' roads west of London can be threatening and have been threatening to her before, Esther defends herself by holding on to a clichéd pastoral and seeing that as the 'real country road'.

Dickens cautions his readers against Esther's narrative by the further device of making her forget her geography. The journey begins at the home of Mrs Jellyby, who lives near the Law Courts, just off Holborn, and it ends at 'Bleak House', situated, at this stage in the novel, near St Albans. Esther, Richard and Ada travel via Barnet, crossing 'over a common and an old battlefield' (chapter 6); following this route means going through Highgate, via either Islington or Kentish Town. They could have gone only a short distance west before turning north. Esther, though, seems to go on thinking she is travelling westwards, into the fashionable suburbs near Hyde Park and afterwards into the country beyond, and to think this long after she has changed direction. This mistake – assuming it is hers and not Dickens's – suggests that for her at least a peculiarly intense and highly-charged rurality is connected with the roads west out of London. All routes leaving the East End behind turn, for Esther, into routes west. Consequently, *Bleak House* exemplifies how the western periphery of London was becoming, in Dickens's eyes, the site of a dubious, ruralist desire, which created a country reality in the image of that desire. Beyond it, on the fringes of England, lies a truer rurality whose remoteness suggests that the nearer, ruralist world is created by what it appears to oppose – the voracious power of London.

George Gissing, in many respects a disciple of Dickens, shares his conception of London's western suburbs and similarly contrasts them with an eastward region symbolizing retirement and integrity, only in his case that symbolism is a snare. Gissing's geography is more dichotomized than Dickens's and it provides no escape in either direction – not, that is, until late in his career when the distant west (of Devon, especially) begins to offer a redemptive retreat from a brutal world.[25] Before then, east and west offer different aspects of the same imprisonment.

The impact of this geography can be most easily illustrated by comparing *The Nether World* (1889), and *New Grub Street* (1891). In chapter 19 of *The Nether World*, entitled 'A Retreat', the novel's principal characters – Sidney Kirkwood, Jane Snowdon and her elderly father, Michael – take a holiday, leaving gloomy Clerkenwell for Danbury. Danbury is an actual place near Chelmsford in Essex. The characters have escaped the hideous prison of London and reached, Gissing says, 'one of those quiet corners of flat, homely England, where man and beast seem on good terms with each other, where all green things grow in abundance'.[26] Their holiday offers them the illusion of a benevolent world ('where men and beast seem on good terms with each other'), an illusion which cultivates the idealism that ruins Sidney Kirkwood's life. *New Grub Street* (1891) opens with Jasper Milvain, an accomplished and superficial literary journalist, visiting his mother and sisters at their home on the western side of London. In chapter 3, entitled 'Holiday', Jasper strolls to his favourite spot:

> certain meadows forming a compact little valley [. . .] sheltered from all winds. [. . .] Along the bottom ran a clear, shallow stream, overhung with elder and hawthorn bushes; and close by the wooden bridge which spanned it was a great ash tree, making shadow for cows and sheep when the sun lay hot upon the open field.[27]

Milvain's acquisitive mind looks out for and appreciates expected forms of beauty and pleasure; Esther's generic pastoral recurs, as both content and form in the paragraph echo the predictable quality of Milvain's taste. Coming back from his walk, Milvain notices a donkey:

> a poor worn-out beast, all skin and bone, which had presumably been sent here in the hope that a little more labour might still be exacted from it if it were suffered to repose for a few weeks. There were sores upon its back and legs; it stood in a fixed attitude of despondency, just flicking away troublesome flies with its grizzled tail.
>
> (Gissing, *New Grub Street*, ch.5, p.65)

The narrative of *The Nether World* proves that the country offers images of harmony and cooperation which are deceptive. Here, Milvain is already undeceived; he takes it for granted that the donkey is being rested in order to be exploited. Sidney Kirkwood believes that we can recover the lost paradise where the lion lies down with the lamb. In the country retreat of Danbury, it looks as if capital has miraculously vanished and labour survives unalienated. For Jasper Milvain, on the other hand, country retreats prove that capital is good, both because the city stimulates where the country enervates and because the city provides for the successful these bowers of repose, easily reached by train. This difference is summed up in the chapter titles; country to the west of London has become 'Holiday' whereas Essex offered 'Retreat'.

Gissing's choice of names follows a similar pattern: unlike the other places in *New Grub Street*, Milvain's home is given an imaginary name. It lies near the town of 'Wattleborough', a name which has various associations, 'rotten borough' among them. Kirkwood's Essex is contrastingly 'real': Danbury exists, as do Chelmsford and Maldon, which the characters also visit. The generic quality of the name 'Wattleborough' accords with Jasper's skilled opportunism and conventional cast of mind; consequently, the modernity he represents seems to bring homogeneity and suburban anonymity. Western London carries these associations. Kirkwood's Danbury acquires poignancy by contrast: its being really there – identifiable and visitable – shows the sincerity of Kirkwood's ideals, their power over his vision of actual places. Such sincerity seems a forlorn virtue, unsuited to the automatic self-interest of the modern world and driven into retreat. Essex may be 'real' by comparison with places on London's western fringes but this quality of reality has the terrible consequence of lending substance to un-realizable dreams. The benevolent England of Essex makes one dream of powerful benevolence, an ability to intervene and remain inde-pendent at the same time. It apparently confirms the value of the individual but through this affirmation the individual destroys him or herself in attempting to resist the force of the market.

Both poles of Gissing's east/west geography, therefore, show how modernity and capital erode personhood – to the west, by creating the modern personality of Milvain, which is driving and empty, and to the east by provoking in its opponents a self-destructive idealism. The mixed feelings in *New Grub Street* about Milvain and his apparently more worthy rival, Edward Reardon, reflect Gissing's sense that east is actually no better than west. The integrity it promises is founded on illusions which in turn produce damaging self-deceptions. Ruralism's belief in harmonizing new and old by bringing country and city together seems in Gissing to have produced two oppressive conjunctions: on the western side of London, the new dominates and erases the old, trans-forming virtue into infinite expediency; on the eastern side, country isolates itself from city and, ironically, by doing so succumbs to the city entirely. With decreasing irony and increasing anxiety, Gissing offers as an escape from this deadlock a removal from the sphere of London alto-gether, a flight into rural exile in Devon. This threeway division – east, west and far west – has been seen before in Meredith, Dickens and the period's culture more widely. The distinctive thing about Gissing's geo-graphy is his dark view of the east and the consequent, abreactive embrace of the far west. Both of these matter to Hardy and they evolve from the more pessimistic, conservative strands of novels which employ this geographical pattern – that is, the more disillusioned side of Trollope and Oliphant, in conjunction with the sinister aspect of sensation fiction.

Barsetshire, Carlingford and Armadale

Anthony Trollope evidently located England in its country life: 'the visitors to England who have not sojourned at a country-house, whether it be the squire's, parson's, or farmer's, have not seen the most English phase of the country'.[28] All the Barsetshire novels are set in 'a county in the west of England' which can be reached quite easily by train from London. Although accessible, Barsetshire remains 'purely agricultural' and comparatively obscure, being 'not so full of life, indeed, nor so widely spoken of as some of its manufacturing brethren in the north'.[29] The novels depict a group of interconnected families, who live and work largely within the confines of this sheltered, provincial county. They show the importance of immediate rivalries and opponents close at hand and they rarely mention any part of England except Barsetshire and London. The latter is visited occasionally and is a constant point of reference, partly because the railways now mean that Barchester has to sustain itself against London's encroaching presence. From the first book in the series, *The Warden* (1855), Trollope sets the merits of traditional, local ways against intrusive forces from outside – these are embodied in *The Warden* by the Ecclesiastical Commissioners, ambitious journalists and the pressurising cant of 'Jupiter', Trollope's nickname for *The Times*.[30]

According to Trollope's view in these novels, local community is able to resist the national invader and does so either through benevolence or petty-mindedness. In *The Warden*, Eleanor Harding can conquer and convert the journalist John Bold so that he sees the merits of the old arrangements as far as Hiram's Hospital is concerned. In other visitors, Barchester's sweetness prompts sweetness in return – in *Barchester Towers*, Madeline Neroni is so struck by the sincerity of Dr Arabin's love for Eleanor, now a widow, that she gives up her own designs on him. Mrs Proudie, wife of the new Bishop, is compelled by her love of dominance to become involved with diocesan affairs, trivial and clogging as they might appear to someone determined on advancement in the Church. Barchester defeats her aims by being so relentlessly interested in the small affairs she wishes to control single-handedly.

Still, these conversions do not prevent change: the old, kindly set-up of Hiram's Hospital is swept away in *The Warden* and with it some of the long-standing virtues of Barchester's clerical life. *Barchester Towers*, however, also shows that the local can resist the evils of modernity because it is discreetly linked to the centre. There is a network of connections which counters the railways and these can still be relied on in a crisis. After the death of the old Dean of Barchester, there is an argument over who should succeed him. Septimus Harding, the representative in *The Warden* of the old, the settled and the accepting, lobbies on behalf of Dr Arabin, a candidate whom the novel admires. He does so

by travelling to Oxford, where he enlists the help of the Master of
Lazarus College; and from there to Westminster, the centre of the 'cleri-
copolitical world'. Barchester, like Lazarus, rises again and makes local
opinion powerful in London. It becomes a check on the new centralizing powers, tempering their arrogance and working within the old but
still potent system to diminish their impact.

This incident typfies the workings of Trollope's conservatism, which
seeks to direct attention to the socially reticent, on a personal and
national level, so that their easily ignored virtues can be retained.
Harding's loyalty to the old coupled with his purposeful dealings with
the new express the possibility of harmonizing the two, a harmony put
forward in a more traditional way in *The Warden* by Eleanor's marriage
to John Bold. Such a harmony persists, usually unnoticed, in Barsetshire. Old and apparently quaint figures among Barchester's clergy can,
sometimes, improve decisions in London. The Church and the 'purely
agricultural' are both recommended by this: they allow a degree of inter-
change to survive between province and capital. Furthermore, the
Church's way of doing things reaches into the processes of government
– it is the Prime Minister who makes major ecclesiastical appointments
– and this enables Trollope to imply that what is good in one may be
good in the other, that the nation as a whole would benefit from being
organized as the Church is.

Later in the series, Trollope's confidence in the power of the old to
withstand the new gradually diminishes and, in line with this, Barsetshire is divided in half, east and west. The eastern part becomes 'more
purely Conservative than the western' because 'the residence of two
such great Whig magnates as the Duke of Omnium and the Earl de
Courcy in that [western] locality in some degree overshadows and
renders less influential the gentlemen who live near them'.[31]

Barsetshire corresponds, roughly, to Wiltshire or Hampshire and one
effect of this division is to move its quintessential area back to the centre
of the country, back to the heartland of the ruralist tradition, which
included Trollope's mother.[32] The division also expresses anxiety about
that tradition's survival. West Barset, colonized and overrun by the new
pseudo-aristocratic plutocracy, is drawn into closer contact with London
despite lying further away. And, as P.D. Edwards insightfully remarks of
Framley Parsonage (1861): 'while West Barset is becoming less and less
self-contained, the eastern half of the county [. . .] is contracting and
consolidating, becoming more exclusive and intransigent'.[33] The dis-
turbed balance of the later novels confirms the nature of the earlier,
harmonious relation which Trollope sees as disappearing – a meeting of

old and new in the ruralist world of central southern England. The geography Trollope uses to indicate the disturbance has the second effect of suggesting that the old has been encircled; a movement farther westward has been blocked off and the inspiriting hopes have been disappointed which that movement embodied. Barset no longer sits comfortably and vaguely in a large, loosely connected region of the south that extends as far as Devon, its extensiveness suggesting a natural dominance and the westerly trajectory carrying connotations of the heavenly.[34] Its idyllic earthly paradise still exists (just about) in East Barset but has become more confined, more isolated and more likely to fester.

Margaret Oliphant's Carlingford has in some respects a more forward-looking spirit than Barchester, yet it is a variant on the same theme – a conservative vision of rural England, in which the country to the west of London demonstrates the workings and benefits of a provincial localism.[35] Esther's remark in *Bleak House* that 'It was delightful to see the green landscape before us and the immense metropolis behind' gives an optimistic account of London's outskirts as the meeting-place of town and country. Mrs Oliphant's *Chronicles of Carlingford* (1863–76) express the same hope for places within reach of London. While amused by their staid quaintness and willing to show their parochial stuffiness, she maintains, nonetheless, that in such places town and country rejuvenate one another.

Carlingford is Oliphant's name for a small town somewhere on the Great Western Railway, reached by changing at Didcot Junction. Never precisely identified, it approximates to Abingdon, Wantage or Wallingford – most nearly to the last, perhaps, because Wallingford is nearest the Chilterns and Carlingford's MP is Mr Chiltern.[36] Oliphant gives less emphasis to geographical connections and locations than Trollope does but Carlingford's general position is consistently maintained. Moreover, *Salem Chapel* (1861), the first full-length novel in the series, lends symbolic resonance to the westerly; the book's opening sentence reads: 'Towards the west end of Grove Street, in Carlingford, on the shabby side of the street, stood a red brick building'; this, the dissenting chapel of the title promises much to the novel's protagonist, a clergyman for whom it is his first congregation. He falls in love during the novel with 'Lady Western', a young dowager out of his reach, and the novel shows his gradually renouncing this fanciful love and seeing the limitations of his flock, the dissenters who 'led the van of progress generally' although, in Carlingford, 'there was certainly an exception to be made'. From the suburban west of London, places further west express romantic, perhaps fanciful aspirations. These collapse under a 'shabby' reality and the hero retreats eastwards, first to Folkestone and later London.[37]

Within Carlingford, however, it is possible, although to a limited extent, to bring romance and reality together. *Miss Marjoribanks* (1866) ends with the marriage of the eponymous heroine and her cousin, who has come home from India having made his fortune. In the course of the book, Miss Marjoribanks, though a stranger and the daughter of a Scot, has made herself into a hostess and social lynch-pin, achieving her last and greatest success in running the election campaign of an apolitical MP, 'an independent candidate, unconnected with party' whose slogan is 'the right man for Carlingford'.[38] Proof that she is being rewarded by the perfect marriage appears when, soon after the wedding, she sees an estate named Marchbank advertised for sale. It is the same estate that her late father had always wanted to buy. She and her newly-rich – though not excessively rich – husband buy the estate and set about improving it. Surname and place-name are pronounced in the same way despite their different spellings. (It is not clear when the reader understands this; different ones will at different times, some from the outset.)[39] By marrying her cousin, Oliphant's heroine keeps her maiden name and now by moving house she becomes Mrs Marjoribanks of Marchbank. Continuity in society and complete identification between landowner and property are expressed by this, in the half-unspoken way characteristic of the book's oblique presentation of its most serious concerns.[40]

The novel, that is to say, is fully in favour of the pattern in which social mobility produces and renews social stability – in this instance, the cousin replaces the father and the couple fulfil paternal desire, using new money to purchase their family estate. Carlingford's nearness to London opens it to the enlivening and restorative influence of the Marjoribanks, who become gradually established as a new, enlightened and 'improving' gentry, practising the English virtues of their adopted home.[41] Oliphant's novel makes a claim, reminiscent of Howitt, that modernization preserves and revives the best of the past – an argument that suits Carlingford's location on the western outskirts of London. There is no reason, Oliphant argues, why local patriotism cannot survive these changes: independent MPs who put their constituency first can still be elected and new money (from India not Manchester, trade not manufacture) can be fully integrated into old structures. Carlingford survives, reinvigorated and not suburbanised, and the book celebrates its unchangingness while encouraging it to change.

The last in the series, *Phoebe, Junior* (1876), situates Carlingford again between town and country and tells a similar story of a strongminded young woman. Phoebe Beecham's mother (also Phoebe, hence the title) married the dissenting minister at the end of *Salem Chapel*. At the opening of *Phoebe, Junior*, Oliphant narrates her and her husband's subsequent move to London and their rise in wealth and status. These mean that, when their daughter Phoebe returns to Carlingford to nurse her grandmother (and guard her and her parents' inheritance from grasping relatives still living nearby), she has to bridge a large gap in class, manners and expectations. Less native than Miss Marjoribanks and more ill-at-ease, Phoebe eventually marries up and out, choosing Clarence Copperhead (the son of the most wealthy member of her father's congregation in London) while aware that Reginald May, himself a clergyman and son of a vicar in Carlingford, has fallen in love with her too. Miss Marjoribanks's project of reforming Carlingford is replaced by Phoebe's struggle to reform her fiancé's father, who thinks her a very poor match. Phoebe's cleverness, honour and fortitude win out over his vulgarly brazen social climbing and although this victory is achieved in Carlingford, soon afterwards she leaves, re-entering 'the regions of the great' (as her grandparents call them) and abandoning both town and novel. In her future life, she is visible only to the initiated as the ghostwriter of her husband's parliamentary speeches.[42]

This second generation novel, written ten years after the other Chronicles, follows Trollope in its declining confidence about local provincialism. Carlingford is the scene of Phoebe's victory; Mr Copperhead's wealth exerts less power there and Phoebe's character is allowed to come to the fore. The country town provides an opportunity for her to reveal her intelligence, education, generosity and ironic self-awareness.[43] Moreover, the family is, to a degree, reconciled – her grandfather solves the finanical crisis threatening to engulf Mr May, Reginald's father, and speaks of his granddaughter in the last chapter as 'a wonderful girl'. That accomplished, though, the heroine leaves her adopted, semi-rural retreat behind. Reginald May is powerless to keep her. The optimistic side of the book declares that, in her own person, Phoebe represents and inhabits the social middle ground – a source of harmony, sense and reconciliation which is still visible in and secured by Carlingford – yet can now perform on a wider stage.[44] The more doubtful feeling in the book is that some precious qualities in country life are being lost: excluded, embarrassed and worn away.

That doubt is reflected in the novel's sense of west. 'Lady Western' from *Salem Chapel* is referred to again, as 'Lady Weston', one of the previous owners of Phoebe's grandparents' house. Her 'extravagant reign', however, has ended long ago. Oliphant also introduces an aristocratic family, the Dorsets, who live at 'the Hall, Easton'. The daughters are both old maids and their father is found completely at a loss early in the book when he visits a ball in London given by the Copperheads.[45] This patterning of west and east recalls that of *Salem Chapel*, but the romantic possibility of the west now lies in the past. The east (of 'Easton') which lies to the west ('Dorset') resembles Trollope's East Barset. Both represent an old-fashioned, country world which has grown sadly lifeless. As Carlingford in this novel diminishes before the apparently unlimited power of London so Phoebe returns there (whereas Miss Marjoribanks moved into the nearby countryside); similarly, Carlingford no longer leads into the west, there being nothing worth looking for there any longer.

One can find in sensation fiction a comparable set of feelings about east and west. Wilkie Collins and M.E. Braddon observe established geographical conventions, often with exaggerated respect, and bring to them a distinctive feeling about east. In *Lady Audley's Secret* (1862), Braddon locates Audley Court in Essex: 'A glorious old place – a place that visitors fell into raptures with; feeling a yearning wish to have done with life, and to stay there for ever, staring into the cool fishponds.' She draws out the implications of this description a few pages later: 'The very repose of the place grew painful from its intensity, and you felt as if a corpse must be lying somewhere within that grey and ivy-covered pile of building – so deathlike was the tranquillity of all around.'[46] Similarly, Wilkie Collins associates eastern England with treacherous stability. A long section of *No Name* (1862) takes place at Aldeburgh, Suffolk (spelt Aldborough by Collins), a place where 'local traditions are, for the most part, traditions which have been literally drowned' because of 'the extraordinary defencelessness of the land against the encroachments of the sea'. Villas have established a precarious foothold 'close on the margin of the sea', amidst the remnants of the old settlement, 'the tiny Gothic town-hall of old Aldborough – once the centre of the vanished port and borough', 'a deserted martello tower' overlooking the sea's 'work of devastation'.[47]

In *Armadale* (1866) an idyllic Somerset is contrasted with the Norfolk Broads, a 'watery solitude':

The shore in these wild regions was not like the shore elsewhere. Firm as it looked, the garden-ground in front of the reed-cutter's cottage was floating ground, that rose and fell and oozed into puddles under

the pressure of the foot [. . .] grassy places, on which strangers would
have walked confidently, where the crust of earth was not strong
enough to bear the weight of a child over the unfathomed depths of
slime and water beneath.

Literally unreliable, like the landscape of Aldborough, the Broads are
wilder, more remote and desolate. 'No sign-post was to be seen; the
country on either side was lonely and flat, intersected by broad drains
and ditches.'[48] East is not the same in the two novels: Aldborough's
newly sprouted villas correspond to Magdalen's quickly adopted per-
sonas; both look out warily towards the more powerful sea and
Magdalen finally marries a sailor, Captain Kirke, changing and regaining her identity at the same moment. *No Name*'s concern with the competing demands of modernity and integrity finds an equivalent in
Armadale, although the later, extraordinarily elaborate novel uses
doubles and dreams to ask questions about how personhood coexists
with multiple layers of being and awareness. Eastern England isolates
the self in a remote, lonely and exposing landscape and then shows it
to be, perhaps, no more than a thin crust with 'unfathomed depths of
slime and water beneath'.

Mrs Henry Wood, whose geographies are generally vaguer, follows the
associations of west and east present in her contemporaries: West Lynne
is a bustling, gossipy country town where elections are held and arrests
made; at East Lynne, a country house, domesticity is infected by deceit
and children die (*East Lynne*, 1861, chs 52 and 62). It may be too that
Henry James was recalling this geography when he located the haunted
country house of *The Turn of the Screw* (1898) in Essex.[49] Wilkie Collins's
work responds to the familiarity of this pattern. Part of the effect of
geographical details in his novel, arises from the feeling that they are
ubiquitous and predictable. His novels are characterized by their use
of highly specified locations, often identifiable ones, in combination
with a geographical pattern which has almost allegorical force.

'Blackwater House' in Hampshire, for instance, the home of Sir
Perceval Glyde in *The Woman in White* (1860) occupies the centre
ground of England, rather as Raynham Abbey does in Meredith's *The
Ordeal of Richard Feverel*, published the previous year. It too proves
suspect and, again as in Meredith, Collins habitually places a purer alternative further west – northwest in *The Woman in White* in Westmorland; due west in *No Name* in the Somerset retreat of Combe-Raven; and
in *Armadale* in Somerset again – 'the Somersetshire shores of the Bristol
Channel' where the hero grows up. These secluded spots are safer if

lying beyond the railway: in *No Name*, Norah's and Magdalen's illegitimacy does not trouble the family until their parents, Mr and Mrs Vanstone, travel up to London by train. The Armadale retreat lies further out, more than a day's walk beyond the railway; consequently, when Ozias arrives, Armadale's rival and double, he is weakened and unthreatening. Likewise, travelling to 'Limmeridge House', the alternative to 'Blackwater House' and to London in *The Woman in White*, involves a journey by train northwards to Carlisle and then one westwards by carriage, towards the shores of the Solway Firth. The second stage proves that the house will be a place of safety. In Oliphant and Trollope, railways provide a link to the capital which does not compromise the stability of the provincial centre. At least, the invasion can be accommodated. Sensation fiction believes instead that the worlds before and after railways are irreconcilable. Collins's novels press towards the country's western limits, 'beyond railways', following and exaggerating the conventional search for an inviolable tranquillity which this direction figures.[50]

His exaggerations give the impression that the conventional associations of places, particular those in the west, are over-familiar. The landscape of innocence, like innocence itself, can and has been replicated. For instance, in *No Name*, Mr Vanstone goes on a second journey by train soon after his return from London and his discovery that his daughters are illegitimate. He travels a short way down the line, hence further west, towards 'Grailsea' and is killed in a railway accident 'near Grailsea station'. News of his death closes one chapter, the next begins:

> The sun sank lower; the western breeze floated cool and fresh into the house. As the evening advanced, the cheerful ring of the village clock came nearer and nearer. Field and flower-garden felt the influence of the hour, and shed their sweetest fragrance.

In the same chapter, Mrs Vanstone, griefstricken at her husband's death, herself dies and with her their unborn child:

> Her child survived her till the evening was on the wane, and the sunset was dim in the quiet western heaven. As the darkness came, the light of the frail little life – faint and feeble from the first – flickered, and went out. All that was earthly of mother and child lay, that night, on the same bed.[51]

Everything is for effect here: the heavily paused sentences ('flickered, comma, and went out'), the insistent emotiveness of the alliteration and the calculated deployment of sentimental cliché. Geographical association, likewise, is brought into play – death and sunset come, as often, together; the western breeze is typical in possessing a soothing freshness and sweet fragrance. And, in the same way that Collins's style deliberately overplays its hand, his geography is suspiciously apt. He allows one to feel that the fresh, western breeze brings into this house its customary but now horrible sweetness.

Similarly, the name 'Grailsea' is sardonic. It evokes the Arthurian connections of the west and unsettles them by becoming the scene of a railway accident.[52] It sounds as if the Arthurian numinous may be vulnerable to intrusive modernity and survive only in names. In addition, the name itself begins to sound artificial or invented, an effect heightened by the actual existence of 'Nailsea', a town in northwest Somerset, between Bristol and Clevedon, served by a station on the Great Western line. Collins places Combe-Raven near the real Nailsea, so that some readers at least would register its transformation into Grailsea.[53] Turning 'nail' into 'grail' would be good marketing and Collins's name begins to look like a comment on the processes of marketing. This part of the Arthurian west is subject to deployment and manipulation, being no longer any different from the sentimental rhetoric that Collins has readily available.[54]

An over-familiar pattern is also one you can find in miniature almost anywhere. In *Armadale*, the pattern of east and west established across England as a whole appears on the Isle of Man, visited early on. On their first evening there, Allan and Ozias look around Castletown, 'the metropolis of the Isle of Man', in search of entertainment. Castletown lies on the eastern side of the island and its landscape is made characteristically eastern: 'a view of a flat coast to the right, and a view of a flat coast to the left. [. . .] The prevalent colour of the town was faint grey'. Disappointed by the town's desolate emptiness, the men return to their hotel to ask for advice and are told that the 'finest coast scenery in the island was [. . .] to the westward and the southward'. Allan, Collins says, 'jumped at the proposal, and in ten minutes more, he and [Ozias] Midwinter were on their way to the western wilds of the island'.[55] From here, they take out a boat and are marooned overnight on the wreck of the ship, *La Grâce de Dieu*, which has already been the scene of events crucial to the plot. While on board, Allan has the portentous dream whose meaning and interpretation govern so much of what follows. West and East, wildness and deadness, discovery and disguise are the polarities around which Collins constructs the novel, manipulating and fixing geographical associations into a neat, claustrophobic pattern.[56]

If, then, the sensation novel takes the conventional geography of west and east and sticks to it absolutely, the rigidity of the patterning has different consequences in Braddon and Collins. After *Lady Audley's Secret*, Braddon's work tends to punish and suppress rebellion. She thrillingly reveals its dangerous presence before re-establishing the accepted state of things. The way she uses the received geography assists in this process: England's conventional layout is made to seem natural so that, for example, the association between the West of England and quintessential English virtue is automatic. Like the established order of society and morals, this geography may be forgotten by impetuous youth but it governs the world and determines the true nature of all locations.[57] Collins's novels make the pervasiveness of the conventional structure a focus of attention. Instead of helping to control rebellion, geography now seems inescapable and almost suffocating. Its dominance appears the symptom of a diseased state of mind. Consequently, the mobility noted as a feature of sensation fiction coexists not only with the commodification of landscape (in which all locations are accessible and each provides an opportunity for touristic pleasure) but also, in Collins's case, with a sinister immobility arising from the sense that all locations have preordained meanings. Wherever you go, you travel within a mapped and symbolized world.[58]

Collins sends his characters westwards in the hope of finding an escape from this received world, though along a route which conforms exactly to that world's organization. Escape retreats before them. First undermining and then overleaping the middle ground of Hampshire's rural England, his stories imply the impossibility of a harmonious marriage between modern and primitive, reason and desire, social and individual. These resolutions are always available in his fiction but only as a pervasive image and as a neat conclusion. Moreover, particularly in *Armadale*, Collins psychologizes geography so that the novel is at once less carefree in its movement and more insistent that a place of safety cannot be found – the retreat is always imaginary and persistently imagined. His mobility does not erase place, it highlights and erodes the investment which his contemporaries made in place, particularly in an idea of England, west of London. Meanwhile his strange immobility, which is present in his gloomy eastern landscapes and emerges from his presentation of conventional associations as ubiquitous, draws out the fact that idealized western England is just that – an idealization.

Arguably, then, Collins's sensation fiction dismisses the ruralist aspiration which Oliphant and Trollope, among others, had relinquished more reluctantly. In doing so, it focusses on the contrast between far west (Devon, Cornwall, Somerset) and east, giving little room to the central southern England, west of London, that was the site of Barset and Carlingford. Sensation fiction reuses, therefore, the romance west made increasingly popular during the 1860s and 1870s by the huge success of R.D. Blackmore's *Lorna Doone* (1869), following Kingsley's *Westward Ho!* (1855) and accompanied by Tennyson's Cornish *Idylls of the King* (1859–84). The same opposition gradually comes to dominate Gissing's fiction too, so that a retreat to rural Devonshire turns into the only alternative to London's dreadful corrosiveness. Through this change of emphasis in geography, ruralist hopes may be seen as restricted to the private life as in Gissing or remembered ironically as in Collins. Or, according to Braddon's view of Cornwall in *Aurora Floyd*, ruralism can survive there in a conservative form. Barset and Carlingford (like Howitt's Hampshire) welcome the new and slowly reform it; Braddon's Cornishman, Talbot Bulstrode, is more forceful and himself unaltered by events. It is Aurora, representing new money and London suburbia, who must learn her lesson. This is a more tyrannical and masculinist image of virtuous behaviour and a more authoritarian view of society than either Trollope's or Oliphant's. It finds an equivalent in Collins's sense that geography itself is a tyrant. Consequently, while Collins's east undermines or melts personality, his west seems to dictate the terms on which personality can be gained. In this he reacts against a belief more widely present in the culture that the far west provides a source of sound guidance and true selfhood. He notices that this praise of the west is a kind of conquest; England's wildest places are civilized by being granted a civilizing influence.

The Return of the Native: facing east and west

Dorset falls into neither the central southern west of Barset and Carlingford nor the remote west of sensation fiction. Sometimes, it is drawn into the first: Dinah Craik's *Agatha's Husband* (1853) celebrates an 'old house on the Dorset coast', at 'Kingcombe Holm', located near Corfe Castle in the Isle of Purbeck. The house is an idyllic retreat beyond the 'sharp bleak wind' of the moors you cross on the way from London, a sheltered spot like those celebrated by Mitford, Howitt and their successors. Ruralist Hampshire, therefore, can just about be stretched into Dorset but more often Dorset represents the backward and unmodernized, sometimes obstinately resistant to change, as in Trollope's *An Eye for an Eye* (1879), sometimes sadly left behind, as in Oliphant's *Phoebe, Junior*. It illustrates by contrast the social harmony and blend of old and new achieved by ruralism. Significantly, too, it lies to one side of the route into the west (along the Thames valley and down into Devon and Cornwall) which expresses the aspiration towards a harmonious, integrated life – a route which at times confirms ruralism and at others leaves it behind as a lost cause. Dorset is western but, by and large, it does not fit. Meanwhile, in sensation fiction, the county hardly features at all (as far as I know) and certainly does not form part of the mystical west made up of Devon, Cornwall and, to a lesser extent, Somerset.

Sensation fiction arises out of the mobility made possible by train travel and its exclusion of Dorset may reflect how the railways bypassed the county, removing it from the 'West Country'. *The Mayor of Caster-bridge* reflects on how the new transport system both modernized Dorset and turned it into a backwater. *The Woodlanders* shows that, for Hardy, ruralist writing had a similar impact. Whether rural places expressed directly the harmony of old and new or showed the damaging conse-quences of remoteness from the modern world or represented a vaguer sense that the countryside was delightful, they were drawn by this writing into a ruralist world and made to conform to its expectations. Backwaters implied a modernizing agenda. In Trollope's and Oliphant's version of ruralism, country places are replaced by country towns and cathedral cities; these are inhabited more than visited. The tactic of both novelists is to embrace the quaintness of the ruralist image and then to reveal its merit. Whether provincial cities are 'really like that' or not, they can tell us how the whole country ought ideally to be arranged.

Hardy was always personally rather hostile to Trollope and no better than ambivalent about Oliphant. His novels attack the clergy repeat-edly and through them the role granted to provincial life by Trollope, Oliphant and by the geography they use. The disagreement is made explicit in *Jude the Obscure*, discussed in a later chapter. Before then, it emerges secretively via Hardy's depiction of a region that is not so much a backwater as somewhere simply different. Wessex's remoteness allows it to stand on an equal footing with other places, different and yet no different, a region but not a province and named after a kingdom.

The following chapters discuss the emergence of this regional Wessex in Hardy's novels, from the pseudo-sensation fiction of *Desperate Reme-dies*, through the complicatedly pastoral world of *Far from the Madding Crowd* and into the anti-ruralist polemic of *Jude*. These analyses are also informed by the personal element in Hardy's geography – its participa-tion in a secret autobiography. In this regard, Henchard's circling of Elizabeth-Jane is exemplary. Hardy, like Henchard, resists the integra-tion of a rural world into a wider scheme of things by building it out of personal attachments. Nonetheless and not surprisingly, the distinctive Wessex which Hardy creates out of his opposition to ruralist geography and to that of sensation fiction modifies those geographies' sense of east and west. This is especially clear in *The Return of the Native*.

As is obvious perhaps, *The Return of the Native* describes a clash between the up-to-the-minute and the outdated, Paris and Egdon. Clym's return home brings the one into the other. And, as has been pointed out before, the novel seems at once to accept the conventional view that Egdon is behind the times and also to query it. Gillian Beer remarks:

> As readers, we are shifted unendingly between microscopic and telescopic, between very old dialect words and very up-to-date references, particularly in relation to Eustacia. So within the individual observer or reader the phases of past cultural development are enacted synchronically through the language of the novel.

These different phases are present to the reader 'not in sequence only but alongside and in contestation with each other', partly because the novel's language shifts in register so drastically and partly because it contains an 'allusive system' which 'disequilibriates any easy developmental assumptions the reader may bring to the text'. Beer is reluctant to claim that Hardy throws off all of his Victorian assumptions ('In Hardy's imagination, as in that of other Victorian writers, return is not possible without the idea of retrogression') and for this reason she emphasizes how the synchronic perception is 'enacted' within the reader.[59] Readers can gain the synchronic point of view which Hardy was still reaching for as he wrote the novel. The novel's geography corresponds to this reading of its language, contributing to the book's realisation of co-present historical periods. In my opinion, however, it also brings out something more radical and controlled: Hardy's conscious scepticism about progress and his hostility to 'Victorian' ideas.

Egdon Heath is characterized as northerly – the home of wild mallards who bring with them 'an amplitude of Northern knowledge', it is a landscape as gaunt as Thule or Iceland.[60] Eustacia, banished from Budmouth to Egdon, is exotically southern ('One had fancied that such lip-curves were mostly lurking underground in the south as fragments of forgotten marbles [. . . .] Her presence brought memories of Bourbon roses, rubies, tropical midnights'); she yearns to return there and looks southwards, towards her 'native place', Budmouth.[61] In the original 1878 version, this trajectory is made more emphatic by Hardy's references to 'Southerton' where Thomasin was to be married to Wildeve. After 1895, 'Southerton' was changed to 'Anglebury', corresponding to Wareham. The original name suggests southerly associations, even a southerly direction even though Wareham in fact lies east of the heath-lands Hardy made into Egdon, on their southern border.[62] Egdon seems to be defined against an exotic, fashionable south, creating a polarity similar to the one established in *The Mayor of Casterbridge* between the warm south of Weatherbury and Melchester to the north which is a snowy and unfeeling barracks-town.

North–south is complicated by the novel's preoccupation with move-ments east and west. J. Hillis Miller has discussed the novel's map, designed by Hardy himself for the first volume edition, and the relation of topography to wider issues raised in the book.[63] He points out that the map places east instead of north at the top. Hardy rotates the conventional orientation through ninety degrees, partly for practical reasons – to fit the length of Edgon Heath most economically onto a printed page – but partly too for thematic ones. Miller discusses the novel's 'complex solar poetry' in which many different figures are asso-ciated with the sun and human life is seen as both generated and destroyed by its power.[64] The sun and the orientation of the map seem to me to be connected.

Characteristically, it is Clym who travels east and west across the heath – from Blooms-End on its westernmost edge, he walks eastwards, at first towards Mistover Knap where he courts Eustacia and later to the cottage in Alderworth where they live after marrying.[65] Other people cross it in other ways: Wildeve usually moves north, from the Quiet Woman Inn on the southern side, first towards Mistover Knap, later towards Alderworth; on her marriage to Clym, Eustacia moves from her north–south alignment (between Mistover Knap, Blackbarrow and the Quiet Woman) to her husband's east–west world, the question in their married life being whether or not Eustacia will visit her mother-in-law at Blooms-End. She gives up her 'independence' not for the life of a lady's companion in Budmouth but for life as a daughter-in-law, caught up in the tensions between mother and son.[66] Similarly, marriage to Wildeve removes Thomasin from Blooms-End (west) to the Quiet Woman (south) and Clym's return moves him from Budmouth (and Paris beyond) back to Blooms-End, returning from south to west. (Newson's move in *The Mayor of Casterbridge* from Falmouth (west) to Budmouth (south) is the reverse of this and, accordingly, it is a move into the future.) The Yeobrights inhabit therefore an east–west world whereas outsiders like Wildeve and Eustacia think in terms of north–south. They look to a world beyond the borders of the heath, while the Yeobrights either dwell contentedly within Egdon's world or in Clym's case seek to re-enter it. So Clym's promise to open a school in Budmouth seems doomed by the geography of the novel as well as by Eustacia's character and his own poor eyesight.

Commanded by the sun, the east–west axis is subject to and expressive of time. For people out on the heath, the sun's position tells the time, day by day. More widely in the period, looking westward was associated with both future and past – places where civilization would flourish next and those still untouched by advancing modernity. It offered the freedoms of possibility and of escape. Looking eastward is a look into the finished and static, into a present already caught in the past, into the Gothic rigidities of sensation fiction. Blooms-End conveys stasis in the novel and Hardy emphasizes the eastward outlook of the house.[67] From it, Mrs Yeobright looks towards the eastern side of the heath, visualising her son's wedding, his imprisonment in what she believes a bad marriage and hers in her regret. She hears, caught on the easterly breeze, 'The ringers at East Egdon [. . .] announcing the nuptials of Eustacia and her son' (Hardy, *Return*, Bk. 3, ch.7, p.214). Later on, Clym finds in the house only recollections of his dead mother; it has become for him a house that looks into the past. Because of this, Hardy upsets conventional associations – journeys west in the novel lead to Blooms-End, to neither a hopeful future nor a pristine past but only to retrospection. This suits Hardy's map for the novel in which going west means going down – into blocked depths. On maps oriented north–south, movement east and west resembles movement forward or back (on the level or along a line of print).[68] By making this axis the vertical, Hardy makes progressive movement appear to lead nowhere.

The geography of east and west in the novel is also complemented by the ferocity Hardy lends to the setting sun. Its light does not lead from this world into another, showing a glimpse of the future and eternity; rather it assaults the living who walk towards it, flattening out the environment through which they move. When Eustacia and Clym are courting, they part at sunset:

> The sun, resting on the horizon line, streamed across the ground from between copper-coloured and lilac clouds, stretched out in flats beneath a sky of pale soft green. All dark objects on the earth that lay towards the sun were overspread by a purple haze, against which groups of wailing gnats shone out, rising upwards and dancing about like sparks of fire.[69]

Eustacia is wrapped up by the sun's luminous rays as she leaves and Clym becomes 'overpowered' by the dead flat of the scenery: 'it gave him a sense of bare equality with, and no superiority to, a single living thing under the sun' (Hardy, *Return*, Bk. 3, ch.5, pp.204, 206). Conventionally, sunset is more uplifting; on Egdon it creates a consuming mist. Briefly lit by its fire, like the Keatsian wailing gnats, people are quickly 'wrapped up' – extinguished and lost. Clym seems to have entered a world in which aspiration is useless and the progressive aspiration to improve matters particularly so. Retrogression and recovery seem, however, just as impossible: his journeys into the heart of the heath always lead eastward from Blooms-End. Partly this implies the backwards, return journey which Clym wants to make. Yet it is in the east that Clym falls in love with a fashionable, modern 'town' girl and finds himself fixed in his present-day self by her expectations of him. He even knows, as he marries and moves east to settle at Alderworth, that his relationship with Eustacia will not develop; that it has, in a sense, no future.

Journeys of return can be figured as either eastward or westward; what one returns to changes with the direction. Clym's romantic sensibility and his desire to re-enter his pristine home suit a westward direction; by reversing it, Hardy suggests the impossibility of Clym achieving his aims and consequently the limits to retrogression. He returns only to his own, modernized self with its limitations and weaknesses; this is what has become native to him and is inescapable.[70] There is an implicit refusal here to believe either in progress or in the possibility of return – to innocence, to origin, to old-world rustic charm. East and west carry these resonances but have been turned upright so that the scope they normally offer disappears. Clym's experience follows a path that runs up and down, up and down, although he thinks of it (and Hardy's readership would think of it) as running along an axis that stretches forward and back, into past and future, away from the confining here and now. Likewise in the novel, human lives seem to consist in a momentary uprightness rising out of a flat surface – Eustacia appears in this way near the beginning – or in a standing figure resisting the flattening power of the sun and surrounding nature. People in the novel stand up to assert their dominion, govern for a time and then, inevitably, fall down. Egdon's flatness gives prominence to the upright human form while its summit on Rainbarrow expresses the power over themselves and others which people aspire to. When dead, people become the uppermost layer in the strata of history: thin, flat and motionless; while alive, they constantly magnify their own size, creating worlds around themselves circumscribed by their own interests. Hardy's vertical orientation of east–west on his map and his placing of Blooms-End in the west but facing east both contribute to the sense conveyed by the novel as a whole that the sequentiality of human experience creates illusions of movement forward and back, of progress and return, of power and its loss. In fact, the book argues, lives are momentary events, incidents not careers.

By placing Alderworth and Blooms-End at opposite ends of the heath, Hardy also suggests the self-involvement shared by Mrs Yeobright and her son, the self-isolating conflict between them which makes Egdon, as they experience it, an enlarged domestic space. Clym's removal to Alderworth creates a larger, disproportionate arena for a family row. Small human woes and a massively indifferent natural world seem overlaid upon one another as if to show, one might suppose, the foolishness of people's self-concern. Actually the result is rather different and more sympathetic. Mrs Yeobright's last journey to be reconciled with her son and his wife lies along the route between Blooms-End and Alderworth in an easterly direction. Her exhausted return, convinced her son has rejected her, follows the same track westward into the setting sun. On her way back, she lies down to rest near a patch of thyme:

> She leant back [. . .] and the soft eastern portion of the sky was as great a relief to her eyes as the thyme was to her head. While she looked a heron arose on that side of the sky and flew on with his face towards the sun. He had come dripping wet from some pool in the valleys, and as he flew the edges and lining of his wings, his thighs, and his breast were so caught by the bright sunbeams that he appeared as if formed of burnished silver. Up in the zenith where he was seemed a free and happy place, away from all contact with the earthly ball to which she was pinioned; and she wished that she could arise uncrushed from its surface and fly as he flew then.
>
> But, being a mother, it was inevitable that she should soon cease to ruminate upon her own condition. Had the track of her next thought been marked by a streak in the air, like the path of a meteor, it would have shown a direction contrary to the heron's, and have descended to the eastward upon the roof of Clym's house.
>
> (Hardy, *Return*, Bk. 4, ch.6, p.282)

Laid low physically by the heat and the demands of the journey, Mrs Yeobright is forced to abandon the aspirations towards self-betterment and escape which she shares with her son and is partly responsible for instilling in him. In a sense, she abandons time and instead lies down on thyme. The herb's name does appear to be a pointed choice. Mrs Yeobright cannot follow the heron into the 'free and happy' air and on its journey into the west – a journey that transfigures the bird into a luminous, mythical creature. Her mind returns to Clym, going straight and quickly in the opposite direction. East dominates west; personal attachment prevents freedom and motherly love proves stronger than a desire for progress.

The passage illustrates how Hardy manipulates the conventional associations of east and west. It shows too Mrs Yeobright coming down to earth literally and metaphorically, finding Egdon to be different and separate from the concerns which govern her sense of it. It could be read as a moral lesson, chastening her ambition and encouraging 'wise passiveness'. Other parts of the book suggest, however, that Mrs Yeobright's self- and human-centred point of view is unavoidable while she lives: self-elevation followed by prostration is experienced by several of the characters and prostration, with the new sense of personal and human smallness it brings, also brings death. Mrs Yeobright dies a few hours after lying down; Eustacia, who is similarly brought low, commits suicide and Clym newly convinced of his own worthlessness seeks death without success. It seems inevitable that, while they live, Hardy's characters are condemned to the trajectories of progress and retrogression even though both directions lead nowhere. They cannot help but inhabit the east–west axis which brings with it exaggerated ideas of your own importance and power – exaggerations which time and the sun pitilessly uncover at the end.

The pathos of this is itself a form of resistance to another version of progress; the moral advance through experience towards wisdom which one might expect does not occur. Instead, Hardy suggests a different form of movement within the landscape which implies a different self-understanding. Diggory Venn proves to be the most mobile of the characters. His work as a reddleman takes him in and out of Egdon, crossing from one side to the other; his interest in Thomasin and her family takes him to all quarters of the district and beyond.[71] This mobility is combined with an unusual generosity. Rather than seek to win back Thomasin, he tries to make her as happy as possible in the life with Wildeve which she prefers. Instead of attempting to determine the future in the light of his own past, Venn adapts to the moment; Wildeve's mortal enemy, he is in many ways Clym's opposite. He manages, for example, to change himself with relative ease into a reddleman, 'one of a class rapidly becoming extinct' and then change back into the dairyman he had been before, with the difference that his profits from the reddle trade allow him to buy the farm his father 'had in his lifetime'.[72] Hardy's references to extinctions and the dodo in connection with the reddleman, Venn's apparent self-improvement and upward mobility, plus Thomasin's departure from the heath in order to marry him, all lead one to think of him as an example of Victorian progress. Yet these elements in his characterization also point in the opposite direction: he has not advanced, he has only regained his father's place (Miss Marjoribanks by contrast attains what her father had always desired). Likewise, Thomasin has lived on the edge of the heath all her life and in this respect North Shadwater is not very different from Blooms-End. The movement she makes resembles Diggory's travels around the heath while a reddleman. Rather than being a migration away (as the proposed move to Southerton with Wildeve would certainly have been), it is a move within her world.

Diggory's character corresponds, therefore, to the presentation Hardy selects for the dialect of the novel and the way the book's varied language suggests many different historical periods coexisting at once. His presence implies, moreover, a way of being where, in the absence of progress or development, coexistence survives. Moving around the heath and living at various different points in it, Venn avoids the axis of time, escaping both the aspiration towards modernity and the abreactive recoil away from it. His cunning is animal yet he is the kindliest and most humane of the characters; not putting himself forward socially, he is often seen lying low to the ground, hiding in bushes and setting traps to trip up his self-important, ambitious rival. Erratic and even eccentric, Venn possesses the same 'eclectic independence' which marks other occasions in Hardy when the provincial is preferred to the metropolitan or national. In a novel so concerned with the march of time, Venn's character resists the future by ignoring it. His provincialism is not antique so much as everyday and, to that extent, timeless.[73] He has the self-containment of the rustic chorus and of the landscape where they live, plus the will and determination which in Eustacia, Wildeve and Clym produces various forms of self-aggrandizing conceit. Consequently, he counters the strand in the novel which implies that people overestimate themselves to the extent that they are self-aware. A fatalistic pattern of rising and falling, aspiration and prostration is linked to the east–west axis of the book. It is answered by Venn's travels around and about, his unpredictable movements which have a pattern of their own.[74]

5
Rural Encounters

Hardy's *Return of the Native* reorients east and west in order to question widely-held beliefs which that trajectory conveyed. Aspirations towards transcendence and self-transcendence, towards personal and social advancement, both arising from the ambition to take command of time and 'make history' – all these are linked to movements westward and eastward and all are challenged by the novel. Of course, east and west were connected by the cultural geography of Hardy's day to other concerns as well: a ruralist desire to make the counties west of London into an image of social harmony which could help confirm national order; and, overlapping with this, sensation fiction's psychologized geography in which the far west suggests possibilities of escape and integrity, compromised as these associations may be by overfamiliarity. *The Woodlanders* shows how pointedly Hardy could parody the language of ruralism, with its presumption and idealization. The present chapter reads *Far from the Madding Crowd* as an inquiry into ruralist assumptions both about rustic communities and social structures and argues that *Desperate Remedies*, a novel plainly indebted to sensation fiction, questions the genre's assumption that geographical location is merely symbolic.

Consequently, in both these novels, visitors to a rural world discover a clash between expectation and material; the places they visit are at once ordinary and distinct. In that respect, places resemble other people, equal to the self and separate from it. Geographies can imply societies, therefore, and *Far from the Madding Crowd* finds a new – regionalist rather than ruralist – account of society through a new way of constructing geography. Secondly, though, geographies may be seen as personal. The ordinary distinctiveness of other places resists the ambition of a ruralist or a sensationalist to make everywhere conform to a preconceived geography. In the same way that Hardy maps his personal

Wessex onto a map of England that is standard and perfectly recognizable, so people generally will construct individual geographies amidst
the powerful forces of cultural expectation fashioning a geography
around them. Hardy's particular sense of how geography may be personal underlies his depiction of Henchard circling Elizabeth-Jane in the
final chapters of *The Mayor of Casterbridge*. Chapter 6 goes on to suggest
that the same interest governs *A Laodicean* and can be seen informing
the development of Wessex from *Wessex Tales* on.

Roads, trains and *Desperate Remedies*

Desperate Remedies was written while Hardy was still working as an architect, work which involved his travelling around Dorset and sometimes
beyond to out-of-the-way parish churches. These journeys would often
have meant travel by train and then by carriage, as was the case in his
journey to St. Juliot in Cornwall in 1870 and 1871 (see *Life*, p.67). Wilkie
Collins's sensation novels suggested that places beyond the reach of railways remained safe from the predations of a corrupting outside world.
Travelling by road that bit further beyond the railway line promised to
transport you into an older time and place, which could be either more
innocent or more primitive or both. *Desperate Remedies* concentrates
its action on Carriford and Knapwater House, which lie close to one
another and are based on places near to Hardy's birthplace: Kingston
Maurward House and the villages of Lower Bockhampton and West
Stafford. Unusually for Hardy's novels, though, this area is reached by
train, from the station at 'Carriford Road' which is a short ride away
from both village and country house.[1] *Under the Greenwood Tree, Far from
the Madding Crowd* and *The Return of the Native* are set in and around
the same scenes but trains do not feature, so there is no felt contrast
between the two modes of travel.[2]

As in *The Mayor of Casterbridge*, Hardy chooses places which railways
have bypassed – Carriford, though served by the station, has nevertheless been robbed of its role within the mainstream of national life. 'The
Three Tranters Inn' in the village

> was an uncommonly characteristic and handsome specimen of the
> genuine roadside inn of bygone times; and standing on the great
> highway to the South-west of England, (which ran through
> Carriford,) had in its time been the scene of as much of what is now
> looked upon as the romantic and genial experience of stage-coach
> travelling as any halting-place in the country. The railway had

absorbed the whole stream of traffic which formerly flowed through the village and along by the ancient door of the inn.[3]

The stables have become silent and empty, overgrown with grass, and the inn-keeper would be 'empty-handed' did he not extend 'his agri-cultural business' – a process partially responsible a little later for burning the inn to the ground. The 'general stillness pervading the spot' and the collapsing roofs, 'sunk into vast hollows till they seemed like the cheeks of toothless age', convey a sinister melancholy familiar from Collins. Beyond the railways' modernity lies this disregarded, poignant, rather threatening little place.

Hardy heightens the effect by making two of the most important women in the novel, Cytherea, the heroine, and later, Eunice, wife of the hero/villain Aeneas Manston, arrive at the station and find no-one to meet them. Each woman is a stranger: Cytherea comes originally from 'Hocbridge', miles away, and is lodging at 'Creston', modelled on Weymouth; Mrs Manston has arrived from London. The moment of their arrival becomes, through the delay, a moment when they face something unknown and unfamiliar. For Mrs Manston particularly, it is a miserable arrival: she looks 'up and down the platform, dreary with autumn gloom and wind' and strains her eyes 'into the gloom of the chilly night', starting to suspect that her husband's non-appearance proves he no longer loves her. In fact, as Hardy has already told us, Manston has simply misread the timetable; similarly, the reason why Cytherea is left to herself on the platform is that her driver has been getting drunk in the 'public-house close adjoining'. Sinister meanings may be imagined, not least by the reader of this sort of fiction, where actually a preoccupied self-involvement is at work: Manston's 'inspec-tion was carelessly made' while he drank his morning coffee; the driver was drowning his sorrows.[4]

The novel as a whole is preoccupied with arrivals similar to this, inter-ested both by what culture railway transport brings with it and what assumptions the railway traveller makes about the world beyond. Near the beginning of the novel Cytherea and her brother Owen travel to Creston, where he has received a promise of work as an architect, assist-ing in the practice of 'Mr. Gradfield'. Cytherea plans to look for work as a governess.[5] 'The whole town is looking out for us,' Owen says to himself throughout their journey. On arriving, 'He called upon Mr. Gradfield – the only man who had been directly informed of his coming – and found that Mr. Gradfield had forgotten it' (Hardy, *DR*, vol.1, ch.2, s.1, p.22).[6]

Likewise, Cytherea's advertisements bring no response until she has tried three times, on each occasion offering to do more menial tasks. When she does at last find work, as Miss Aldclyffe's maid, she learns almost at once that it is as a result of private recommendation, made by Edward Springrove who is in love with her:

> 'Oh, yes,' she said, 'of course.' Her thoughts had run as follows [. . .]
> Edward knew I was going to advertise for a situation of some kind.
> He watched the *Times*, and saw it, my address being attached.
> He thought it would be excellent for me to be here that we might meet whenever he came home.
> He told his father that I might be recommended as a lady's maid [. . . .]
> 'His father told Mrs. Morris; Mrs. Morris told Miss Aldclyffe.'
> The whole chain of incidents that drew her there was plain.
>   (Hardy, *DR*, vol.1, ch.5, s.2, pp.68–9)

Outsiders' largely unconscious belief in their own special importance is twice disappointed here, in Cytherea's case with the added feeling that you will not be noticed at all until you have made some sort of personal impression on a native – that is, with somebody who has connections. In part, Hardy is making quite a familiar point about the discrepancy between merit and success and the difficulty outsiders face in breaking into a settled and self-contained community. He is also interested, however, in the fact that the world beyond the railway is assumed by visitors to be different, being seen as backward and hostile or idyllic and delightful. A geography common to sensation fiction and ruralist writing locates it in these ways. It turns out, however, to be little different from anywhere else.

One proof of this is the repetition of similar events in London. Later in the novel, Miss Aldclyffe advertises for a land steward. Although she receives many replies from suitable candidates, she chooses Manston, to whom she has sent a copy of the advert anonymously. She secretly notifies Manston in London and Manston sends a letter of application from Liverpool. Despite the best efforts of a worthy lawyer (in quite a funny scene), several far more well-qualified candidates are passed over because Miss Aldclyffe, who is connected to Manston, is determined he should have the post. On the larger stage of England, as in Creston, private motives control success and failure.

Similarly, in the closing sections of the book, Hardy narrates a number of chases, either of Manston or by him. Manston tries to intercept an incriminating letter by taking the mail-train out of London and then walking with the postman to the remote letter-box where it is delivered. He succeeds in obtaining the letter but only after an undignified scramble in the mud, searching for the key to the box. The whole episode is narrated in extraordinary detail, in part reflecting Manston's skill and in part registering the intricate particularity of the local world which the railway and the sensation novel enter. Manston, another outsider, seems to be being brought up against the strangeness of remote places and shown how, when seen close to, they reveal hidden extents and recesses. The received geography is replaced by a more intimate, material one. This contrast could itself be put to use by a broadly pastoral perspective and made to confirm that rural life contains face-to-face relations and complex social structures whereas town life produces deracination and anomie. Again, however, Hardy sets up a contrast between train and road, metropolitan and rustic, which he goes on to disturb.

Although, for example, Manston's ingenuity as a pursuer does succeed, nothing comes of it – a second letter which he does not know about arrives safely and leads to his exposure. By balancing his villain's vile success with the resourcefulness of his virtuous opponents, Hardy prevents Manston from becoming either the rapacious violator of a rural community or its defeated invader. Hardy sets him instead on a level with the people who gradually start to resist him by acting in similar ways: Cytherea, who travels by train to visit Manston's local rector, Mr Raunham, and charms him into helping her; Owen, who tracks down the local newspaper reporter in order to find out more about the death of Manston's wife; Edward Springrove, who follows Manston and Cytherea by train to Southampton in order to prevent their going on honeymoon. Later on, in an exact reversal of Manston's search of the country, Edward pursues Manston's trail through the lodging-houses and pawnshops of London.

Tracking, pursuit and avoiding discovery become more and more frequent as the novel reaches its climax, suggesting that Hardy is both employing and countering the geography of sensation fiction. Springrove plays a similar role to that of John Hartright in Collins's *The Woman in White* and his search through London recalls searches in *No Name*. In Collins, these journeys and pursuits confirm (with whatever degree of archness) the accepted valuations of city and country – the first is seamy and corrupt, the second idyllic and / or Gothically imprisoning. In *Desperate Remedies*, Hardy unsettles these polarities and, in some respects, a kind of flatness is the result: Owen's early disappointment at finding that his arrival has been forgotten typifies the novel's suggestion that everywhere is equally indifferent to outsiders and equally closed to them. How different it may be is not visible. And, because what characterizes the new place cannot be seen at once, the conventional assumptions visitors make are almost inevitable and almost always misleading. Furthermore, the equivalence of everywhere corresponds to the self-concern everyone usually displays.

In the final passages of the novel, it is true, this point tends to get lost. Instead, Manston's increasing isolation is set against the heartening team-spirit shown by Springrove, Owen Graye, Cytherea and the rector; generally a more traditional narrative structure takes over. The book ends with the villainous Manston, sophisticated and metropolitan, unmasked by the newly forming community, based in the country. The conventionality of this division of the novel's world is confirmed by the routine quality of Manston's final confession to the murder of his wife. It is paralleled in Dickens's *Hard Times* where the villain Bounderby is isolated and exposed while Stephen Blackpool is rescued from a derelict mineshaft by communal effort.

Such an ending is typical of sensation fiction in being broadly conservative and reassuring. It makes it easy to forget the novel's disturbance of other conventions of the genre, including its geography. Much in the layout of Knapwater House and its surroundings evokes sensation fiction. There is a 'gushing waterfall [. . . .] Black at the head, and over the surface of the deep cold hole into which it fell' and a creaking waterwheel, 'which the coachman had said would drive him mad'.[7] Cytherea, on the night of her arrival, luxuriates in the terror and gloom these sounds evoke. Over the course of the story, her experience leads from such Gothic trappings, intensely and weirdly realized by the novel, towards a more active engagement with the world nearby. She begins to move around the local district, living in it and coming to understand the various characters who make up the community. Moving from one geography to the other – from the preordained patterns of sensation fiction to the local knowledge of an inhabitant – is matched by a move from passivity to agency. Cytherea and Owen are both pushed by events to act for themselves and this contributes to their gaining the kind of geographical knowledge that locals possess – locals who are equally and just as self-interestedly acting for themselves.

Although, then, it adopts at moments sensation fiction's construction of the relation between country and city, the book works more usually (and more originally) with complex oppositions between action and inaction, progress and repression. These, according to *Desperate Remedies*, are universal polarities, ones which 'country and city' attempts to command and delimit. That is to say, the deepest feelings in the book surround the question of getting on in the world, of self-advancement and integration into society. These could easily be mapped onto an opposition between rural and urban, so that, for instance, the journey to the city became a crucial stage in life, a turning-point in the *Bildungsroman*. Hardy is more engaged, however, with the universally present pressure to get on and pursue one's own interests even while social interaction is one of the conditions of existence. The book implies that using an opposition between country and city may be attractive as a way of dividing up the world precisely because it distracts attention from these uncomfortable facts of life.

Far from the Madding Crowd: stars, constellations and Herbert Spencer

Commissioned by Leslie Stephen after he had come across *Under the Greenwood Tree*, *Far from the Madding Crowd* appears to be the earlier novel's successor. The 'short and quite rustic story' of *Under the Greenwood Tree* seems the natural precursor to the 'pastoral tale', *Far from the Madding Crowd*.[8] The later novel often continues to be seen as 'Hardy's sunlit pastoral of English rural life'[9] and certainly it invokes the scenes and vocabulary of the ruralist tradition. John Goode, Marjorie Garson and Joe Fisher, however, have all recently argued against the well-established account of the novel as a celebration of agricultural life, seeing its pastoral elements as both consciously deployed and subverted.[10]

In some respects, the novel's geography corresponds to the pastoral readings it has received: the Great Barn on Bathsheba's farm near Weatherbury provides an image of permanence appropriate to 'these nooks' where 'the busy outsider's ancient times are only old, his old times are still new' and 'his present is futurity'.[11] The Weatherbury district is contrasted firstly (and mostly) with Melchester, where Sergeant Troy's regiment is barracked and where Fanny goes in search of him; it is compared secondly with Bath, where Troy and Bathsheba marry. Sophisticated and alluring, Bath makes Weatherbury uncomplicated and undeceitful; the bleakness of the Melchester barracks in chapter eleven gives greater emphasis to Weatherbury's warmth, fecundity and kindness. As Rosemarie Morgan has pointed out, from the 1895 edition on, Hardy tended to replace references to Melchester with references to an unspecified town 'many miles north of Weatherbury'.[12] Apart from moving the cruelty and coldness of the place further away from the

centre of Wessex, these changes bring out the north–south contrast of
the book, conforming its geography more closely to that of Elizabeth
Gaskell, George Eliot and the Howitts, fitting the pastoral of Weatherbury into a conventional, national geography.

In other respects, however, the novel's geography contributes to the
sense that it is deliberately unsettling pastoral conventions and ruralist
feeling. The opening chapters show Gabriel Oak tending his flock on
Norcombe Hill, meeting Bathsheba while she is living nearby with her
aunt, proposing to her and being rejected. When many of his sheep are
accidentally killed, Oak is forced to give up farming for himself and offer
himself for hire as a shepherd. Bathsheba has already left the neighbourhood of Norcombe Hill and travelled to Weatherbury, 'more than
twenty miles off'. Oak follows her. The rest of the action takes place in
Weatherbury and its environs but Norcombe remains a point of reference and refuge. Bathsheba retreats there to visit her aunt when Troy is
presumed dead; earlier, when he is proving a bad husband, her regrets
about the marriage join to a nostalgia for Norcombe:

> That she had never by look word or sign encouraged a man to
> approach her, that she had felt herself sufficient to herself, and had
> in the independence of her girlish heart fancied there was a certain
> degradation in renouncing the simplicity of a maiden existence to
> become the humbler half of an indifferent whole, were facts now
> bitterly remembered. O if she had never stooped to folly of this
> kind, respectable as it was, and could only stand again as she had
> stood on the hill at Norcombe, and dare Troy or any other man to
> pollute a hair of her head by his interference.
>
> (Hardy, *Madding Crowd*, ch.40, pp.239–40)

By comparison with Norcombe, Weatherbury is a place of interference,
compromise and bitter mistakes. Indeed, rather than inhabiting a
rustic paradise, both Gabriel and Bathsheba have been driven out of
Eden – Gabriel by financial ruin, Bathsheba by suddenly inheriting
wealth.

Consequently, Gabriel's journey to Weatherbury and his reception
there have a double aspect; they are comparable to Lockwood's intrusion into a provincial 'nook' and at the same time they are an entry
onto a wider stage of life – one in which Gabriel's own insignificance
and powerlessness become obvious. Moreover, the same is true of
Bathsheba even though she looks to Gabriel as if she has adapted
perfectly to the new conditions. Initially a May-queen, governing

the rustics with generous charm, Bathsheba is also made, through Troy's seduction, to recognize the power of her own sexuality. The reader, although mostly closer to Gabriel's centre of consciousness, sees the experience of both these characters as partly quaint and partly terrible.

Norcombe's presence, therefore, before and behind Weatherbury enables the novel to prompt reflection on the ruralist world-view it caters to. Joe Fisher and John Goode have seen this reflection as fundamentally hostile; both writers bring out the critical, sometimes caustically satirical undertones of the novel, reading Hardy as covertly hostile to his readership and the conventions of pastoral which it demanded. Certainly in chapter 17, the novel sounds prickly towards the 'Genteel strangers, whose god was their town, who might happen to be compelled to linger about this nook for a day' (Hardy, *Madding Crowd*, p.104). There are several other comparisons of town and country in this part of the novel (see pp.100 and 106); this one focusses on Boldwood, 'the nearest approach to aristocracy' in the district and the focus of interest for 'Genteel strangers'. At this stage in the narrative, Boldwood is beginning to turn into Bathsheba's obsessive lover, the change showing the superficiality of the visitors' expectations. They are mentioned here as so many Lockwoods to Boldwood's Heathcliff.

Despite this, however, the novel cannot be read very satisfactorily as just a satire on pastoral or ruralist perspectives, with their ignorance and self-ignorant complacencies. That is to say, quaintness and pain do not oppose each other like illusion and reality, pretence and truth. The rustic clowns (Jan Coggan, Joseph Poorgrass, Jacob Smallbury, Laban Tall and so on) exist alongside the at times frighteningly intense feelings of Boldwood, Bathsheba, Troy and Gabriel. Entering the Weatherbury world, as Bathsheba and Gabriel do, the reader is confronted by constantly altering perspectives – altering as characters change, altering between characters or groups of characters. The primary question seems to be less about uncovering truth amidst falsity than about coordinating many different points of view. The novel's concern with the management of farms, with how one person can best govern a team of workers, is of a piece with its central characters' experience of encountering and negotiating with a rural society that can be bafflingly varied. Cytherea in *Desperate Remedies* gradually attracts a group of people around herself, forming a team and miniature community. Bathsheba finds herself amidst an already existing group whose differing needs and shortcomings she must address. The oppositions in the first novel lie between fictional and real strangeness; in the latter, the difficulties involved in encountering the real are considered via the contrast between solitary autonomy and the demands of a society.

Arriving at Creston shows Owen and Cytherea how little other people care about them and implies how easy it is to make fanciful assumptions about unknown places. In the same way, settling in Weatherbury brings Bathsheba into a ruralist paradise but one where she must act and one which looks to her less perfect than the place she has left. The reader's likely ruralist feelings about Weatherbury correspond to some of Bathsheba's nostalgia for Norcombe. Consequently, her experience in the narrative challenges those assumptions from a subjective and objective direction – both as they are felt inwardly and as they operate externally. In addition, Hardy develops related concerns already present in *Desperate Remedies*. It seems from the two novels that, where sensation fiction, according to Hardy, encourages passivity, ruralist writing imagines organic communities in which selfhood and will are virtually absent. Weatherbury, though, is experienced by Bathsheba and for that matter Gabriel as a place where personal will is thwarted by other people's. Its community is made up of different selves, competing and conflicting with one another. The distinctiveness of a locality is discovered here, in ways reminiscent of *Desperate Remedies* and hostile to the ruralist assumptions of a visitor. At the same time, the ruralist question about how a society might best be established is taken up and given a new solution.

Clocks and stars, with which the novel seems oddly preoccupied, are included so often because they contribute to Hardy's thinking about the social world. In the opening chapters, Norcombe Hill gives Gabriel an unsurpassed view of the night-sky:

> he stood and carefully examined the sky to ascertain the time of night from the altitudes of the stars.
>
> The Dog-star and Aldebaran, pointing to the restless Pleiades were half way up the southern sky, and beneath them hung Orion which gorgeous constellation never burnt more vividly than now as it swung itself high above the rim of the landscape. Castor and Pollux with their quiet shine almost rested on the ground: the barren and gloomy Square of Pegasus was creeping round to the north-west; far away through the plantation Vega sparkled like a lamp suspended amid the leafless trees; and Cassiopeia's Chair stood daintily poised on the uppermost boughs.
>
> 'One o'clock,' said Gabriel.
>
> (Hardy, *Madding Crowd*, ch.2, p.12)

Another description, nearly as detailed, occurs earlier in the chapter and Oak's ability to 'ascertain the time of night from the altitudes of the stars' is put to use again in chapter six. Later, in chapter fifteen, Matthew Moon placates Oak, who has recently returned from a visit to Norcombe, by admiring his power to 'tell the time as well by the stars as we can by the sun and moon' (Hardy, *Madding Crowd*, p.97). At the same time, Gabriel carries 'by way of watch what may be called a small silver clock' which 'had the peculiarity of going either too fast or not at all'. This timepiece is mentioned at the novel's opening and then largely forgotten, replaced by the more accurate timepieces of the Weatherbury world. Clocks and churchbells prove authoritative there, a fact which Hardy emphasises at moments of crisis or cruelty: Jan Coggan carries a watch which strikes the hours when he and Gabriel are following Bathsheba towards Bath; Troy's forced wait for Fanny at the altar is made agonizing by the clock at the church's west end mercilessly ringing the quarters; Fanny, desperate to reach Casterbridge, hears a town clock strike one 'in entombed tones'.[13]

Through the opening passages Hardy seems carefully to establish qualities in Norcombe which are recalled later in the novel by a succession of contrasts: clocks in Weatherbury work while – or 'so that' – the stars become a matter of indifference. Bathsheba, infatuated by Troy and threatened by Boldwood, sees within the 'green and pellucid expanses in the western sky': 'indecisive and palpitating stars. She gazed upon their silent throes amid the shades of space, but realised none at all. Her troubled spirit was far away with Troy.' (Hardy, *Madding Crowd*, ch.30, pp.181–2).

Much of what happens in the novel involves the anguish of commitment: Boldwood's exposure to the passionate love he has never experienced before; Bathsheba's similar discovery of the power Troy possesses over her and the loss of independence that it brings; Gabriel's inability to break free of Bathsheba or leave Weatherbury even when Troy has supplanted him in her affections; and lastly Troy's own 'romanticism', his belief (however brief and self-dramatizing) that he loves Fanny Robin. Behind and before these stands life in Norcombe which for Gabriel offered the chance at least of working for himself, a comparable independence to what Bathsheba remembers of the time when no man ruled or owned her.

The stars above Norcombe Hill are linked to the breadth of vision this freedom brings. In one of their early conversations, Bathsheba tells Gabriel that out of doors she finds it hard to think: 'my mind spreads away so' (Hardy, *Madding Crowd*, ch.4, p.27). Her feeling for Troy prevents that 'spreading away', so that she can no longer 'realise' any of the stars.[14] In line with this, Bathsheba finds herself made 'wild and perturbed by [. . .] new and fevering sequences' (ch.29, p.170) and Boldwood is drawn out of 'the spherical completeness of his existence' into a world of successive events:

> then she turned away. Boldwood dropped his eyes to the ground and stood long like a man who did not know where he was. Realities then returned upon him like the pain of a wound received in an excitement which eclipses it, and he too then went on.
>
> (Hardy, *Madding Crowd*, chs 14, 18, pp.87, 113)

As is also the case in *The Return of the Native*, sexual attraction and love are continually associated with lights – a light through the trees, which Gabriel mistakes for a star, proves to come from the shed where Bathsheba and her aunt are milking. Bathsheba carries a 'dark lantern' when she meets Sergeant Troy in the wood: 'A hand seized the lantern, the door was opened, the rays burst out from their prison, and Bathsheba beheld her position with astonishment' (ch.23, p.142). This bursting forth of light figures sexual awakening and the perplexed self-recognition it brings, in which Bathsheba sees herself as vulnerable because carrying within herself unsuspected extremes of feeling. The fearfulness of this moment links Bathsheba to Boldwood for whom also excitement eclipses pain – the pain which reasserts itself when the excitement has passed. The stress on light in these incidents means also that the word 'eclipses' can almost be taken literally. The lovers in the novel appear like heavenly bodies, points of light moving around one another, drawn out of their proper orbit and cast into shadow, outshone or eclipsed.

Their turmoil seems the more poignant because the reader can recall Gabriel's rapt and practised attention to the stars above Norcombe Hill. These were varied, individuated and at the same time grouped into constellations: Castor and Pollux produce a 'quiet shine'; Vega sparkles like a lamp; Aldebaran points to the restless Pleiades. The 'twinkling of all the stars seemed to be but throbs of one body, timed by a common pulse' while, because of the sky's remarkable clarity:

> A difference of colour in the stars – oftener read of than seen in England – was really perceptible here. The kingly brilliancy of Sirius pierced the eye with a steely glitter, the star called Capella was yellow, Aldebaran and Betelgeux shone with a fiery red.
>
> (Hardy, *Madding Crowd*, ch.2, p.9)

Unity and individuation seem to coexist in the night-sky, kingly separateness within one body. Between these extremes (of single stars and
the whole sky), the constellations seem as recognisably individual as
the named stars and as united as the whole. Observing all this, Gabriel
sees the sky firstly as 'a useful instrument' and then, standing still
and regarding it 'in an appreciative spirit, as a work of art superlatively
beautiful' (ch.2, p.12).

The action of *Far from the Madding Crowd* might seem to suggest that
this ideal balance of sociality and individual differentiation cannot be
realized in the adult world of will, possessiveness and sexual desire.
Norcombe's sky becomes a social ideal of independence joined to community which desire prevents. If this is the conclusion then people in
adult life prove to be more similar to the planets, the moon or comets
than to the stars – adult experience is fluctuating, unreliable and com-
petitive; individuals overlap with one another, clash; passions flare up
and disappear. Hardy certainly makes comparisons to this effect:
Gabriel's face is like the moon, one of the rustics is Matthew Moon (and
he can tell the time by the moon), Boldwood thinks of women as
'comets of [. . . .] uncertain aspect' whose orbits may be 'as geometrical,
unchangeable, and as subject to laws as his own, or as absolutely erratic
as they superficially appeared'. Similarly, Troy's swordplay looks to
Bathsheba like 'the luminous streams of this *aurora militaris*'.[15] Nonetheless, Hardy does suggest a form of relation between adult individuals
which is close to that of the stars in their constellations.

After their quarrel in chapter nineteen, Gabriel leaves Weatherbury
and moves to 'Nest Cottage' across the valley. The day after his departure, Bathsheba's sheep break into a field of young clover – a crop which
is poisonous to them. Without skilled assistance, they will all die and
no-one possesses the requisite skills except Gabriel. Bathsheba's dependence on him is made painfully clear and, after a struggle, she gives way
and sends for his help:

> Bathsheba watched: so did all the rest. [Laban] Tall cantered along
> the bridle-path through Sixteen Acres, Sheeplands, Middle Field, The
> Flats, Cappel's Piece, shrank almost to a point, crossed the bridge,
> and ascended from the valley through Springmead and Whitepits on
> the other side. The cottage to which Gabriel had retired before taking
> his final departure from the locality was visible as a white spot on
> the opposing hill, backed by blue firs. Bathsheba walked up and
> down. The men entered the field, and endeavoured to ease the
> anguish of the dumb creatures by rubbing them. Nothing availed.

Bathsheba continued walking. The horse was seen descending the hill, and the wearisome series had to be repeated in reverse order: Whitepits, Springsmead, Cappel's Piece, The Flats, Middle Field, Sheeplands, Sixteen Acres.

(Hardy, Madding Crowd, ch.20, p.122)

Meticulously going through 'the wearisome series' of fields evidently heightens the suspense, imitating Bathsheba's anxious impatience. Initially, though, sensing his advantage, Gabriel refuses: as Laban reports, 'He says he shall not come unless you request him to come civilly in a proper manner, as becomes any person begging a favour.' Bathsheba, though resenting Gabriel's humiliation of her, writes the desired formal request and adds at the bottom: '*Do not desert me, Gabriel!*'. In this context, Hardy's way of describing Laban's ride may be seen as bringing out the brute fact of the distance involved, indicating that Gabriel is no longer at Bathsheba's beck and call. He cannot come 'instantly' as she demands, there are too many fields in between.

As 'a white spot on the opposing hill, backed by blue firs', Gabriel's cottage also resembles a star hanging low in the sky (in the same way that Bathsheba's shed had looked like a star early in the novel). This similarity gives the impression that Gabriel's reluctance partly arises from his desire to get his own back but it also suggests an equality between them, an equality which his demand for a civil request asks her to acknowledge.[16] There is still a clash of wills going on. Gabriel is taking revenge to some degree for Bathsheba's refusal of him; Bathsheba, although she does ask more humbly, still resists coolness – the passionateness of 'Do not desert me' reminds Gabriel of the devotion he has felt before and may still feel. ('Shall I beg to a man who has begged to me!' Bathsheba exclaims.) Nonetheless, amidst its possible coerciveness, the phrase also allows for a sense of mutual dependency. It begins to suggest the form of friendly marriage which Gabriel and Bathsheba establish as the novel ends. 'Theirs was that substantial affection' or 'good-fellowship' which arises when people 'associate [...] in their labours', 'the romance growing up in the interstices of a mass of hard prosaic reality' and producing 'the only love which is strong as death – that love which many waters cannot quench, nor the floods drown'.[17] The transition in this passage from the soberly understated to the rousing and deeply-felt reflects the same interest as the earlier episode shows in joining equality and passion. The wearisome list of fields provides one instance of the 'mass of hard prosaic reality' such love continually encounters and, indeed, depends upon. Norcombe's constellations look by comparison enviably free and unencumbered; the distances between the stars may be almost unimaginably large but the eye connects them effortlessly and instantly. Even so, Hardy does suggest a starlike quality to Gabriel, living in his cottage across the valley. His geographical self-establishment offers an equivalent to the status he asks for in his relations with Bathsheba; it prefigures too the relative social and financial autonomy he has gained by the time he marries. A constellated interdependence seems the foundation of their marriage and it requires a perception of landscape which respects distances. These distances reflect the continued separateness of the lovers and, what one might call, their mutual independence.

The simple listing of the fields contributes, then, to Hardy's suggestion of a more equal footing for their relationship by expressing the material distance between them. Gabriel cannot instantly be summoned; he inhabits a space of his own which needs to be reached and from which he will need to travel.[18] Similarly, in *Desperate Remedies*, locality is not easy to reach; Manston has to accompany the postman every single step of the way if he is to obtain the particular letter he wants. Additionally, in the later novel, Gabriel's independence combines with Hardy's naming of the fields to create the sense that they too form part of a world, peculiarly and particularly understood by its inhabitants. A visitor would not know these names or be struck by them, prosaic indicators that they are: 'Middle Field', 'Sixteen Acres', 'Whitepits'. The description adapts to the scale at which farmers perceive their land and the kind of interest it has for them. Both are unexpected for visitors and readers alike, I suspect. Likewise, the stress placed on the distance travelled takes the reader aback, as Hardy's description suggests a landscape refusing to conform to expected forms of description and yet plainly unexotic. One is part of it or not and that separateness corresponds to the one dividing Bathsheba and Gabriel. The reader will need to address the landscape civilly and in a proper manner if s/he is to see it properly, in its ordinary strangeness.

The nearest equivalent in the novel to this incident occurs when Fanny Robin is struggling towards Casterbridge, pregnant and exhausted. Getting from one milestone to the next, then from post to post along a railing, calculating the distance in miles then yards then steps: all these are emphasized in the narrative and bring out Fanny's subjection to the physical demands made by distance on her body. Increasingly tired, she tricks herself into keeping going by telling herself that the end of her journey lies only five posts further along the railing; once she has reached that point, she tells herself it is another five and so on. Hardy comments:

> Faith in what she had known all the time to be a fable had given her strength to come a quarter of a mile that she would have been powerless to face in the lump. The artifice showed that the woman, by some mysterious intuition, had grasped the great paradoxical truth that blindness may do greater things than prescience, and the short-sighted than the far-seeing; that limitation, and not comprehensiveness, is needed for striking a blow.
>
> (Hardy, *Madding Crowd*, ch.39, p.232)

These sentences resemble many in Hardy's *Life* and his other fiction where the disadvantages of awareness are observed and bemoaned. Within *Far from the Madding Crowd*, they further the contrast between Norcombe and Weatherbury, between wide, independent, spreading vision and the obsessions compelled by love and the will to live. The lights of Casterbridge look to Fanny at first like an 'aurora' guiding her; later when 'individually visible', they appear like 'fallen Pleiads' (pp.230–31, 234). The course of her love affair with Troy (from enthralled delight to personal encounter to betrayal) is recalled by this sequence; so is its similarity to Bathsheba's experience and to Gabriel's ecstatic sense of freedom on Norcombe Hill, something remembered now as an impossible, youthful dream.[19] The conclusion seems to be that Norcombe is defeated by Weatherbury, innocence by experience, private freedom by subjection to social pressure. This, though, is not the whole story.

Fanny, the most isolated figure in the book, is not deserted by it. Socially disgraced and exiled, she is given two chapters almost exclusively devoted to her – this one and chapter eleven; they lend weight to her experience while their imagery suggests an equivalence between Fanny and Bathsheba which conventional morality and most nineteenth-century novels would deny. Both chapters also exist curiously disconnected from the rest of the novel – they could be left out and the story survive intact.[20] Their inclusion, coupled with how they represent Fanny and her feelings, imply a desire to acknowledge the distinct experience of others, whether morally respectable or otherwise. Following Fanny along the road is analogous to following Laban's ride back and forth through the fields; both incidents contribute to the perception that other people are independent from each other and, simultaneously, parts of the same world.

The imaginative sympathy Hardy's narrative structure works towards is practised within the story by a stray dog; this creature appears out of the darkness, approaches Fanny and allows her to support herself upon its back. With its help, she reaches the Casterbridge workhouse and gains shelter; its lovingkindness (although the word does not occur) comforts and effectually assists her, prompting her affection in return. Bathsheba learns in the next chapter of Fanny's death in the workhouse and Hardy says that she 'had begun to know what suffering was, and she spoke with deep feeling' when imagining Fanny's last hours (Hardy, *Madding Crowd*, ch.40, p.241). The dog's behaviour foreshadows Bathsheba's concern while its relation to Fanny curiously resembles Gabriel's and Bathsheba's earlier, when the sheep are endangered. The animal offers help and, at the same time, it is looking for affection; Fanny, lying exhausted on the verge, 'looked up to [the dog] just as in earlier times she had, when standing, looked up to a man' (ch.39, p.233). The dog seems both to serve her and stand over her, her (male) master and her (animal) helper, while its selflessness is not actually disinterested but arises from the hope of satisfying a natural need for affection. Similarly, with Gabriel and Bathsheba, the servant becomes master, the man is commanded by the woman and passion and civility cannot be disentangled. These events show Hardy reaching for a form of equality, one in which both sides at once give precedence to and govern the other. This balance allows for a devotion which avoids overwhelming or consuming the person to whom devotion is given. Amidst unity of purpose, cooperation and mutual dependence, independence persists.[21]

The novel, therefore, seems to be searching after equality in sexual relations and extending sympathy to all regardless of their supposed moral worth. The same endeavour can be found in Hardy's depiction of the novel's rustic chorus, figures who are apparently of less importance than the major characters and figures whom it is easy to relegate to the past, to the generically determined and to the stereotypical. Hardy allows room for such assumptions and challenges them, with the result that his own ideals of conduct and perception have a social dimension and are not limited to the personal life. The novel, in other words, suggests a way of thinking about regions, provinces and nations, taking issue with ruralism generally and the philosopher Herbert Spencer in particular.

Its chorus of pastoral rustics are old men who behave like children; they seem to be unmarried, with the exception of Laban Tall, who is hen-pecked, and their lives take place outside the realm of Eros. The name 'Weatherbury' suggests wethers, castrated sheep, and Weatherbury's society divides into those who are possessed by sexual desire (the major characters) and those who are not (the rustics).[22] The latter are also disorganized, liable to panic in a crisis and in need of Gabriel's commanding leadership whenever fires have to be extinguished or sheep saved from death. The rustics also display, however, great mutual forbearance and understanding, particularly in humouring the maltster. Similarly, Joseph Poorgrass's cowardice coexists with his genuine good sense, including that of the novel's last words: 'But since 'tis as 'tis, why it might have been worse, and I feel my thanks accordingly' (ch.56, p.353). Poorgrass is always being given remarks of this kind; this one seems especially laughable and especially just. Hardy provides many moments when the rustics are the object of contemptuous amusement and many others too when they appear to express an ideal of social relations, visible in their behaviour and experienced through the genial laughter it provokes. Poorgrass and Jan Coggan both emerge from the group and gain a degree of respect from the other characters (and the reader) while still winning their affection.

Uncertainty, then, surrounds what status the rustic characters should be granted – foolish or wise, worthy of respect or condescension, a chorus of types or a collection of emerging characters. Hardy shows the implications of this instability by the comparisons he uses to describe the rustic world. When Bathsheba's corrupt bailiff is sacked and she takes over the running of the farm, the workers are summoned to meet her:

> A crooked file of men was approaching the back door. The whole string of trailing individuals advanced in the completest balance of intention, like the remarkable creatures known as chain salpae, which, distinctly organized in other respects, have one will common to a whole family.
>
> (Hardy, *Madding Crowd*, ch.9, p.68)

The procession seems characteristic of primitive life-forms, such as Chain Salpae, in which 'distinctly organized' individuals are subsumed in the will common to the whole. Salpae are microscopic, aquatic organisms; they live sometimes separately, sometimes linked together. They were used by Herbert Spencer in his essay 'The Social Organism', their form of joint life providing an analogy for an early form of human society. Spencer is scientifically detailed about them: when linked up, he states, there 'exists a vascular connection between them and a common circulation'; each individual is biologically connected to the group which forms a 'compound animal'.[23]

In a later scene, Sergeant Troy intervenes to help Bathsheba hive a swarm of bees. He has to dress up in her beekeeping outfit, which makes him look ridiculous but he successfully completes the task, bringing order to the farm and asserting his dominance over its previous mistress. Hardy compares the bees' swarming to the formation of stars:

> A process was observable exactly analogous to that of alleged formations of the universe, time and times ago. The bustling swarm had swept up the sky in a scattered and uniform haze, which now thickened to a nebulous centre: this glided on to a bough, and grew still denser, till it formed a solid black spot upon the light.
>
> (Hardy, *Madding Crowd*, ch.26, p.157)

In part, this passage reproduces ideas about erotic relations which occur elsewhere in the novel. When he has caught the bees, Troy climbs back down the tree, 'holding the hive at arm's length, behind which trailed a cloud of bees'. This cloud foreshadows the '*aurora militaris*' of his sword exercise, performed in the next chapter. The bees' 'uniform haze' condenses to a 'nebulous centre' and then becomes 'still denser'; likewise, Bathsheba is 'enclosed in a firmament of lights and sharp hisses' and gradually focussed upon, until climactically Troy kills a caterpillar resting on her bodice. Fanny Robin's sight of a 'distant halo' or 'aurora' over Casterbridge which gradually turns into 'lights [. . .] individually visible' echoes these earlier formulations of attraction and commitment. The link is the more visible because Hardy connects Bathsheba's and Troy's courtship to the stars: Troy's swordplay 'resembles a sky-full of meteors close at hand' and the bees, swarming, condense like stars, becoming first a nebula and then 'still denser'.[24] Though connected to the novel's other representations of sexual desire, the bees' swarming also links up with the salpae. Swarms and chain salpae are both, in a sense, 'compound animals', and both are mentioned at points in the novel when a natural unity is being brought under the command of a single person: Bathsheba is about to take control of the farm; Troy hives the bees. Likewise, bees and nebulae are also discussed by Spencer – in this case, in his 'The Nebular Hypothesis' which like 'The Social Organism' was published in 1868 in *Essays, Scientific, Political, and Speculative*, a copy of which Hardy owned.

In 'The Social Organism', Spencer gives equivalents in the animal kingdom to various forms of human society: protozoa and thallogens are equated with the structureless society of Bushmen, amoebae with Aborigines; hydrae, hydrozoa, zoophytes and salpae represent various stages in the emergence of nations from groups of tribes. 'The Nebular Hypothesis' principally elaborates the French astronomer Laplace's theory that 'stars result from the aggregation of diffused matter'.[25] Spencer describes this as a process in which atoms are drawn closer and closer together by gravity until some of them 'suddenly enter into chemical union', a process 'accompanied by great and sudden disengagement of heat'. When cool, these 'newly-formed binary atoms' precipitate and aggregate, first into clouds, then into spiralling nebulae which gradually coalesce so that at their centre stars are formed. Bees come up, though quite incidentally, in Spencer's discussion of nebulae.[26] A similar vocabulary is used in both essays with the result that processes of both biological evolution and star formation are connected to an idea of natural progress from lesser to greater complexity. Particularly in 'The Social Organism', the same supposedly natural progress is seen at work in the historical process of nation building.

According to Spencer, greater complexity in an organism reduces the independence of the separate segments; the organism is no longer an aggregate of similar cells but, instead, 'the internal organs are no longer uniformly repeated in all the segments'. Cells specialize and contribute to the whole, just as in nations: 'along with the growth of a central power, the demarcation of these local commmunities becomes relatively unimportant, and their separate organizations merge into the general organization'.[27] England, Wales, Scotland and Ireland are subsumed in the United Kingdom; and the same principle of progress can be seen 'on the Continent, in the coalescence of provinces into kingdoms'. 'Coalescence' is a favourite word for Spencer, used here for the precipitation of stars from clouds of gas and for animal life – microscopic units aggregate into 'organized groups' which multiply before 'coalescence into compound groups'. Spencer's essay instinctively celebrates the emergence of greater complexity, of 'organization' (another word he applies in all three areas). But the celebration occurs alongside his insistence that analogies between social and animal organisms always break down:

It is well that the lives of all parts of an animal be merged in the life of the whole; because the whole has a corporate consciousness capable of happiness or misery. But it is not so with a society; since its living units do not and cannot lose individual consciousness; and since the community as a whole has no corporate consciousness.[28]

For Spencer, progress means ever-increasing social complexity, the merging of the local into the central and the 'coalescence of provinces into kingdoms'; at the same time, he declares that 'The corporate life must [. . .] be subservient to the lives of the parts, instead of the lives of the parts being subservient to the corporate life.' Provinces and local communities inevitably disappear yet 'the lives of the parts', including presumably the lives of individuals from the provinces, must be preserved. The principal conclusion Spencer draws from this clash between increasing social complexity and individual experience is that personal liberty needs to be defended against the encroachments of centralized state power. He makes no comment about where his account of progress will leave the provincial individual, whose regional autonomy vanishes while his or her personal liberty must be kept intact.

Far from the Madding Crowd is addressing this difficulty, I think; Hardy admired Spencer but scarcely ever agreed with him. The novel's ruralist vocabulary brings with it progressive assumptions according to which the rustic world is inevitably on the wane. According to ruralism, the best outcome for town and country will be for them to merge – town will enlighten country and country purify town. Remote and autonomous rural communities are viewed with alarm and their primitive life is seen as barbarous. Hardy's writing, like the book's geographical pattern, registers these assumptions neither accepting nor explicitly rejecting them. Similarly, his comparisons with bees, nebulae and salpae invoke the ideas of progress and national structure which underlie Spencer's thought. Calling the rustics salpae seems to confirm that they are primitive; similarly, Troy seems to be the more advanced individual bringing order to the swarm of bees. Yet Troy turns out to be brutal and, oddly, innocent as well – gaining self-understanding concurrently with Bathsheba; meanwhile, the social relations among the rustics prove to be 'remarkable'. The 'compound animal' which Spencer places low on the scale is elevated in Hardy's representation of their form of community, where unity of action instead of depending upon the absence of individuality coexists with it. Living units do not lose individual consciousness and are not submerged in the whole they collectively constitute, yet they behave with 'one will'. Hardy's wording brings them forward as a curiosity before showing how they are more (and more significantly) remarkable than that, worthy of greater attention than this kind of comparison would normally encourage.

Hardy draws attention to microscopic life elsewhere. The closest equivalent to this passage comes in *A Pair of Blue Eyes*, vol.1, ch.13 when

Stephen Smith visits Henry Knight's London flat. Knight owns an aquarium in which every evening 'the many-coloured zoophytes' were lit by a sunbeam and 'put forth their arms [. . .] the timid community expressed gladness more plainly than in words'. A few pages later, Knight shows Smith the view from his window, an alley thronged with surging crowds and 'a babble of tongues'. This – Knight's 'Humanity Show' – becomes visible when the sunbeam has faded and 'the zoophytes slept'. Hardy unsettles assumed hierarchies again here: the primitive organisms grow superior to the people outside the window; their 'timid community' seems at first a consciously quaint description and becomes a more serious one when compared with the amorphous, brutalized crowd. As in *Far from the Madding Crowd*, a pastoral style (this time used to depict an aquarium) diminishes its subject and then reveals the injustice of diminishing it, so making it hard to judge relative importance or worth. The terms Hardy employs for the 'zoophytes' may reflect to some degree Henry Knight's characteristics – his condescension towards Smith and his lofty fascination with the crowd – but they may accord as well with the readership's habits of mind when imagining 'timid communities'.[29]

Far from the Madding Crowd argues overall that the qualities found in the primitive life-form and in the rustics are the same as those seen by Gabriel in the constellation. These people and the world they inhabit can be regarded either as a primitive life-form or as an ideal of community, just as the rustics themselves appear ambiguously, perhaps innocent of, perhaps beyond, sexual passion. The novel's pastoral seems to be both what Eros destroys and what successful sexual relations need to regain. Consequently, local, step-by-step knowledge of place and of its material, separating distances provides here, not an image of division but rather a means of expressing how individuals may be joined into communities, their individuality uncompromised and their communality preserved. The list of fields dividing Gabriel's star-like cottage from Bathsheba's farm articulates a form of social life, in which people can live together as the stars do in a constellation.

Hardy's concerns overlap here with the geographer Doreen Massey's: 'What gives a place its specificity is [. . .] the fact that it is constructed out of a particular constellation of social relations, meeting and weaving together at a particular locus.'[30] Her mixed metaphor (in which a constellation meets and weaves) shows her trying to express the existence of agency within determining structures, resisting both stability on the one hand and free mobility on the other. Hardy discovers something similar to a constellation in the layout of English fields and he shows passionate, capricious people to be comparable to stars. These metaphorical comparisons reach towards the paradoxical coexistence of agency and constraint, equality and passion. Massey regards this paradoxical view as an advance on earlier, over-simple ones. Hardy has greater yearning after the state of unconstrained, asocial independence: the youthful world of Norcombe in *Far from the Madding Crowd*. Both writers, however, share the sense of adult identity as formed within webs of interaction, webs which may be oppressive but may also form patterns in which selfhood and society are reciprocal. Moreover, like Massey, Hardy is making a point about nationality. His allusions to Spencer draw attention to the relation between centre and periphery, a dominant centralizing power and the independence of localities. Certainly, these invocations of Spencer imply that the primitive and the advanced cannot be differentiated as readily as one might suppose. Not only do they live in the same habitat, the primitive may also be more advanced than the culture which replaces it. In this respect, the novel offers a critique of Spencer's progress and of Victorian self-confidence more generally, raising the questions about history's relation to culture which are explored more deeply in *The Return of the Native*. At the same time, Hardy is implying that, *contra* Spencer and in line with Massey, England might best be seen as a constellation.

Personal geography

Local knowledge, as exemplified by the field-names of Laban Tall's ride, is gained through an immediate, sometimes arduous encounter. What is learned is, moreover, useless to anyone outside a very small group, indeed to almost anyone apart from the person concerned. Hardy chooses in this episode an instance of the local shading into the personal. He does so because his concept of local independence follows the same pattern as that of personal independence. Places within countries and communities within nations are treated in the same way as individuals within groups. And not only are places distinctively different, though interconnected; individuals have distinctive geographies which coexist with the consensual ones created by a culture. That is evident among the characters: Bathsheba's Weatherbury differs from other people's, whether locals or visitors, because of her connections with Norcombe. Eustacia constructs Egdon Heath around her desire to be in Budmouth or Paris, Clym around his desire to re-enter the past; Thomasin inhabits an Egdon familiar from childhood and her parents' childhood. It is also the case that Hardy's 'Wessex of the Novels' is a personal and autobiographical environment; its relation to national geographies corresponds to Hardy's sense of himself as a member of a society.

Michael Rabiger, in a discussion of the autobiographical roots of Hardy's novels, makes a similar point about his and their geography:

> Many apparently minor details of Hardy's broad terrain of Wessex are actually found near Bockhampton, so that Hardy's Wessex may first have evolved less as an organising device than as a necessary enlargement to mask the archetype's tellingly localised origins.[31]

This implies that Hardy's Wessex bears the imprint of his psychology, betraying the deepest structures of his personality and his attempts to disguise them. Rabiger's language, like that of many other critics, suggests real 'origins' for an imaginary Wessex. He implies that, once the minor details have been traced back to Bockhampton, they reveal the true meaning of the fiction. My disagreement with this account stems from the feeling that Hardy's imaginary world and the actual places where he lived, though separable, remain in relation with one another. His sense of a personal geography, in other words, is coloured by his awareness of being changeable and of constantly reconsidering places. Wessex does not disguise localized origins so much as consider the clash between a local beginning and an adult life led in relation to a national society. Because Hardy was conscious of himself as a person engaged by a modern world in some ways at odds with his background, the interplay between Wessex and Dorset, altering over the course of his career, shows several versions of his endeavour to accommodate modernity to a sense of place. More generally, he recognizes that places are altered by changing views, moods and opinions. His geography reflects his indebtedness to impressionist painting and corresponds to his presenting in his novels a 'series of seemings' rather than a consolidated or authoritative account of the world.[32]

Desperate Remedies is explicitly concerned with the process of adapting to the demands of adult life. It suggests, more optimistically than many of Hardy's later works, that personal independence can be reconciled with social advancement. This optimism emerges through the novel's presentation of uncanny stillness and rapid movement. Movement may be fulfilling but may also be a dull, mechanical grind; stasis may be suffocated lethargy or it may be visionary. The book prefigures Hardy's later work because of these ambiguities; it also tends to resolve them in favour of independent movement and secretly connects such movement with Hardy's work as an architect.

Just before their first kiss, Edward and Cytherea are involved in a slightly tense and driven talk about careers and success. 'But will you not try to get on in your profession?' Cytherea asks him. 'Try once more; do try once more.' After a few more exchanges, Edward 'looked into the far distance and paused' – a pause which is repeated in the surroundings:

> the sea glided noiselessly, without breaking the crest of a single wave, so strikingly calm was the air. The breeze had entirely died away, leaving the water of that rare glassy smoothness which is unmarked even by the small dimples of the least aërial movement. [. . .]
>
> At length she looked at him to learn the effect of her words of encouragement. He had let the oars drift alongside, and the boat had come to a standstill. Everything on earth seemed taking a contemplative rest, as if waiting to hear the avowal of something from his lips.

He makes his avowal: 'he appeared to break a resolution hitherto zealously kept. Leaving his seat amidships he came and gently edged himself down beside her upon the narrow seat at the stern'.[33] 'Encouragement' leads ironically to drift and then to love, as if she had encouraged him sexually rather than offered him, as she meant to, encouragement in his career. Edward's action arises too from a double negative – he cannot refuse any longer – and though there are reasons in the plot for this, it lends a kind of willing passivity to what he does. It is as if he gives in to the stillness.

When, later on, Cytherea is courted by Manston, she finds herself once again enclosed by an impressive, disabling quiet:

> Cytherea and Manston walked into the porch, and up the nave.
>
> They did not speak a word during their progress, or in any way interfere with the stillness and silence that prevailed everywhere around them. Everything in the place was the embodiment of decay
>
> (Hardy, *DR*, vol.2, ch.4, s.8, p.235)

It is here that Manston finally extracts from her a promise to marry him, having pressured and harried her (with Miss Aldclyffe's help) for weeks past, often employing the same emotional blackmail Alec d'Urberville uses on Tess. A third example comes a few pages later, on the morning of her wedding day, when Cytherea wakes from bad dreams to find the landscape eerily silent after an ice-storm:

> A shoot the diameter of a pin's head was iced as thick as her finger: all the boughs in the park were bent almost to the earth with the immense weight of the glistening incumbrance: the walks were like a looking-glass.
>
> (Hardy, *DR*, vol.2, ch.5, s.1, p.242)

The noises overnight which had entered her dreams are now explained as the sound of branches splitting away under the burden of the ice. There are literary echoes in all these incidents: the boating scene recalls both Byron and Shelley; the church feels spookily gothic and Cytherea's dream seems a variant on Lockwood's nightmares near the beginning of *Wuthering Heights*. They exhibit, however, a repeated pattern of contrast between stillness and drive; each stillness exists amidst a different pressure – the pressure suffered by Edward and Cytherea in their dealings with the world's demands; the pressure exerted by Manston's 'hot voluptuous [. . .] passion' which 'at times radiated forth with a scorching white heat' (Hardy, *DR*, p.226); and in the last case the self-determination of Cytherea's rival for Edward's hand.

This contrast emerges when a conversation among the servants on the same morning reveals that Adelaide Hinton, previously engaged to Edward, has married someone else. Clerk Crickmay brings the news: 'Whilst Master Teddy Springrove has been daddlen, and hawken, and spetten about having her, she's quietly left him all forsook. Serve him right. I don't blame the little woman a bit.' The cook, running the kitchen and keeping Crickmay in his place, remarks with dry approval, 'Just like her independence' (Hardy, *DR*, pp.245–6). It is, of course, ironic that at the moment when Cytherea is about to marry Manston, whom she does not love, the obstacle to her marrying Edward 'quietly' removes herself. The irony, though, is pointed and instructive, more comic than the bereft ironies of Hardy's tragic novels. All around Edward and Cytherea, other people are making their own lives. The novel's hero and heroine seem required to come to terms somehow with the need to act. The book presents stillnesses which may be either rapture or decay (or incarceration) and opposite them movements which may be violently wilful or the result of a straightfoward 'independence'.

Independence is admired too in Edward; in the boating-scene, he tells Cytherea off for being concerned about what onlookers might think about the 'absurd directions' in which they have gone while out on the water. Cytherea feels 'the delicious sensation [. . .] of being compelled into an opinion by a man she loved' and compares him to her brother.

> Owen [. . .] would not have had the intellectual independence to answer a woman thus. She replied quickly and honestly – as honestly as when she had stated the contrary fact a minute earlier – 'I don't mind.'
>
> (Hardy, *DR*, vol.1, ch.3, s.2, p.45)

Likewise, Edward's track in the water is decisive; once Cytherea is no longer steering, 'they sped in a straight line towards the shore' (Hardy, *DR*, p.45) and Cytherea, faced with the prospect of losing him, intervenes; they turn round again, go back out to sea and she resumes steering.[34]

It is in accordance with this strand of the novel that Owen Graye goes lame soon after arriving in Creston, undergoes several operations and recovers towards the end. Regaining his power of walking coincides with his helping to uncover Manston's past and with professional success: he is offered 'superintendence, as clerk of works, of a new church, which was to be built in the village of Palchurch' (Hardy, *DR*, vol.3, ch.2, s.1, p.293).[35] The straight line of Edward's rowing seems analogous to the means whereby people recover, assert themselves and prevent suffering. The ice-storm seems, similarly, to epitomize the attraction of a state where action is not possible, where an outside power – be it fate, circumstance or Eros – determines your future. What is unusual in Hardy is not so much the questions raised as the degree to which the novel endorses a positive and volitional solution, a solution which corresponds to the novel's willingness to celebrate the swift, straight lines of Creston as much as the intricate, winding recesses of Carriford, fully known and recognized only by 'natives'.[36] Likewise, the novel works to balance the drive of plot with the stillness of the visionary moment, articulating through the competition between these two elements the clash between professional and personal, social and individual, world and home. Adelaide Hinton's 'independence', entering the novel from an unexpected, previously neglected quarter, connects this ideal to remoteness and provinciality.

'Hinton' may not be entirely an accidental name. It is quite frequent as a place-name in Dorset: Piddlehinton is the example located nearest to Bockhampton; there are also Hinton Martell and Hinton Parva, north of Wimborne, Tarrant Hinton near Blandford and Hinton St Mary just to the north of Sturminster Newton. Interestingly, I think, a few miles east of Hinton St Mary lies the village of Manston. John Hicks, for whom Hardy was working, at least part-time, between 1867 and 1869, built two new churches in this area in 1867: one, All Saints, in Stour Row and another in Compton Abbas West (sometimes known as West Compton).[37] The train route from Dorchester was via Wareham and Wimborne, where you would change onto the Dorset and Somerset Railway running northwest through Blandford and Sturminster Newton. Compton Abbas is most easily reached by road from the station at Blandford, Stour Row from Sturminster Newton. A turnpike road, in this case the road to London, connected Dorchester and Blandford but the roads from Blandford north along the route of the railway line are minor and indirect; no turnpike connects Dorchester and Sturminster direct. The building of the Dorset and Somerset Railway in 1860–2 may have opened up the district for restoration work and the Bridport line, built in 1857, may have done the same for that part of the western parts of the county where Hicks has work restoring churches at the same time. Certainly there is a correlation between architectural work and new railways.[38] Whether Hardy helped Hicks with these projects and made the journey is unknown, but he must have travelled in the same direction in 1869 when he was working on St Mary's, Turnworth and writing the novel. Turnworth lies on the southern side of the same railway line, the nearest station being at Shillingstone, half-way between Blandford and Sturminster.[39]

Michael Millgate finds convincing evidence that Hardy wrote *Desperate Remedies* with the manuscript of his first unpublished novel, 'The Poor Man and the Lady', open beside him.[40] The hero of 'The Poor Man and the Lady' is 'Will Strong' (changed to 'Egbert Mayne' in 'An Indiscretion in the Life of an Heiress', the short story Hardy published in 1878, based on 'The Poor Man and the Lady'). The name 'Manston' similarly, stresses and queries the virility of Hardy's hero. Read in this light, the name fits with the novel's wider inquiry into the relations between worth and masculinity, masculinity and physical/sexual power.[41] Still, the coincidence between these names and places Hardy may have visited as an architect while working on the book is congruent with the book's interests. When connected to the place, the name Manston carries a reminder of Hardy's own experience travelling into new places, gradually becoming more familiar with them and attempting to alter them. Manston's role not only as the rival of Edward Springrove but as the antithesis of Owen Graye becomes clearer when the secret connection between his invasiveness and Hardy's work as a travelling architect comes into view.

The same is true of Adelaide Hinton if her name is seen as also referring to a place connected with Hardy's travels. Adelaide Hinton and Aeneas Manston (drawn together by the rhythmic and alliterative similiarities between their two names) epitomize the alternative modes of self-determination – one is independent, the other amoral and self-seeking.[42] Hardy, when thinking how to distinguish between these two, may have been drawn back to his own experience as an architect (which is plainly visible in *Desperate Remedies*) and to the places and journeys it involved. In other words, the secret geography of *Desperate Remedies* continues the novel's inquiry into professionalization. It is also foreshadows Hardy's later employment of place-names in the creation of a personal geography.

As Hardy's fictional Wessex place-names became more well-established and consistent, he often transferred real place-names to his characters. This can secure the topography for the interested reader, where Hardy's fictional place-names may leave doubt; it also suggests an identification between the character named and the place, one which may carry a subversive implication. As Hutchins's *History and Antiquities of Dorset* indicates, many Dorset place-names include the family name of the lord of the manor; so, for instance, in *The Hand of Ethelberta*, the heroine's family name of 'Chickerel' suggests that she and her relatives are more rooted and more aristocratic than Lord Mountclere or Lady Petherwin because 'Chickerel' is a village northwest of Weymouth.[43]

The inclusion of the names Manston and Hinton in *Desperate Remedies* has a somewhat different effect, but one that is also evident in Wessex as Hardy later constructed it. Their names suggest a geography that is not only personal but thematic and secretive. In other words, places come into the novel from Hardy's experiences at or near the time of writing; their connection to his life governs his treatment of them and influences the meaning they have within the fiction. This is true not only of *Desperate Remedies*. The majority of Hardy's novels have as their principal location(s) the place(s) where Hardy was writing them.[44] Until he settled at Max Gate in 1885, Hardy and his wife lived nowhere for more than two or three years. With several exceptions, his work before 1885 centres on where he is living and after 1885 on places he has recently visited. In this respect, his practice as a novelist parallels his work as a travelling architect; each place gives scope for one principal novel and after its completion Hardy looks elsewhere – either when younger by moving house or when older by visiting another part of the county. Furthermore, each locality is linked to a particular period in his life, becoming charged with his preoccupations while he was in it and writing about it. The larger geography of Wessex, into which by various adjustments Hardy fitted nearly all his writing, can therefore be seen as in some respects an autobiography – a means of organizing his sense of himself as well as of making his *œuvre* consistent in its topography.

6
Wessex, Elusive and Independent

Elusive places in *Wessex Tales*

In the original versions of the *Far from the Madding Crowd* (in manuscript, serial and its first volume edition), Norcombe Hill is located quite vaguely – the distance from Weatherbury is specified but the direction is not. Little or nothing is said about surrounding places. In the 1895 edition and thereafter, Hardy gives Norcombe's location as 'north-east of the little town of Emminster' and crossed by the 'highway between Emminster and Chalk-Newton'; Emminster is the Wessex name for Beaminster; Chalk-Newton refers to Maiden Newton, so this area corresponds to the high ground near Toller Down. The villages of Corscombe and Norwood lie nearby and could have been the basis of Hardy's fictional name. If they are the source, then Hardy must have had this district in mind in 1874, although he chose not to identify it.[1] It is a district of crucial importance to Hardy's Wessex – to its geography and that geography's significance. Clearly, the changes Hardy made to the novel in 1895 fit it into the geography of Wessex as a whole, specifying a fictional place which the reader can identify with an actual one. He brings it, however, into a part of Wessex which has similar associations and resonances to those Norcombe possessed originally.

When Gabriel arrives at Casterbridge hiring fair, farmers think of Norcombe, where he has come from, as 'a long way' away; he is told in the same episode that it is 'Five or six miles' from Casterbridge to Weatherbury and that Shottsford, the place he is headed for, lies 'Eight miles t'other side of Weatherbury'. Placing Norcombe at a vaguer distance separates it from this group of linked-up places. Similarly, the maltster, when listing the villages where he has worked, nods in the direction of most of them as he speaks of them; he does not do so when mentioning Norcombe. People come and go from Norcombe yet it seems to lie just off the map (Hardy, *Madding Crowd*, chs 6 and 8, pp.36, 57). The Wessex edition clarifies these uncertainties by placing Norcombe on the map; at the same time, Hardy chooses for Norcombe a part of Wessex that is particularly connected in his writing with vagueness and elusiveness. This preserves the clash between two worlds – Norcombe and Weatherbury – which is present in the original version of the novel where the geography is much sketchier.

Hardy shows a frequent interest in this northwesterly corner of Wessex and in the journey to and fro, northwest to southeast, that connects it to Bockhampton – a route which follows the course of the river Frome. *The Woodlanders* and Hardy's short story 'Interlopers at the Knap' are the most striking instances of his choosing this area and connecting it with elusiveness. Both also endow the district with personal meaning. Hardy's fondness for the area is evident: he cited the view from 'Toller Down to Wynyard's Gap' as one of the finest in Dorset (*Personal Writings*, p.233); his tendency to evoke it via names is frequent: 'Tollamore', Hardy's name in 'An Indiscretion in the Life of an Heiress', for what later became Mellstock, may be an indication of his thinking early on about the Toller Down region and, even, of his lending importance to the north-west/southeast trajectory prominent in the later narratives. Furthermore, as in *Desperate Remedies*, a surprising independence manifests itself in elusive places and little-noticed people like Adelaide Hinton.

The name Hinton means a 'Farm or estate belonging to the religious community' and reappears, slightly altered, in the 'Hintocks' of Hardy's *The Woodlanders*. 'Ock' means 'oak' so that the name 'Hintock' links trees and community, going to the heart of that novel's concerns.[2] The Hintocks, though, have proved uniquely difficult to locate: Denys Kay-Robinson calls 'the country of *The Woodlanders*, the most elusive of the regions in which the Wessex novels are set' and F.B. Pinion shows that the difficulty arises because Hardy transferred the setting eastwards, from an area around Melbury Osmond to one close to Minterne Magna, north of Cerne Abbas. His reason for his doing so is, according to Pinion, a desire to avoid giving offence to the Ilchester family, who lived at Melbury Osmund House. Offence might be taken if they were linked to the disreputable Mrs Charmond who lives in the equivalent house in the novel. Such a concern can be seen at work in the changes Hardy made to his short story, 'The First Countess of Wessex' when he published it in serial form in December 1889. Pinion suggests that Hardy is foreseeing similar difficulties with *The Woodlanders* and forestalling them. 'We can immediately discount the theory,' he adds, 'that he wished to divert the reader's attention from his links with Melbury Osmund' – that is, Hardy's family connections with the area.[3]

There are other possible reasons: Melbury Osmond lies near to the railway running from Weymouth to Yeovil, whereas Minterne Magna and Cerne Abbas are further away from any contact with the railway network. The isolation of the Hintocks would be more difficult to establish if they were identified with a place right beside the railway line. Moreover, the sense of family connection was very strong for Hardy and it plays a part in the geography of both novel and short story. Hardy's mother was born at Melbury Osmund and one branch of his Hardy ancestors also owned land nearby: Hutchins gives a pedigree of the 'le Hardy' family under the entry for Melbury Bubb, a village a mile or two south of Melbury Osmund, and connects them with 'Toller Welme and Wolcomb-Matravers', villages nearby (Hutchins, *Dorset*, IV, p.433). In Hardy's *Life*, he mentions a visit to Evershot (two miles south of Melbury Osmund) made in September 1888, eighteen months after *The Woodlanders* was published and while he was writing 'The First Countess of Wessex':

> The decline and fall of the Hardys much in evidence hereabout. An instance: Becky S.'s mother's sister married one of the Hardys of this branch, who was considered to have demeaned himself by the marriage. 'All Woolcombe and Froom Quintin belonged to them at one time,' Becky used to say proudly. She might have added Up-Sydling and Toller Welme.[4]

The first three of these lie southeast of Melbury Osmund, the last to the southwest. Melbury Osmund lies just off the the road from Dorchester to Yeovil (the present-day A37); Up Sydling and Frome St. Quentin straddle the same road on a section known as 'Long Ash Lane' where it follows the track of a Roman Road. The district and the roads to it are full of reminders of both his remote ancestry and his immediate family. It may also be that Hardy's architectural work took him in that direction. Hicks and later Crickmay restored churches in three main areas of Dorset: to the east around Wareham; northwards in the area between Sturminster Newton and Shaftesbury which *Desperate Remedies* secretly refers to; and to the west in an area between Bridport and Beaminster. Hardy's journeys as a young architect's clerk to make 'surveys, measurements and sketches of old churches with a view to' their restoration (*Life*, p.35) would have taken him from Dorchester northwest, familiarizing him with this area of Dorset linked to his family.

Pinion dismisses the idea that family connections are the reason for the doubtful locations of *The Woodlanders* on the grounds that Hardy did write elsewhere about an identifiable 'King's Hintock', corresponding to Melbury Osmund, specifically, in his short stories, 'Interlopers at the Knap', first published May 1884 and included in *Wessex Tales* (May 1888) and 'The Duke's Reappearance', first published December 1896 and collected in *A Changed Man* (1913). This argument is unconvincing because, particularly in 'Interlopers at the Knap', Hardy is again confusing about the precise location of the Hintocks, altering names and topography in successive editions; in fact, as Pinion recognizes, 'King's Hintock' does not receive that name until 1912.[5] In revising the story's topography, Hardy made it conform more accurately to the layout of Wessex as it had developed in his other writing but the more consistent fictional geography continues to obscure the real one which, in the 1884 serial, had been secretly and exactly followed.[6] For example, in the same way that *The Woodlanders* moves the Hintocks eastwards, in 'Interlopers at the Knap' the route taken to reach them changes from 'The north-west road from Casterbridge' to 'The north road' even though the name of the road is changed from the imaginary 'Holloway Lane' to 'Long-Ash Lane', this being the actual name of the 'north-west' road. 'The north road' leads via Cerne Abbas to Minterne Magna, hence to the changed site of the Hintocks, but it is not 'Long-Ash Lane'. In all versions, though by differing means, Hardy keeps the geography unusually muddled – it is possible to discern similarities between the Hintocks and both Minterne Magna and Melbury Osmund but the identification is far less straightforward than is the case with almost anywhere else in Wessex.

The confusion in the topography reflects both narratives' concern with the obscurity and remoteness of out-of-the-way places. 'Interlopers at the Knap' and *The Woodlanders* both begin with visitors getting lost on their way to the Hintocks. Whatever need he may have felt to prevent the Ilchester family from being scandalized, Hardy's principal concern seems to have been the presentation of elusiveness via a confused geography. Family connections would, to my mind, have been related to this: 'Interlopers at the Knap', the first of Hardy's works to mention the Hintocks, opens with Farmer Darton travelling from the south of the county towards the Knap in Hintock. The Knap is the home of Sally Hall to whom the farmer intends to propose. Hardy's father travelled from Bockhampton to Melbury Osmund on the eve of his wedding to Hardy's mother and, according to Millgate, resembled Farmer Darton very nearly: 'Family tradition concurs in the insistence upon the bridegroom's hesitancy and in the anecdote about climbing a signpost in order to read it in the dark' (*Hardy: A Biography*, p.15). The story, in other words, closely follows events intimate with Hardy's life and can be read as an inquiry into origins, origins which prove elusive and mysterious, as perhaps they must. Evershot's Wessex name is 'Evershead' and 'Head' is the maiden name of Hardy's paternal grandmother. The name thus draws the other side of Hardy's family into this part of Dorset. 'Evershead' might also mean 'the head, the source of eternity' and the choice is justified by the fact that the river Frome rises near to the village. Travelling from Stinsford towards Melbury Osmund takes one back up the river to its source. A journey in this direction is linked with a particular moment of family history and associated more generally with beginnings.

It is appropriate, therefore, that when Farmer Darton and his companions lose their way to the Knap it is because they find a signpost whose names have become illegible: 'Not a letter, sacred or heathen – not so much as would tell us the way to the great fireplace,' Darton's companion Japheth declares. 'Either the moss and mildew have eaten away the words, or we have arrived in a land where the natives have lost the art of writing.' Faced by this, Darton decides to 'take the straightest road'. The incident closes with 'the ironical directing-post' left behind; it remains 'holding out its blank arms to the raw breeze, which brought a snore from the wood as if Skrymir the Giant were sleeping there' (Hardy, *Withered Arm*, pp.253–4).

There is a comic edge to all this, as the prosaic rustics, carrying a turkey in a basket, find themselves in the surroundings of a school-boy adventure yarn. Hardy's momentary parody of one genre is coupled with more threatening hints: Japheth exclaims about 'the great fireplace' and Darton seems unconsciously to share the fear that these roads lead to Hell when he chooses the 'straightest' one.[7] A similar balance of tones characterizes the final sentence which juxtaposes the 'blank arms' held out 'to the raw breeze' with 'a snore from the wood'.[8] Bleakness is comforted by quaintness but both persist. The snore, too, comes from 'Skrymir the Giant', the sleeper in Norse mythology whom not even Thor could awaken. Skrymir evokes a still more distant past and his presence suggests that the characters have entered a world whose depths can never be sounded – there is always another, lower layer of time to be uncovered and none of the layers will give up their secrets, however thoroughly you quarry them. Personal origins are tied together with a world that possesses (or has returned to) an original primitiveness. The sudden disappearance of secure historical foundations corresponds to the vertiginous quality of any search for personal roots in family history.

At the centre of this inchoate, blank world, the story discovers Sally Hall who, because of various interruptions and 'interlopers', never marries Farmer Darton or indeed anybody else. She leads instead a life of happy 'independence' – a word which recurs with reference to her. Independence which was practised by Adelaide in her decision to marry now seems possible in the single life and, perhaps, only there, only in obscurity. Sally's behaviour remains as praiseworthy as Adelaide's but it is odder, running counter to the traditional path of worldly success for a woman. The difference in this respect between *Desperate Remedies* and 'Interlopers at the Knap', written nearly fifteen years later, could be read as an index of Hardy's growing disillusionment with marriage or, more generally, with movement and progress. It might be thought to exemplify his gradually increasing investment in the virtues of a secluded, rural life free from ambition or mobility.

Sally herself is strikingly and uncomplicatedly successful in business. This suggests that her ambition has not been thwarted, it has simply chosen another direction. Nonetheless, there are other aspects of *Wessex Tales* which could support the view that Hardy has grown more nostalgic about the past and less confident about the future: 'The Three Strangers', the first story in the collection, presents overbearing forces of law entering a rural community, a community which conspires at the end to protect an escaped criminal whose actions seem defensible. With the rustics' help, the 'clever sheep-stealer' evaporates into the landscape:

> his marvellous coolness and daring in hob-and-nobbing with the hangman [. . .] won their admiration. So that it may be questioned if all those who ostensibly made themselves so busy in exploring woods and fields and lanes were quite so thorough when it came to the private examination of their own lofts and outhouses. Stories were afloat of a mysterious figure being occasionally seen in some old overgrown trackway or other, remote from turnpike-roads, but when a search was instituted in any of these suspected quarters nobody was found.[9]

The final sentence here carries an ingenious and evasive double-meaning: 'nobody was found' perhaps because the search was something of a pretence (as the previous sentence suggests) and perhaps because the sighting was also fabricated (with the aim of demonstrating to authority the continuing vigilance of the neighbourhood).

Perhaps too, the 'mysterious figure' had become rather elusive, slipping between the gaps in the community – the gaps between those who knowingly let him go and those, not in the know, who cannot find him. He is 'afloat', like the stories about him, liberated by connivance.

Likewise, the final story, 'The Distracted Preacher', looks back fondly to the days when the authorities turned something of a blind eye to the smuggling that was 'second nature' to the villagers. In the present of the story's close, however, 'it is all over': 'The officers have blood-money for taking a man dead or alive, and the trade is gone to nothing. We were hunted down like rats.' Lizzy, who says these words, soon after agrees to marry Stockdale, the preacher distracted by her before, and they go away:

> He took her away from her old haunts to the home that he had made for himself in his native county, where she studied her duties as a minister's wife with praiseworthy assiduity. It is said that in after years she wrote an excellent tract called *Render unto Caesar; or, the Repentant Villagers* [. . . .] Stockdale got it printed, after making some corrections, and putting in a few powerful sentences of his own.[10]

The disruption of an earlier society by the blinkered forces of law and religion is presented in the straightening out of Lizzy: when she is uprooted, she becomes 'assiduous' and her language is corrected. The dry, sardonic humour of this closing paragraph is turned into more difficult and painful irony when juxtaposed with the earlier speech – 'making some corrections' and 'putting in [. . .] powerful sentences' reveal their self-ignorant cruelty by being placed alongside 'hunted down like rats'.

The endings of the two stories, coming first and last in the collection, suggest a further, historical narrative. Lizzy and her fellow-smugglers are hunted remorselessly down whereas earlier, in 'The Three Strangers', overgrown trackways become the haunts of ghostly escapees, protected and welcomed by a more flexible and morally perceptive society. The sequence of the collection replicates the historical sequence in which the hangman who cannot capture his victim has been replaced by the officers who can and the preachers who do the same to the womenfolk. Throughout the collection, moreover, language seems implicated in the acts of oppression typified by the 'innocent' Stockdale; he corrects his wife's writing whereas the Hintocks lie beyond the reach of words, in a land before or after writing. Similarly, in 'The Withered Arm', Hardy draws attention to the prison facade, visible from Egdon Heath and 'bearing the inscription, "COVNTY JAIL: 1793."' These inscribed capitals, decorating 'a classic archway of ashlar', assert the same power of government that cracks down on smuggling and, in 'The Melancholy Hussar of the German Legion', executes deserters. Stockdale and Lizzy are reminiscent of Henry Knight and Elfride Swancourt in *A Pair of Blue Eyes*. There is 'a hard square decisiveness in the shape of [Knight's] sentences, as if [. . .] they were not there and then newly constructed, but were drawn forth from a large store ready-made'. Confronted though, at the end, by Elfride's death, Knight's voice becomes 'mild and gentle as a child's'. The confrontation occurs when he and Stephen Smith are shown the inscription for her coffin, a piece of writing Hardy introduces into the novel in the black-letter text of the supposed original.[11]

Nonetheless, *Wessex Tales* presents more than an elegy for a vanishing way of life and expresses more than the desire to escape from the forward-marching world of language into the silences of vision and stillness. The geography of 'Interlopers at the Knap' draws the collection away from the southern coast of the county which dominates the other stories so that the Hintocks offer a different environment – originary, unmappable and unidentified – which at once corresponds to Hardy's family home (Melbury Osmund) and is an alternative to the places he is personally more familiar with (the Frome valley, the Channel coast). As well as rounding out the collection's picture of Wessex as a whole, 'Interlopers' challenges the perspective that structures the other stories, both individually and collectively. Its distinctiveness, apparent in its geography, is confirmed by Sally's resolute decision not to marry.

In the story, Sally is robbed of her intended husband by the accidental appearance of Helena, her sister-in-law, dressed in a gown intended for Sally herself. Darton sees Helena wearing Sally's dress and falls in love with her; when she is left a widow, they marry. Two other stories, out of the collection's original five, involve usurpation or displacement of a similar kind: Rhoda in 'The Withered Arm' is supplanted by the new wife, Gertrude; in 'Fellow-Townsmen', Mr Downe instead of Mr Barnet marries Lucy Savile. Rhoda and Gertrude, Sally and Helena seem doubles of one another, opposed and conjoined.[12] The outcomes though are not the same: in 'The Withered Arm', rivalry reduces both women to violent, withered versions of their earlier selves; more mutedly in 'Fellow-Townsmen', Mr Barnet and Lucy are abandoned at the story's end to weary solitude, he travelling the world, she lingering in an empty, over-large house. In 'Interlopers at the Knap', the ending presents an image of contented singularity.

After her marriage to Darton, Helena sickens and dies; Darton as a widower woos Sally again, visiting her for the final time on 'a bright day late in May' and travelling along a road that is 'scarce recognizable as the track of his two winter journeys'. She refuses him, kindly but firmly demanding that he never asks her again. The story ends by stating 'that Sally, notwithstanding the solicitations her attractions drew down upon her, had refused several offers of marriage, and steadily adhered to her purpose of leading a single life'.[13] Sally is endowed by the cadences of this conclusion with a nobility that has been belied earlier on by her straightforward, practical character. As is often the case in Hardy's work, the remote place turns out to be both less and more peculiar than a visitor imagines – the puzzle of finding Hintock is removed and the greater, plainer puzzle of Sally's self-sufficiency and steady purposiveness takes over. Not apparently trying to punish Darton or embittered by her experience, Sally simply behaves in this way. The writing is more concerned to have us credit what happened than to offer an explanation for it. In the last clause the rhythm of 'adhered to her purpose' is repeated in 'of leading a single', like a repeated phrase in music; consequently, the word 'life' makes a peculiarly intense affirmation when it completes the sentence and the story. Elsewhere, especially in respect of young women, Hardy feels the poignancy of their having only one opportunity to live; Sally sounds determined to take her chance and lead the one life available to her as well as keen to avoid marriage.

In part, this ending suggests, like other stories in the collection, that 'primitive' rural communities allow for more varied (and progressive) forms of social life than do other supposedly more advanced ones. Sally in Hintock is approached but unmolested by the men she attracts; she can exercise choice in her sexual affairs and be accepted as a single person, a householder and successful business woman. Her freedom and independence continue the collection's polemic against hangmen, central authority and preachers like Stockdale. However, coupled with the story's geography, its ending also draws attention to the self-contained quality which people possess. Sally has no airs, yet such an unpoetic person remains quite obscure to other people – her motives, aims and desires are impossible to reach or map. Tracking her down on a dark, wintry evening presents difficulties emblematic of those encountered in trying to fathom her nature yet the first is possible and the second is not. You cannot discover where you come from: there seem an infinite number of possible origins and the self evaporates among and between them. At the same time, you can neither deny nor comprehend the fact of your own, individual being. There is both boldness and simplicity about Sally's presence in the same way that her strong-mindedness is carried lightly. These qualities come through more fully because she appears out of the blank obscurity of the Hintocks, the more self-possessed because she is untroubled by the mysteries which surround her.

A Laodicean: geographies of provincialism

'The Distracted Preacher' was written at the same time as Hardy was researching *The Trumpet-Major* and takes place in the same southerly district of the county, the downland on the Channel coast. The other stories in *Wessex Tales* suggest comparable links: 'The Withered Arm' revisits the landscape of Egdon Heath first used in *The Return of the Native*; 'Fellow-Townsmen' and 'Interlopers at the Knap' echo, respectively, *The Mayor of Casterbridge*, in plot, and *The Woodlanders*, in location. Hardy's choice of stories for the collection allows it to move through miniature versions of the various landscapes of his Wessex novels.[14] *Wessex Tales* can be read as offering a summary of the different ways of addressing his native country which Hardy adopted in different novels. The different approaches to Wessex include not only those of the 'Novels of Character and Environment' and the 'Romances and Fantasies' but those of the 'Novels of Ingenuity' as well – novels often thought of as the ones Hardy needed to relegate or remove if Wessex were to be self-consistent and conform to late nineteenth-century expectations. Sally Hall's determined independence, in other words, although it contrasts most immediately with Grace Melbury's re-acceptance of her estranged husband Edred Fitzpiers at the end of *The Woodlanders*, has as its nearest equivalent the heroine of one of the 'Novels of Ingenuity', Paula Power, who in *A Laodicean* (1881) becomes uncharacteristically decisive in the novel's closing chapters.

There are other similarities between the two: 'Interlopers at the Knap' and *A Laodicean* both discover the resolve of a woman and both take place somewhere hard to locate. 'Stancy Castle' is located in Hardy's 1895–6 edition of *A Laodicean* on the north Somerset coast (that is, in 'Outer Wessex'); there it can be identified with the actual Dunster Castle. Originally, though, the identifications are less clear. Though Dunster Castle is one source, resemblances have also been found between Stancy Castle and Corfe Castle, inland from Swanage. (The castle had featured, much more recognizably, in *The Hand of Ethelberta*, where it was named 'Coomb Castle'). Somerset is suggested by the name of the hero, George

Somerset, yet Casterbridge lies within easy reach, although it is not clear in which direction; 'Sleeping-Green', one of the novel's locations, is the actual name of a village north of Wareham (now known as 'Slepe'). The principal towns in the novel are 'Markton' and 'Helterton', neither corresponding to an actual place.[15] Taken together, these aspects of setting and place-name give the sense that, overall, topography is being deliberately unsettled.

This is a more marked innovation given the novels Hardy had written most recently beforehand: in *The Return of the Native* (1878), Hardy created in Egdon Heath a mapped terrain that closely resembled Piddletown Heath, near Bockhampton; in *The Trumpet-Major* (1880), he accurately reproduced the geographical situation of historical events during the Napoleonic War. *The Return of the Native* was published with a map in 1878 and 1880; *The Trumpet-Major* used real place-names when first published; these were replaced by Wessex place-names in 1895–6. In his next novel, *A Laodicean*, he made it impossible to find the places he was talking about, even supposing they existed. A similar sudden change in style had happened in the 1870s when, after his first success with *Far from the Madding Crowd* (1874), Hardy refused to continue writing rustic novels and published instead, *The Hand of Ethelberta* (1876), a social and satirical comedy, set as much in London and Normandy as in Dorset.[16] Coming after the profoundly topographical *The Return of the Native* and the self-consciously traditional regionalism of *The Trumpet-Major*, *A Laodicean* could be seen as a comparable abreaction. However, as is true of 'Interlopers at the Knap' within *Wessex Tales*, *A Laodicean* feels more successful than that and better positioned. The novel like the story seems to comment on Hardy's rustic world, throwing into relief the genre he is seen as writing within.

Hardy is reported to have said in 1900 that *A Laodicean* 'contained more of the facts of his own life than anything else he had ever written' (*IR*, pp.63–4). This is the more striking because usually he denied any autobiographical element to his work. In the *Life*, he is at pains to maintain that even *A Pair of Blue Eyes* is purely fictional and does not 'show a picture of his own personality as the architect' (*Life*, pp.76–7). Probably, too, Hardy is willing to suggest *A Laodicean* is autobiographical because doing so diverts attention from his more famous rural novels, scotching the idea that they are autobiographical and that he is therefore a rustic simpleton. *A Laodicean* claims in its sub-title to be '*A Story of To-day*'; it makes much of telegraphy, photography and continental travel, combining these with both explicit and implicit discussion of current issues: debates about architectural styles, colonialism, 'Modern

England' and Matthew Arnold's analysis of 'Pagan and Medieval Religious Sentiment'.[17] Identifying *this* novel as based on the facts of his life gives the impression that Hardy was, as a person, familiar with and involved in contemporary life.

The novel was written in London and for most of the time during its composition Hardy was ill, unable to go outside or, for a considerable period, even to rise from his bed. This incarceration prevented his researching a new novel, certainly not to the extent he had for *The Trumpet-Major*; nor could he retreat into the country to write, as had been the pattern early in his career when he was living in London.[18] Being thrown back on his own resources – his personal library as well as memories and experience – coincided with an increasing dissatisfaction with London life. In May 1881, as soon as he was back on his feet and the novel finished, Hardy began looking for a house in Dorset; in June, he and Emma moved to Wimborne. His concern with his place or lack of it in London is reflected in his re-reading of Arnold, especially Arnold's 'The Literary Influence of Academies' – an essay Hardy reacted against forcefully in a note from the winter of 1880–1:

> Arnold is wrong about provincialism, if he means anything more than a provincialism of style and manner of exposition. A certain provincialism of feeling is invaluable. It is of the essence of individuality, and is largely made up of that crude enthusiasm without which no great thoughts are thought, no great deeds done. (*Life*, p.151)

The assertiveness of this entry stands out all the more because the *Life* is otherwise so carefully temperate and so reluctant to exhibit drive or will. Declaring Arnold to be simply 'wrong' removes any doubt and hesitation on the matter; Hardy's bold and unkind frankness exhibits the 'crude' provincialism which the entry praises. *A Laodicean*, from its title on, is concerned with attaining this decisiveness, with the processes that bring hesitancy to an end and with the advantages and vulnerability of such a provincial tone of mind – its capacity or otherwise to come to terms with London and produce '*A Story of To-day*'.

George Somerset is found, at the novel's opening, making 'a summer circuit in the west' in order to make sketches of English Gothic architecture. Somerset, like Springrove in *Desperate Remedies*, is caught between architecture and literature, between dreams and practicalities, and the 'sketching circuit' is undertaken as a 'contrite return to architecture' after two years spent dabbling in poetry. Somerset's situation and character fits the image of himself Hardy constructs through the *Life* and the other young men of his novels, such as Clym Yeobright, caught uncertainly between the pressure to make something of themselves and the felt need not to. It is, however, a more curiously precise portrait than earlier ones; the opening pages are demandingly thorough (not to say dull) about Victorian architects and architectural styles. More precisely still, the preference for English Gothic echoes Hardy's account in the *Life* of Raphael Brandon, quite a famous architect for whom he worked in London in May–August 1870, when *Desperate Remedies* had been written but not published, and when Hardy had met Emma but not decided on marriage (see *Life*, pp.79–80). Somerset's first appearance recalls this period in Hardy's life, its uncertainties, lassitude and efforts to regain momentum; its long-forgotten disputes over styles of Gothic and their supposed 'principles'.

Other periods, however, are also recalled: as Hardy mentions in the *Life*, the novel's Baptist minister, Woodwell is 'Among the few portraits of actual persons in Hardy's novels' (*Life*, p.35), being based on the Rev. Frederick Perkins whose sons, Alfred and William, argued with Hardy about adult baptism (see *Hardy: A Biography*, p.64). As with Somerset's architecture, his elaborately detailed debate with Woodwell about the Established Church, Paedobaptists and Baptists recalls an incident from Hardy's own experience and one which is virtually repeated in the *Life*. Exceptionally, the novel seems legible via the autobiography. More than that, Woodwell is linked to Hardy's thoughts about provincialism.

The novel states several times how worthy of respect Woodwell is despite the triviality of the differences in opinion he makes so much of. He is, for instance, an impressive speaker:

> He was gifted with a burning natural eloquence, which though perhaps a little too freely employed in exciting the 'Wertherism of the uncultivated' had in it genuine power. He was a master of that oratory which no limitation of knowledge can repress, and which no training can impart.
>
> (Hardy, *Laodicean*, Book. 3, ch.4, p.180)

'Wertherism of the uncultivated' comes from Hillebrand's article on 'Modern England' (which Hardy was reading at the time). There the phrase refers disparagingly to Methodism; in the novel, the quotation's learning and its impressive origins signal a sophistication which has to concede, nonetheless, Woodwell's 'genuine power'. Likewise, Hardy's second sentence begins in superciliousness and ends in respect. The 'crude enthusiasm', which Hardy sees as the essential quality of 'invaluable', heroic provincialism, appears again in Woodwell's 'burning natural eloquence'; it proves Hillebrand mistaken in the same way that Hardy declares Arnold wrong.[19] Woodwell's name may be making a similar point: recalling restoration comedy, 'would well' primarily suggests the character's good intentions; 'wood' can also mean 'mad', however, so that 'woodwell' values the eccentricity which academies frown upon, connecting it to a rural place – a well in a wood. Such eccentricity possesses and exerts 'genuine power', Hardy says, using a word which resonates in a novel whose heroine is named Paula Power.

In Paula's character, Hardy presents a 'Laodicean' – someone who, until the novel's closing sequences, appears unable to determine her own conduct, being spontaneous and easily influenced, or at worst just weak. These traits of character are the more obvious because she occupies a prominent position in local society, having inherited the wealth and influence acquired by her father, John Power, a builder of railways.[20] The plot uncovers her strength and shows her future husband George Somerset also becoming gradually less hesitant and ineffectual. The two of them plan at the close to build in place of the castle, which has been burnt down, a 'mansion of independent construction hard by the old one, unencumbered with the ghosts of an unfortunate line' (Hardy, *Laodicean*, Book. 6, ch.5, p.378): the ghosts, that is, of the de Stancys whose portraits filled the castle and who, in the shape of Captain de Stancy, tried to press Paula into marriage. Similar to *Desperate Remedies* in its employment of sensation novel elements, *A Laodicean* echoes that novel again in its conclusion. A newly-married couple takes possession of a country property – the woman doing so by resisting the 'rightful' owners, the man by proving his professional worth. Paula's rejection of Captain de Stancy repeats Cytherea's of Manston (whose suit is supported by Miss Aldclyffe); Somerset's defeat of the rival architect, Havill, repeats Owen Graye's increasing success as an architect, itself a corollary of Edward Springrove's effectiveness in tracking Manston. In the same way that Cytherea and Edward bring the outside world of Creston (Budmouth) and beyond into the world of Knapwater House, Paula and George plan a modern house, eclectic and 'independent'. And, as is the case in *Desperate Remedies*, this course of action is 'straight': George tells Paula that she should not regret giving up her medievalism but embrace the modern: 'since it is rather in your line you may as well keep straight on'. Her 'line' is as straight as Edward's course across Weymouth Bay and it should now replace the ghosts of the de Stancys, 'an unfortunate line'. The building of a new house recalls the landscape of *Desperate Remedies* where again there are two mansions, one old and one new. Miss Aldclyffe lives in the new mansion and has recently renovated the old one for Manston to live in, 'restoring' where Paula and George are building anew.

The novel's affirmation of youth's power to overcome established institutions brings it close not only to *Desperate Remedies* but to *The Hand of Ethelberta* and *Two on a Tower* as well. Ethelberta is trapped by her seedy, aristocratic husband but goes on to dominate him, conquering her husband as earlier she conquered London. Lady Constantine, in *Two on a Tower*, deceives a Bishop into marrying her when she is pregnant by another man, the ardent astronomer, Swithin St Cleeve. There is a price for these victories: Lady Constantine is prematurely aged by her miserable marriage to the Bishop and her despair of regaining Swithin; Ethelberta, though victorious, is hardened by the battle, more severe than her mother would like and unattractive to her former lover.[21] In *A Laodicean*, the costs are harder to see: Paula accepts the modern despite voicing in her last words regret that the castle has been burnt and that George is not a 'de Stancy'. Whimsical disappointment is, however, in character, proving that, although she can be determined when she has to, she remains spontaneous and many-sided.

More troubling is the fate of Charlotte de Stancy, Paula's friend and the first person George meets when, early in the novel, he enters the castle. Soon after hearing that Paula and George are to marry, Charlotte writes to Paula announcing that she will soon 'steal from the world [. . .] for whose gaieties and ambitions I never had much liking' and will join a 'Protestant Sisterhood'. Her withdrawal into a High Anglican convent confirms her connection with a medievalism that the novel is rejecting; it seems at first of a piece with the captain's disgrace and the castle's destruction. Charlotte, though, has been treated more sympathetically throughout and been involved in an intense, sexually-charged friendship with Paula. Her withdrawal implies that some kinds of eccentricity (such as transgressive sexuality) withdraw before a victorious modernity. Speaking as she does in terms of 'gaieties' and 'ambitions', Charlotte also echoes Hardy's autobiographical hesitations about the behaviour required by the social world. Her action means that a contrary feeling begins to colour the novel's conclusion, as if getting rid of a corrupt aristocracy and a bogus medievalism brought with it the rejection of something more genuine and more odd – its forced retreat into, what Charlotte terms, a 'secluded home'.[22]

Charlotte does not say where she is going: the 'Protestant Sisterhood at——' will be her 'resting-place till the great rest comes'. She retreats into a death-like placelessness to escape the forward-planning married couple, who will tend to 'keep straight on' since that is 'rather in [their] line'. Her removal is the equivalent in the novel to Ethelberta's hardness and Lady Constantine's worn-out despair; it shows the cost of successful adaptation to 'the science of climbing' (*Life*, p.54), a cost that is largely unfelt in *Desperate Remedies*. The secludedness of Charlotte's future home and its indefinition also connect with the novel's geographical uncertainty as a whole. Stancy Castle and its surroundings are quiet and remote; their geography is reasonably well-defined within the novel but cannot be traced back to a single, actual original. At the end of the novel, Hardy sets beyond this place a further recess – Charlotte's convent – which is unnamed and unlocated within either the novel's geography or that of the real world. This contrast brings Stancy Castle nearer by comparison and makes its imaginary topography seem less generic.

As a result, success and modernity seem to involve a coming into the world, geographically as well as socially. Charlotte's retreat resembles that of the sheep-stealer in 'The Three Strangers' and, even more closely perhaps, Henchard's journey into Egdon Heath to die. Meanwhile, the other aspect of the ending – Paula's and George's determined, brave engagement with the future – catches the same balance of feeling as dominates the end of 'Interlopers at the Knap'. There Sally sustains herself even when Hintock has become (on Darton's last visit) visible and easily found; Paula and George aim to do the same in a place which similarly, because of Charlotte's departure, has drawn closer to the world. Both novel and short story ask whether a balance can be struck between old and new, similar to the balance which Hardy later located in his early life, when he was working as an architect in Dorchester while still living at home. *A Laodicean*'s hostility to medievalism rejects the widely-held belief that Gothic architecture could bring about such a balance. Instead, Hardy argues, people are required to embrace progress or retreat from it. Ambivalent feelings surround this requirement but it cannot be shirked; both the Gothic revival and medievalism more broadly are being presented by the novel as evasions.

It remains uncertain, though, whether embracing the modern allows for a continued relation to the old, the rural, the private and the secluded. *A Laodicean*, in the confidence of its closing scene and in its 'independent construction' of a mansion (and a novel) 'eclectic in style', suggests for a moment both that it may be possible and how it may be done. Independence and eclecticism imply together a free choice among possibilities, wedded to none. They approach the same mobile and self-sufficient position as Hardy adopted when he was moving as a young architect to and fro between Dorchester and Higher Bockhampton. Provincialism of this kind, autonomous and discriminating, is as Hardy wrote at the same period, 'of the essence of individuality'. It depends upon and produces a 'burning natural eloquence', independent of what instruction can impart; at the same time, it entails a wilful, eclectic sometimes contrary reluctance to obey the rules or accept the authority of 'principles' in art.[23]

A position like this continually runs up against the contradictions of the novelist's profession and the ironies of self-promotion. It must ask as well what society or nationality can possibly be formed from a group of people who obstinately remain individuals. *A Laodicean* addresses these concerns through its plot, characters and its allusions to academic discussions of such issues. Its geography does the same. As has been said, locations in the novel are confusing: where real equivalents for them can be found, they are scattered around various parts of the West Country. However, as in *Desperate Remedies*, hints exist of a personal connection. Between 1854 and 1859, Hicks rebuilt the chancel of the church in Powerstock, a village northeast of Bridport and southeast of Beaminster. In 1870, Crickmay restored the north aisle of St. John the Baptist, Buckhorn Weston, a village between Sherborne and Gillingham. Hardy was working for both at the relevant times. Powerstock, according to Hutchins, 'belongs to the Earl of Sandwich and the Duke of Cleveland, representatives of Harry Paulet, Duke of Bolton'; he includes a pedigree of the De Paulets in his account of the village.[24] The conjunction of names recalls Paula Power. The railway branch line from Maiden Newton to Bridport, completed in 1857 (during the restoration work), had a station near Powerstock and on a hill above the village lay the ruins of a castle. Buckhorn Weston, where the later restoration work took place, lies very near the border of Dorset and Somerset (the nearest town being Wincanton), and right beside the London and South Western line. Buckhorn Weston tunnel nearby is one of the longest railway tunnels in the county. In the novel, George and Paula visit and admire a railway tunnel and the railways visible from the castle go, it is said, to London.[25] Furthermore and rather strangely, on the first series Ordnance Survey map of the area (which Hardy would have used), a farmhouse on the edge of the village and abutting the railway is named 'Dunster'.[26]

Neither place nor both together form the location of the novel, which remains geographically eclectic. The similarities between them and elements in *A Laodicean* imply instead that, while writing the book in London, Hardy recollected his working life of ten years earlier and the journeys around Dorset which he made, or others in the office made. In this respect the names of characters and the geographical details extend the personal references present in Hardy's allusions to English Gothic and behind these to Raphael Brandon. Likewise, the novel's revival of elements from *Desperate Remedies* continues into its geography which draws on the same part of Hardy's life and raises the same issues of power versus seclusion, action versus passivity. Powerstock's alternative name was 'Poorstock' (used by the Ordnance Survey map) and the double name epitomizes the complications addressed by this novel among others by Hardy – the relation between poverty and power is considered, moreover, by a plot first used in 'The Poor Man and the Lady', while Paula Power's name echoes 'poor' and 'power', Powerstock's name and one of the book's concerns. Hardy, as 'The Poor Man' indicates, was conscious of coming, in some people's eyes, from 'poor stock'.

Furthermore, just as *A Laodicean* addresses a more acute and more troubled sense of modernity's impact than does *Desperate Remedies*, so it employs a geography which inquires into how geographies are made. The novel's geography, in other words, corresponds to its advocacy of provincialism as the source of individuality. Fragments of personal association occupy the same landscape as the stereotypical and generic: so, 'Markton', the conventional country town, and 'Sleeping-Green', whose name offers the clichéd image of rustic tranquillity, both contain personal memories for Hardy of Powerstock, Buckhorn Weston and other places like them. Actual places are alluded to – Somerset, Dunster, Corfe Castle – yet the novel will not attach itself to them; it shifts these names from the actual towards the generic as much as the names wed the novel to real locations. The effect of this is clearer when the novel's place in Hardy's output is considered.

The settings of *The Return of the Native* and *The Trumpet-Major* squared, although in different ways, with a part of the country which was already publicly identifiable as, to some degree, Hardy's when the novels were first published. *A Laodicean* is loosed from that south Dorset context and, simultaneously, its personal elements become both more secret and more pervasive. Where the two earlier novels followed the maps of history, either ancient or more recent, *A Laodicean* is mapped by the novelist's choice which, like George Somerset's sketching tour, is the product of both whim and practical good sense, both self-indulgence and self-interest. Hardy is preoccupied in *The Return of the Native* with the overlaying of historical strata within a single landscape. In *A Laodicean* this interest becomes autobiographical as Hardy creates an environment in which several periods of his life are combined – his time with Hicks, that with Crickmay, his early married life at Swanage, in the Isle of Purbeck, near Corfe Castle, his time in London working on the book and revisiting his home county through the pages of Hutchins. Moreover, in the same way that George and Paula grow into greater independence (in part by travelling abroad), so the novel's created world acquires substance by standing alongside the real places of the Rhine valley and Normandy. Making up a world – out of conventional elements, tourist attractions and private associations – creates an environment which attains the same status as real ones do. Hardy's world in *A Laodicean* competes with the outside world from which it picks and chooses.

The optimistic note on which *A Laodicean* concludes, casting off medievalism and accepting the costs of progress, upholds the possibility of eclectic independence. A provincial setting, generically idyllic and overfamiliar, can be made into a personal world. The plot argues this and so does the book's geography, especially as it was first published in 1881. The considerable alterations, however, which Hardy made to the novel's settings, when it was included in the Wessex edition of 1895–6, would seem to imply its exceptionality – the difficulty of fitting its geography into the Wessex Hardy was presenting through the new edition. The revisions may also be taken to imply a change in Hardy's thinking about personal independence; indeed, both of these can be seen as occurring together. In my opinion, however, *A Laodicean* is characteristic of the Wessex edition rather than being exceptional.

If the Dorset world Hardy presents in his novels frequently contains autobiographical references, their hiddenness within the text corresponds to the elusiveness and the immediacy of self – its retreat before inquiry and its inescapable presence. The existence of these allusions within the place-names of *Desperate Remedies* and *A Laodicean* extends the autobiographical elements of those novels into their geographies. Each novel addresses how young people can assert themselves within the public, social world. The later novel's conclusion that power and integrity can survive through a particular type of provincialism has as its corollary Hardy's creation of an unidentifiable, individual world situated amidst the 'real' one. In addition, the obscurity of Stancy Castle has an equivalent in the short story, 'Interlopers at the Knap', in Sally

Hall's barely discoverable home. Sally's determined self-sufficiency manifests again the qualities Hardy admired in provincialism, which on this occasion he brings into Wessex. The anomalous, topographically inaccurate geography of 'Interlopers at the Knap' (and later *The Woodlanders*) repeats the combination of elusiveness and presence which is explored through the non-Wessex geography of the original *A Laodicean*. Identifiable parts of Hardy's Wessex, therefore, possess *A Laodicean*'s eclectic independence. The valorization of eclecticism and independence can be found in Hardy's more conventionally rustic novels, beginning with *Far from the Madding Crowd*, through their use of pastoral conventions, their many-layered landscapes and through Hardy's suggestions in each about how local relates to metropolitan. More surprisingly, perhaps, the same stance emerges from the collected edition, both in the changes Hardy made for it and in the map he drew. Hardy's Wessex as a whole may be seen as an enlargement of *A Laodicean*'s independent provincial world, rather than being a toning down or a denial of it.

Constructing Wessex

Recent criticism of Hardy has, by and large, been hostile to 'Wessex', seeing it as a late addition, superimposed on the original variety of his novels and fitting them to the needs of his late nineteenth-century audience. Peter Widdowson presents the process as adaptive: 'Hardy himself bowed to public desires enough to revise his novels and add new prefaces making the Wessex he had invented more prominent in the stories and more easily located by pilgrims.' Wiener identifies these 'public desires' as, in particular, the wish for images of secure national identity at a time of domestic and international tension.[27] The same pressure is evident from contemporary and twentieth-century criticism which fashions Hardy into the novelist famous for celebrating a timeless, rural world. The prominence of Wessex in discussion of the novels arises, according to Widdowson, from this bias in the critical tradition.[28]

Wessex is understood by these accounts as performing the role in Hardy's work which late capitalism and imperialism performed within the culture more widely. Robert Colls sees late nineteenth-century politics as progressively eroding individualism in favour of the nation-state – a nation-state which was increasingly conceived as an organic unity. Geographical studies in the period followed a similar pattern, defining essential England as a single region formed by natural borders.[29] Studies of 'Englishness', like those of Wiener and the essays collected by Robert

Colls and Philip Dodd, regard all the literature of the period as coloured by its imperial ambitions and its concurrent need for a national identity rooted in belonging.[30] Hardy's Wessex supplies another example. The danger of this reading, as far as Hardy is concerned, is its tendency to present him in a pastoral light even while seeking to rid him of Wessex's pastoralism. Hardy's early novels are seen separately from the national conditions which surround them; his later revisions of his output are presented as the result of an oppressive, imperious audience. 'Wessex' is forced upon Hardy in the same way that the needs of 'England' imposed themselves upon rural Dorset both culturally and economically.

Joe Fisher shares many of these views. He argues that Hardy's Wessex offers an 'apparently "natural" context for "natural" characters and dramas, work practices and power relations' – that is, that 'the myth of Wessex' confirms the status quo by naturalizing it. In his view, however, Hardy also 'developed and exploited' the idea as his career went on. He made the most of it in the pursuit of success – 'cultural (and economic) power' – while simultaneously he undermined its values even within his most famous novels, as can be seen from their similarity to his neglected, and explicitly subversive, 'Novels of Ingenuity'.[31] This refreshing account of Hardy's using Wessex to further his career goes along with Fisher's observation of his developing the idea from relatively early on. Although not consolidated into a mapped world until the collected edition of 1895–6, Wessex was becoming an element in Hardy's thinking about his novels and himself as a novelist from fifteen years before at least.

Fisher, however, equates 'the myth of Wessex' with the 'bourgeois fictions' in which, according to him, Hardy traded. Just like the pastoral elements in *Far from the Madding Crowd*, Wessex is something Hardy offers the readers deceitfully, subverting it and its values even as he does so. It seems to me truer to say that, as is the case with pastoral in the novels, Hardy is neither succumbing to an imperialist account of national identity nor showing the hollowness of such an idea. Rather, Wessex resists the national account of place and personhood in order to affirm provincial, eclectic independence – the form of rootedness which the ruralist nationalism of, say, Trollope and Oliphant, parodies and endangers. This becomes clear from the map Hardy draws and its relation to the novels in the collected edition.

In other words, Hardy's creation in *A Laodicean* of an unidentifiable, individual world situated amidst the 'real' one corresponds exactly to the workings of his map of Wessex. The importance of this map should not be underestimated. It first appeared in 1895–6 and again, somewhat altered, in the edition of 1912–13, the second version being modelled on a sketch Hardy had provided himself.[32] Though scaled down and simplified a little, the 1912–13 version was used for the New Wessex edition, published by Macmillan in the 1970s. Subsequent reprints have reproduced the same cartography: where unable to reproduce the accepted map, presumably for copyright reasons, they have published redrawn versions of it. Its continuing, powerful influence is shown by the inclusion of the 1895–6 map in the recent Penguin edition even though the edition reprints Hardy's novels as they appeared when first published in volume form. Although the texts antedate 'Wessex' and have been used partly to attack the dominance of Wessex over readings of Hardy, nonetheless the map appears in every volume.

Though increasingly detailed and elaborate, the map is always relatively spare. It shows with perfect accuracy the outline of an area of south-western England, from Windsor in the east to Barnstaple in the west and reaching as far north as Oxford; Cornwall is inset in the top left-hand corner. River systems are marked, again accurately; county boundaries are drawn in, using dotted lines, and the counties named as 'Outer Wessex', 'South Wessex' and so on.[33] Apart from these, the 1895–6 map includes nothing else except the names of the places referred to in the novels and short stories, plus a few other real place-names: 'BRISTOL', 'BATH', 'NEW FOREST' and others. Capitals indicate real names in 1895–6, lower-case lettering being used for fictitious ones. The primary effect achieved is of separate, seemingly quite isolated places dotted around an empty, featureless expanse. Using this map to guide you through the topography of a particular novel involves finding its different locations and then imagining relations and journeys between them. Rivers suggest routes and connections but they are not followed on a journey from, say, Weatherbury to Melchester, Flintcomb Ash to Emminster or Weydon Priors to Casterbridge.

One consequence of this is an effect similar to the opening chapters of *The Return of the Native*. A blank, extensive environment is given, then 'humanity appears', on a road and moving between points on the ground. There is an elemental, unmarked quality to the land which draws attention to the human movements which cross it, marking on its surface roads, paths and railway lines. This activity is emphasized by the novels and continued by the reader when consulting the map. Readers create imaginatively the routes taken by characters, scoring them on the plain image provided by the map. Secondly, the map is comparatively empty because it includes nothing which does not feature in the novels: the real places mentioned are restricted to those which figure in Hardy's work. Of course, the map is consequently uncluttered and places referred to in the narratives are easier for the reader to locate. It also means, however, that 'The Wessex of the Novels' dominates the region covered by the map. By excluding all the other towns and cities in the area, Hardy's map stresses its limitations and subjectivity. The region itself, with all its other components and settlements, is invoked by the outline of the actual coast and the lines of the river systems. They are recalled, yet Hardy's Wessex remains parallel to them – neither a separate world (like Tolkien's, for instance) nor a world vaguely located somewhere within the real one (as is the case with Trollope and Oliphant). Outline and place-names in Hardy's map juxtapose the claim to universal validity which is inherent in modern cartography with the personal geography of a particular individual. By placing the imaginary worlds of his novels on an ordinary map of England, Hardy does not so much imply an acceptance of and conformity to the geographical and cultural status quo; instead, he suggests the equal validity of his own point of view to that of everyone else, the necessary subjectivity of all perspectives applying also to the one that is validated and enforced by the centre.

Two further related points emerge from Hardy's mapping of Wessex: firstly, in the same way that as a whole the map represents a single person's vision, within it each place is linked to a particular novel. Hardy's novels were by and large written in different places until he moved to Max Gate and each novel tends to be set in a different place. The map, while seeming to unify the body of work, also reveals its bittiness and dispersal. Few places come up in more than one narrative. Mellstock, Casterbridge, Budmouth, Melchester, Egdon Heath and the Hintocks are all exceptions to this, but none of them lies at the centre of more than one narrative, apart from Mellstock, which appears under various different names. Moreover, in collecting his work into volumes, Hardy tended where necessary to move stories to new locations so that they no longer overlapped with others: 'Benighted Travellers', first published in 1881, became 'The Honourable Laura' in *A Group of Noble Dames* and was moved from 'Portpool' (probably identified with Bridport) to the 'Prospect Hotel' on the 'Lower Wessex' (North Devon) coast; 'The Romantic Adventures of a Milkmaid', written in 1882–3 and set around the Froom valley and Casterbridge, was relocated further west into the valley of the Exe. This prevents its occupying the same district as the Talbothays of *Tess*, in the same way that moving 'The Honourable Laura' separates it from 'Fellow-Townsmen', the short story in *Wessex Tales* set in Port Bredy. Neither of these stories is entirely characteristic of Hardy's output, as it is usually portrayed: one is sensational, the other supernatural. Taking them away from the centre of Wessex to its outer reaches helps homogenize and make easily recognizable the centre of his œuvre, as Hardy was constructing it. The same might be said of Hardy's relocation of *A Laodicean* to Dunster Castle on the Outer Wessex (Somerset) coast. Its satirical and sensational elements might appear out of place at the heart of Wessex. Here too, however, Hardy is also avoiding overlap with another novel, in this case *The Hand of Ethelberta*, which features Corfe Castle – one original for Stancy Castle.

With exceptions, then, the places marked on the map are connected with principally one novel or story. This is more obvious in the case of *Jude the Obscure*, for example, than of *Tess* because the main locations of *Jude* lie in the top right-hand corner of the map in a cluster on their own. The same could be said of other outlying places on the map: 'Deansleigh' in Upper Wessex features in 'Lady Mottisfont', the fourth story in *A Group of Noble Dames*; 'Falls Park' in Outer Wessex belongs to the first story in the same collection. More notable places such as Sherton Abbas (Sherborne) and Stourcastle (Sturminster Newton) come up in only one story: *The Woodlanders* in the former case, *Tess* in the latter. In fact, each of the principal locations of *Tess* – Marlott, Trantridge, Talbothays, Wellbridge, Flintcomb Ash, Kingsbere, Sandbourne – relates almost exclusively to that novel and each is carefully marked on the map.[34] Finding the novel's various locations on the map as you read takes you through 'Tess's country', a place separate from that of the other novels, though occupying the same space. One tracks the world of the novel through South Wessex, an area of the map crowded with other, competing worlds.[35]

This means that the map suits each novel and story but does comparatively little to connect the various narratives to one another. They coexist without significantly interlinking or forming a single world. In this respect, the map reflects the self-containedness of the novels. Though a 'series of novels', they do not resemble *A la recherche du temps perdu* or *A Dance to the Music of Time*, or even the more loosely assembled 'Barchester Chronicles'. Boldwood, it is true, appears briefly in *The Mayor of Casterbridge*, but this is the exception, not the rule. Most of the stories do not share characters with other stories; nor, more surprisingly, do they occupy the same places. Hardy seems, indeed, to have taken steps to minimize any repetition of locations. As a result, the map does the opposite of what you might expect: diversity emerges the more strongly because it is seen to persist within and despite a normalizing cartography.

The second point about Hardy's mapping arises from the changes he made over time. The map for the 1895–6 edition is remarkably unadorned; for later editions, Hardy not only updated it (changing, for example, 'Portland' to 'The Isle of Slingers' after *The Well-Beloved* was published) and added further detail – *Jude the Obscure*'s 'Cresscombe' and 'The Brown House' are added near to Marygreen. He also emphasized typographically the difference between real and fictitious names, using italics for the latter and 'Upright old text' for the former. On his own drawing, 'Southampton', 'Bristol' and such like appear in an antique-looking Gothic script; in the 1912–13 edition, this is replaced by what looks like an eighteenth-century font. First series Ordnance Survey maps make use of something similar: natural features are named using lower case italics, towns in italic capitals, while villages appear in an 'upright old text'; only in later series did antiquities begin to be named in an antique script.

Hardy's choice of typography arises principally from his concern to make fiction and reality stand more clearly apart – the earlier version of the map had used capitals for real places, lower case for fictitious ones but the distinction breaks down.[36] The altered typography is in line with Hardy's insistence that his Wessex scenes were never direct or plain representations of places in Dorset.[37] It has the additional consequence of unsettling the usual hierarchy of real and fictional. The map overlays one on the other but neither is obviously prior. Flamboyant italics are juxtaposed with either Gothic script or 'upright old text'; in terms of type, neither seems closer than the other to contemporary normality. The fictional names look exaggeratedly fictional, the real ones antiquated.

In the same vein, Hardy marks places in 1912 by using miniature houses or churches, imitating the conventions of sixteenth- and seventeenth-century county maps.[38] Both these features apparently support the idea of Hardy's accepting and encouraging a nostalgic view of Wessex by making his maps of it visibly old-fashioned. The lettering contributes to this, evoking the conventions of the first series of Ordnance Survey maps which were being replaced from the 1890s onwards.[39] Simultaneously, though, his letterings clash with one another, as much jumbling up the past as helping to fix Wessex in it. Evidently eclectic, Hardy's typography suggests both that the real has no natural authority over the fictitious and that the present cannot position the past. Different periods lie on top of one another in the same area but, as in *The Return of the Native*, they do not come to the surface in reverse chronological order as one might expect. Within its conformity to nostalgic taste, the map hints at Hardy's experience of the Dorset landscape as somewhere containing the traces of many different historical periods – ancient tribes as near and visible as the recently dead.[40]

Similar purposes also underlie how Hardy chooses to represent dialectal forms in the novels. When, for example, *The Return of the Native* was published in November 1878, the unusual sophistication of Hardy's rustic speech was criticized as inconsistent with the book's remote setting: 'the talk seems pitched throughout in too high a key to suit the talkers'; 'We almost always find ideas and words more or less belonging to the stratum of comparative culture, blending with the ideas and words of rough and superstitious ignorance.'[41] Similar objections had been voiced to Hardy's presentation of dialect in *Far from the Madding Crowd*. Answering them, Hardy declared that his policy when representing dialect was to preserve 'the local idiom, together with the words which have no synonym among those in general use, while printing in the ordinary way most of those local expressions which are but a modified articulation of words in use elsewhere'. To transcribe rustic pronunication would be, in his opinion, to 'disturb the balance of a true representation by unduly insisting upon the grotesque element'; after all, 'In the printing of standard speech hardly any phonetic principle at all is observed.'

Phonetic accuracy produces quaintness, an insistence upon the grotesque, but the alternative is equally problematic: presenting rustic accents in standard spellings has the disadvantage of normalizing a distinct dialect which is 'intrinsically as genuine, grammatical, and worthy of the royal title as is the all-prevailing competitor which bears it'.[42] To reproduce this dialect would not do it justice and, at the same time, not reproducing it seems to concede its status as a corruption of the standard. Hardy himself saw Dorset speech as quite otherwise – as a language of its own at least among its older speakers. It is dying out because children educated in national schools have begun to speak a mixture of standard English and Dorset dialect – what Hardy calls, 'a composite language without rule or harmony'. Tess alternates between the two, speaking dialect at home, standard speech in public and to her social superiors.[43]

Evidently designed to prevent his readers from patronizing his rustics as grotesque, Hardy's dialect is both easily intelligible and mixed. '[C]omparative culture' is, as the critics observed, blended with local forms ('words of rough and superstitious ignorance'). In this respect, the dialect is presented in rather the same way as Wessex is mapped – something distinctive stands amidst the received and standard. Ironically, the blending of standard and dialectal presents Wessex speech as the 'composite language' of the younger, nationally educated generation. The penalty for not presenting his rustic characters as 'rustic' and quaint is that Hardy's novels are bound to modernize them. Their standardized language compels this; meanwhile, for Hardy, any attempt to transcribe dialect accurately is inevitably framed by standard English. Accurately presented dialect immediately becomes a variant on the standard form instead of a language in its own right.

The blending which early reviewers complained about has, therefore, a polemical edge to it. It addresses the contradictions present in regional/ provincial fiction from the Romantic period onward – writing, that is, which sought quasi-scientific accuracy in its depiction of rustic life. Comparable to Emily Brontë's aggressively unintelligible dialect, Hardy's way of representing the speech of his rural characters seeks to do justice to them while seeing that justice will be done by an outsider, that vindication involves assimilation. Assimilation, however, also produces a small invasion: the reviewers are offended by the entry of rough words into cultivated language and would prefer to keep them at a distance through thorough-going dialectal transcription. By including them, Hardy is representing as best he may the distinctive form of English spoken by people in Dorset; loyalty to its actual sound is sacrificed for loyalty to its equal worth – its status as a kind of English rather than a dialect of English. The strategy is comparable to that of some contemporary, post-colonial writers whose adoption of standard English infiltrates that language while also appearing to accept its authority.

Moreover, and again like the confusion of period in his map's lettering, Hardy's presentation of dialect in *The Return of the Native* disrupts progress: the *Athenaeum* reviewer claimed that 'The language of [Hardy's] peasants may be Elizabethan, but it can hardly be Victorian'; they talk 'as no people ever talk now'.[44] Part of the accusation here is that Hardy is being over-literary, making his characters speak a kind of cod-Shakespeare (along the lines of a Peter Ackroyd pastiche). Coupled with this is a claim by the reviewer to know exactly how people 'talk now' and an assumption that their language reflects their period. To be real, you have to speak the standard, modern way. This encourages the repression of variant forms; it also employs the idea that you are either in the present or you are nowhere. Hardy challenges this by writing a dialect which is largely intelligible although non-standard; it may not be 'Victorian' English but much of it looks exactly the same. The characters using this language are evidently not modern yet they cannot be secured in a remote past or a yokel backwater; their words suggest that many different present moments coexist at the same time.

The polemical quality of Hardy's dialect in the novels does not diminish as he revises the novels for later editions, even though some of the revisions involve dialect. *The Return of the Native* is little changed in this regard, though it is importantly revised in other ways. In other novels, dialectal forms are subtly and complicatedly altered, more complicatedly than there is room to discuss fully here. These changes tend to allow more phonetic transcription of dialect forms. In the same way that Hardy's 1912 map seems more antiquated than the 1895–6 version, later editions of the novels introduce a greater degree of what could become or could produce quaintness. Phonetic transcription is used, however, of particular characters and for particular reasons: the Penguin editor says of Henchard, for instance, that 'From [the 1895–6 edition] on his "of" is often contracted to "o" and his "ye" more consistently become "ee".' His language becomes more visibly a dialect even as he complains of Elizabeth-Jane lapsing into dialectal forms. In *Tess*, successive revisions increase the number of dialectal forms used by Tess's parents and diminish the number in the speech of Tess herself.[45] Quaintness seems to be acknowledged by these changes, not embraced. Hardy makes use of phonetic transcription to increase the sense of the distance back to the likes of Henchard and Tess's parents, on each occasion juxtaposing their old ways with someone younger who speaks a different language, though not the standard English of the supposed readership.

The reader encounters, therefore, different, jarring worlds of dialect and the effect produced is similar to that of reading Hardy's map and seeing several, discordant geographies occupying the same territory. In neither case is it easy to situate Wessex in the past and the reader in the present or to see its remoteness as peripheral while the reader occupies the centre. Such ruralist assumptions and their successors in 'Englishness' are countenanced but opposed; their nostalgia and nationalism are both questioned. Instead, Hardy's maps and his way of presenting dialect, like his geography, present Wessex as a world of its own amidst the real one; somewhere it is not possible to isolate or absorb, invade or abandon; somewhere separate, equal and coexistent.

7
Wessex and Elsewhere

Mobility and attachment in *Jude the Obscure*

Hardy's last novel is often spoken of as leaving Wessex behind because the Dorset settings which dominate his other novels barely figure. Instead, the action largely takes place in Berkshire and Oxfordshire, on the outer fringes of the region presented on Hardy's map. In the text, nonetheless, Wessex is referred to frequently. Christminster, for instance, is situated 'within hail of the Wessex border': 'and almost with the tip of one small toe within it, at the northernmost point of the crinkled line along which the leisurely Thames strokes the fields of that ancient kingdom'.

Similarly, from Shaston (Shaftesbury), there is a fine view into 'three counties of verdant pasture – South, Mid and Nether Wessex' and the novel's many references to the English counties all conform to Wessex conventions.[1] Evidently, placing Christminster just outside Wessex sets in motion a geographical contrast between the world where Jude grew up and the one he enters; the reader is alerted to the ominous consequences of crossing the border into the outside world. Yet Hardy's conscious overwriting here brings into that contrast a sense of artificiality. The elaborateness has an arch quality as if Wessex were a solemn game in which, almost fussily, well-known places are given false names. The convention makes distinctions between different areas of the country but they seem suspect. The whole idea of Wessex is made grander and faintly ludicrous at the same time; it turns into a convention liable to parody.

Consequently, references to Wessex offer a reminder through the novel of the rural world which it no longer deals in, contributing to its elegaic aspect. At the same time the novel includes within its Wessex world many features absent from earlier Wessex novels. The region is drawn away from its rural associations so that the novel may begin to challenge the readership's assumptions about what Wessex means. This ties in with its publication history: it was serialized in 1894–5; it first appeared in book form as the eighth volume of Hardy's collected edition of 1895–6 and not separately, as had been the case with his previous novels. The last of the 'Novels of Character and Environment', *Jude* appears both to complete Wessex and comment on it, extending and radically questioning the geography it follows so carefully.

A similar effect is created by the titles Hardy gives to the several parts of the book: 'At Marygreen', 'At Christminster', 'At Melchester', 'At Shaston', 'At Aldbrickham and Elsewhere' and 'At Christminster Again'. Charles Lock connects the repeated use of 'At' with the novels emphasis on railway travel which creates 'the distinctively modern paradox of dynamism and passivity'. In *Jude*, people are 'at' places, accidentally and momentarily; they are never 'in' them.[2] John Goode, in his powerful reading of the novel, makes the similar point that

> 'At', the word which links the title of each part, implies a double negation of the subject since although it defines a location it does not suggest, in fact in most cases positively denies accommodation – thus at various stages the characters are placed but have no place.

Appropriately, it becomes a novel 'literally about finding a lodging'.[3] Displacement produces an itinerant way of life in which clearly named locations gradually become little more than names; near the end, they seem synonymous with 'Elsewhere'. Goode suggests that this increasing indifference to the named place can be explained using the sequence of titles. Jude, and later Jude and Sue together, travel:

> from the purely given (Marygreen) to the chosen by gesture (Christminster), the chosen by compromise, blocked gesture (Melchester and even more Shaston), the determined solely by economic necessity (Aldbrickham and elsewhere). The arbitrariness is vital: they both have to go to these places and these places have no meaning for them.[4]

Hardy's place-names show, then, economic necessity gradually conquering: a given place is exchanged first for one Jude chooses freely and then for ones chosen for him more and more imperiously by external forces. The final part of the novel, 'At Christminster

Again', is seen by Goode as a protest against this process of alienated enslavement.

The novel's geography modifies Goode's account rather than over-turning it. The names used in the titles do acquire a weightless speci-ficity as Jude and Sue move from place to place so frequently and so fast. 'At' becomes the indicator of displacement which Lock and Goode both describe while Melchester, Aldbrickham and the other placenames overparticularize, signalling the wish for topographical exactness which the collected edition responds to generally but also implying its super-ficiality. Moreover, there is a movement from 'Marygreen' to 'Elsewhere' and then to 'Christminster Again' which corresponds to the story's depiction of gradual deracination and the 'moves' people make in an effort to resist it. Goode goes wrong, though, in his inclusion of Melchester and Shaston as nothing other than places on the way to Aldbrickham because, although in part they are like that, they also fit into a geographical structure which tells a slightly different story.

Joe Fisher essentially follows Goode in his thinking about *Jude*'s 'topo-graphical structure'. It is, he says, 'very much an imperial model' with Christminster:

> obviously the centre of the empire. Marygreen is the furthest outpost we see, like Hintock an intaking from the wilderness. [. . .] Shaston, Aldbrickham and Alfredston are ranged between. Melchester is the main distributive centre, the place where missionaries and imperial civil servants get their training.
>
> (Fisher, *Hidden Hardy*, p.190)

This is characteristically punchy and invigorating, though Marygreen strikes me as very unlike the Hintocks. Also, like Goode, Fisher is less convincing about the places in between than about the opposition between Marygreen and Christminster.

There are several elements to the geography of the novel which con-tribute simultaneously to the story it has to tell. Marygreen and the fields nearby are not given a very clear or specific location until chapter 3, when Jude walks up the 'long and tedious ascent' to the ridge. Before reaching this point in the narrative, the reader could have found Mary-green on Hardy's map but not until this stage has Hardy drawn atten-tion to the possible significance of Marygreen's position in relation to other places. From the vantage-point Jude gains at the top of the slope, 'The whole northern semicircle between east and west, to a distance of forty or fifty miles, spread itself before him' and, in a sequence of events that Hardy narrates carefully, Jude sees from here, or thinks he sees, the roofs of Christminster lit up by the setting sun:

> about a quarter of an hour before the time of sunset, the westward clouds parted, the sun's position being partially uncovered, and the beams streaming out in visible lines between two bars of slaty cloud. [. . .]
>   Some way within the limits of the stretch of landscape, points of light like the topaz gleamed [. . .] showed themselves to be the vanes, windows, wet roof slates, and other shining spots upon the spires, domes, freestone-work, and varied outlines that were faintly revealed. It was Christminster, unquestionably.
>
> (Hardy, *Jude*, Part 1, ch.3, p.19, 21)

Noticing that this resembles the Bible's heavenly Jerusalem, or the heavenly City uncertainly glimpsed by Bunyan's Christian, or the Promised Land seen by Moses from Pisgah, it is easy to miss its likeness to a scene later in the novel when Sue visits Phillotson in Shaston. He is lying in bed recovering from an illness, partly brought on by Sue's leaving him for Jude. As they talk to one another, Hardy mentions that 'the sun was going down in splendour over the lowlands of Blackmoor, and making the Shaston windows like tongues of fire to the eyes of the rustics in that Vale'.[5] Phillotson cannot see the sunset from where he is lying. Sue, who tells him it is 'like heaven opened', holds a 'swing-glass [. . .] by the window where it could catch the sunshine, moving the glass till the beams were reflected into Phillotson's face'.

The incident links Phillotson to Jude; both are drawn towards unrealizable aspirations and both are in love with Sue; both are also rustics originally and in these scenes they are shown reflections of the westerly sun. The similarities between the two men grow more marked as the novel continues and they attract sympathy for Phillotson at several points; here the pathos of his vulnerability becomes more touching because his experience of Sue resembles that of Jude as a boy, compelled by his vision of the distant city. Marjorie Garson remarks that Jude's 'desire for Christminster is a desire for a transfigured state of being'. Sunset, especially given its associations in Victorian culture, lends it those qualities; an earlier version of the reflection Phillotson sees in the mirror, Christminster also is 'like heaven opened'.[6] Hardy stresses, however, the reflected nature of Christminster's charms, its robes borrowed from the sun, and sets up a contrast between it and the 'ridgeway' that Jude is standing beside: 'This ancient track ran east and west for many miles, and down almost to within living memory had been used for driving flocks and herds to fairs and markets. But it was now neglected and overgrown.' John Goode points out that Jude's first vision of Christminster occurs at a crossroads (where the highway is 'crossed at right angles by a green "ridgeway"') and sees in this a foreshadowing of Jude's Christ-like role. This may be so but Hardy is also opposing the disused route into the west with a city that is lit from the west and mimicking its glories.[7]

Jude stands, in other words, at a point where two versions of the west cross one another and seems condemned to opt for the substitute, reflected version, like Phillotson later, powerless on his sickbed. In the second scene, Sue comforts and tortures him because the heavenly vision she helps him see is offered as an alternative to her presence as his wife. Her action also epitomizes the self-protectiveness which has characterized her relations with him throughout. She retreats behind the glory she shows him. In this respect, Christminster, Shaston and Sue are all the same: they dazzle and lure towards them rustics, including Phillotson and Jude, by seeming to be heavenly, transcendent and westerly and, in each case, they prove not to be so, but only a reflection of those things. The passage where Sue buys statues of Venus and Apollo returns to the idea that sunlight from the west, in this case the southwest, lends objects special attractiveness. As is clear from *A Pair of Blue Eyes* and *The Return of the Native*, Hardy's other novels endow westerly places and light from the west with romance. Particularly in *The Pursuit of the Well-Beloved* (1892), the western is yearned for as an ideal, lost home. *Jude* is distinctive, however, in using reflections to suggest that the western has been taken up and taken over by places at the centre.[8]

It is surprising to bracket Shaston with Christminster because in other respects they seem placed at opposite extremes by the novel. Phillotson is a native of Shaston so that his time there is the only occasion in the book when a character lives 'at home' (until, that is, the very end when Sue returns to her birthplace, Marygreen, to live with him). Phillotson's defiance of convention in freely releasing Sue from their marriage takes place at Shaston as well and, although it does produce a backlash from the town's upholders of respectability, the gipsies who also live there protest against it and offer Phillotson his only support. Shaston is, lastly, the most westerly of the book's locations, the most remote and unvisited and the only one within the boundaries of South Wessex (Dorset), the county where Jude was born and the principal setting for the other Wessex novels. All this suggests that the westerly trajectory of the middle third of the book – from Christminster to Melchester and then on to Shaston – follows a route away from Christminster and back towards some kind of rootedness. It is a journey, therefore, which may lead to some possible alternative to modernity.

For Jude, Sue and more ambiguously for Phillotson as well, this possibility remains out of reach even while they go along the route towards it. Sue, in some ways, brings Christminster into Shaston and precipitates from its amiable stability Phillotson's revolutionary behaviour and the hostile reaction it provokes. If this is the conclusion – that the protagonists cannot go back into a rooted past – then it is foreshadowed as soon as Sue and Jude make the first move on the journey. They settle in Melchester and, on their first day out together, go to visit Wardour Castle nearby. On the way, they hit upon 'the old road from London to Land's End'. They are walking north, from one railway line to another, and the road runs 'due east and west' so that, as in Jude's walk near Marygreen, the road is 'crossed'; it too is disused: 'They paused, and looked up and down it for a moment, and remarked upon the desolation which had come over this once lively thoroughfare, while the wind dipped to earth and scooped straws and hay-stems from the ground.' (Hardy, *Jude*, Part 3, ch.2, pp.137–8).

There is a slightly heartless, cheery intellectualism about their remarking 'upon the desolation which had come over this once lively thoroughfare', brought out by Hardy's parodic diction and by the sense that 'while' they converse they are oblivious to the immediate, desolate surroundings – the straws and hay-stems being blown around in the wind. The repetition of this geographical arrangement (in which the old road is crossed by a modern traveller, east/west by north/south) suggests a link with Christminster, as if not only have its values now been internalized by Jude and Sue – as their remarking upon the desolation implies – but they carry its world and its geography into the recesses of South Wessex and 'unvisited' Shaston.

Looking north from Marygreen towards Christminster, then, means looking towards a substitute heaven. It also reveals a new version of the past, a place whose medievalism invades remoteness. As is clear from Trollope's *Barchester Towers*, Oxford epitomized the belief that old virtues, networks and social structures could act effectually to temper the excesses of the new-fangled. Gothic Revival architecture and Tractarian religion both take up the past, declare they possess its essence and see it as the means of bringing harmony to a troubled present. The modern refines the medieval and the medieval restores the modern to an ordered life. Oxford is connected to these aspirations and its geography suggests that they can have national impact, rather than being confined to what lingers on in secluded Barchester. Ruralism's suburban ideal in which modernity is married to old, renewed sources of stability, particularly focussed on the Home Counties to the west of London and the upper reaches of the Thames. From the escarpment north of Marygreen, Jude sees this landscape spreading around him, right and left, with Christminster/Oxford lying at its heart, the metropolis of the Thames Valley. From this viewpoint, Jude confronts what was perceived as the heart of England, by whose qualities social harmony could best be sustained. It is home to the pastoral nationalism of ruralism and 'Englishness' and is at once idyllic, a powerful enchantment and self-confidently expansionist.

These associations for Oxford and the Thames valley are very strong in the period and Hardy can rely on them quite confidently. Choosing Cumnor, near Oxford, for the place where Phillotson keeps a school exemplifies this process. Hardy gives it the gloomier but still recognizable name of Lumsdon and by this choice of location invokes Matthew Arnold, especially his poems 'The Scholar-Gipsy' and 'Thyrsis', his elegy for Arthur Hugh Clough. Both poems are set in the countryside near to Cumnor. In the novel, Jude and Phillotson both become scholar-gipsies of a kind, though far less blithe and free than Arnold's. Through this allusion to Arnoldian haunts, Hardy can make the novel suggest an attack on Arnold's complacency about people who are excluded from seats of learning.

At the same time, Oxford's ruralist agenda is seen by the novel as already old-fashioned and in decline. Likewise, Jude and Sue, discussing the overgrown road, sound quaint in their earnestness, naïve by comparison with their later selves, even though one of the most poignant aspects of the book is the unchanging sincerity both of them possess. Partly presented as simply a result of their temperaments, this obstinate idealism is also seen as arising out of their involvement with Christminster. Its medieval forms and its medievalist pretensions are both outdated, being swept away by a mobile, acquisitive society, expanding from 'the depths of London' and governed by market forces, not principle. Christminster's increasing irrelevance to the nation emerges in the book as it focusses in Part 5 on Reading, Basingstoke and Newbury (Aldbrickham, Stoke-Barehills and Kennetbridge). Trips to and from London, routes in and out of London, the pressure to conform exerted by one's customers, the need to be married for form's sake if nothing else – all these take precedence over Christminster, home of lost causes, and particularly oppress those like Jude for whom Christminster has become 'a sort of fixed vision'.[9]

A professional and ecclesiastical geography, centred on Christminster and Sue, is replaced with increasing force by a commercial geography centred on Arabella and London. That change is seen as a historical development which leaves Jude stranded in the past despite his conduct making him appear ahead of his time. His work as a stonemason means that he shores up the walls which exclude him and that irony expresses a truth about his submission to Christminster – an outcast, he idealizes what has rejected him. Being a stonemason also resonates with Ruskin's praise, in 'The Nature of Gothic'(published 1853 in *The Stones of Venice*) for the obscure builders of Gothic cathedrals and, consequently, with the Gothic Revival's attempt to recreate organic communities in modern England.

Read in the context of Hardy's personal world, Jude's profession also has the effect of throwing him back a generation: Hardy's father was a stonemason, whereas Hardy himself had risen from there into the profession of architecture. It is well-known that Marygreen, based on the village of Fawley, also has personal resonance for Hardy: his father's mother, Mary, had lived there as an orphaned child. Notably too, Hardy's sister, also called Mary, took a post as schoolmistress in Denchworth, a village just north of Wantage (Alfredston). She had trained in Salisbury at the college which provided the model for Sue's in Melchester. Hardy stayed with his sister at Denchworth in 1863 and 1864, travelling up from London where he was living at the time, and visited Fawley in search of relatives. Strangely too, their younger sister Kate came, aged six, from the family home in Bockhampton to live with her sister in Denchworth (Hardy and Mary were both in their early twenties). Millgate comments about the incident: '[Hardy's mother's] willingness to part with her youngest child at such a tender age suggests (not for the first time) a certain lack of maternal warmth' (*Hardy: A Biography*, p.83). Kate's journey might be seen, therefore, as underlying both Jude's move from South Wessex to Marygreen, where he lodges with his great-aunt, and, more strangely perhaps, Father Time's arrival on Jude and Sue's doorstep, disposed of as an inconvenience by his natural mother, Arabella.

These encoded personal memories are joined in the novel by feelings about Hardy's father, who died in 1892. The novel was written in 1893–4. Millgate reads Jude as modelled to some extent on Horace Moule and Hardy's uncle by marriage, John Antell. The personal associations of the novel's chosen geography also evoke Hardy's father, named Thomas as well, whose mother was Mary Head rather than Jemima Hand. It evokes, in other words, a person similar in some ways to Hardy himself but lacking any connection until his marriage with the sources of independence Hardy found in the parts of Wessex linked to his mother's family: Norcombe Hill and the Hintocks. Rather than an imaginary self-portrait, therefore, Jude can be thought of as a portrayal of what Hardy would have been had his mother been less ambitious for him and less driving, had his mother not taught him early on the need for self-assertion and the merits of cunning. Arabella, likewise, although she cannot be read as a portrait of Hardy's mother, does embody qualities which in some ways he is glad (or relieved) to possess himself, thanks to his mother's influence.

Marygreen's geography works, then, to suggest Jude's susceptibility to a Gothic revival dream of national order, centred on Oxford and the Thames Valley and spreading out westwards, through a 'churchy', Trollopian network, via Melchester to Shaston. Marygreen's position within quite easy reach of the London trains (which stop at Kennetbridge) later shows Jude's exposure to a modern, structureless society in which Christminster has become a lost cause. His arduous walks along the road from Christminster to Marygreen contrast with his ease of movement, using the railways, elsewhere and the similar, fatal ease with which Arabella appears in various parts of the country. Thirdly, Marygreen's location implies that Jude has been denied access to independence, that he is more of a rustic and a 'simpleton' than Hardy was himself, less modern and less worldly-wise.[10]

In these respects, the novel's geography helps to depict a particular cultural moment, in some ways distanced from Hardy's own, in some ways equivalent to his. Hardy describes his early life, working in Dorchester and living in Bockhampton, as allowing him to move from one world, one age to another and back again. Marygreen and Jude are also between worlds – at the edges of both Wessex and the Englishness of the Thames Valley. That betweenness creates paralysis, however, instead of eclectic mobility. In part, the rural world of South Wessex (which is referred to but scarcely entered during the novel) is offered as the lost counterweight to modern respectability and homogeneity: to both the imperial order of Christminster and the orderlessness of commercial London. On the other hand, coming from a rural place like Marygreen can make you, if ambitious, particularly naïve in the face of the demand for conformity. It seems a result of his background as well as his temperament and fate that Jude immolates himself before an illusory ideal. Arabella, who has lived in Aldbrickham before the novel begins, carries on her life more cynically, conforming and indifferent to conformity. In Jude, then, rurality is deracinated; he is caught between the exploitative idealization of the rural, presented by one version of the centre, Christminster, and a debased version of rural earthiness, represented by Arabella and the working class of Christminster and London. The latter is winning out and within it, perhaps surprisingly, a kind of independence survives.

Jude's distinctive position and plight is also brought out through the contrast with his mentor and surrogate father, Phillotson. The novel suggests that, while Christminster destroys Jude, his childlike and simple-minded adherence to an ideal of learning, represented for him by Christminster, nonetheless breathes genuine life into that ideal. Christminster at once symbolizes and extinguishes the belief that life can be lived according to an enlightened, unprejudiced moral code. Such a belief motivates Sue and via her Jude as well. Phillotson's generosity in releasing Sue from her marriage vows evidently arises from the same aspiration, Phillotson's own desire for a principled life. In equal measure, though, it is the result of his rurality.

Phillotson is the character in the novel most frequently linked to his rural roots: he knows his way at night 'without hesitation' around 'a district over which he has played as a boy' and, when chatting with his friend Gillingham, 'Though well-trained and even proficient masters, they occasionally used a dialect-word of their boyhood to each other in private' (Hardy, *Jude*, Part 4, ch.4, pp.228–9). Phillotson's giving-up of Sue may ruin him professionally and later on worsen Sue's feelings of guilt; it may also be an idealistic course which he later regrets. He may even become crueller in going back on his kindness than he would have been had he earlier restrained her from leaving 'with a wise and strong hand', as the vicar of Shaston puts it to him.[11] Even so, the bravery, magnanimity and eccentricity of his action are all respected by the novel. Phillotson achieves, for a while, a form of independent, forward-thinking behaviour which is ideally kind even if proves to be self-destructive.

Hardy points out in the incident that Phillotson's enlightened ideals lead to the same generous action as the disreputable laxity of Shaston's itinerant workers would have done. This is something the reader may recall when Mrs Edlin protests about Phillotson's remarriage to Sue. 'She's [Jude's] wife if anybody's,' Mrs Edlin declares. 'I don't know what the times be coming to. Matrimony have growed to be that serious in these days that one really do feel afeard to move in it at all. In my time we took it more careless' (Hardy, *Jude*, Part 6, ch.5, p.367). Phillotson's age and his surviving connections to his native town place him in an earlier generation from Sue and Jude, in a period when, it appears, you could be quietly revolutionary via your rural independence. He is gradually crushed by the book; Jude and Sue, who are more volatile and more vulnerable, are also destroyed. Although Phillotson's narrative echoes and repeats the extinction of idealism which they suffer, it also achieves temporary success. He gives Jude and Sue their best chance of happiness. Simultaneously, his age places them in historical context, setting in the past the ideal position of 'eclectic independence' suggested by *A Laodicean* and almost achieved again in what Phillotson does – almost but not quite, because Shaston is now a respectable place as well as meeting-place for gipsies. Their and Mrs Edlin's broadminded tolerance recedes further into the past behind him.[12]

Its nearest equivalent in the novel is found in Arabella and the working class of Christminster. Among them Jude finds 'a book of humanity infinitely more palpitating, varied and compendious than the gown life'; the latter being made up of 'a floating population of students and teachers' that is 'not Christminster in a local sense at all' (Hardy, *Jude*, Part 2, ch.6, p.118). Faced by the bleak horror of the book, it is tempting to sentimentalize this praise of ordinary people; Hardy's adjectives – 'palpitating, varied and compendious' – are carefully euphemistic, however, and the characters Jude meets live up to no cosy account of ordinary people. '[S]truggling men and women', they are heavy drinkers and sexually promiscuous. They might also appear another of the book's many contrasts and seem to confirm that in Jude's world there is only unreal purity or squalid debauchery, nothing in between.

Arabella, though, is more complex than this.[13] When as a widow she first meets Jude again, she immediately declares that she must have him back: she throws away the religious tracts which have consoled her. 'Feelings are feelings!' she says. 'I must be as I was born!' Similarly, the power of her last words about Sue ('She's never found peace since she left [Jude's] arms, and never will again till she's as he is now!') arises in part from her having acted on the perception that the same is true of herself.[14] Arabella knows that she needs Jude as a sexual partner and companion and that she too will never be at peace without him. When he has gone, she will of course need and find another, just as she turned back to him only when Mr Cartlett, her second husband, died. Mobility, though, does not rule out loyalty.

Arabella talks as if she remarries Jude only for the advantages it will bring her and she is unambiguously aggrieved when he proves too ill to support her. Likewise the plot structure draws attention away from her motives towards the ironies and pain created by the spectacle of Jude reunited with Arabella when Sue is reunited with Phillotson and giving herself to him sexually. Nonetheless, Hardy suggests as well that Arabella is drawn towards Jude instinctively. Jude's last actions seem governed by his unstinting devotion to Sue – a love which rejects Arabella again in the final chapters. The oddness is that Arabella seems to be motivated by a comparable, lasting desire for Jude.

It is not an equivalent devotion but her recapture of Jude arises from a similar need. In part, that need is evidently a physical one. Consequently, the plain eloquence and the authoritative, final position of her judgement on Sue confirm the impossibility, even the inhumanity of Sue's ideal of passionate friendship between the sexes – of love without possession. Just before remarrying Sue, Phillotson recalls the vicar of Shaston's belief that Sue would have obeyed a 'wise and strong hand'. These words seem to endorse cruelty, naming it 'firmness', and sound like another satire by Hardy on the Church's failure to be Christian. Yet the novel also suggests that Sue does require a structure and will find one where she can, either from a loving husband or from a cruel one, or from a punitive religion. It is not therefore only irony which reverses Jude and Sue at the end, making him as free-thinking as she used to be, nor is Hardy making a simply essentialist, anti-feminist point. Instead, he contrasts Arabella's self-knowledge with Sue's self-ignorance about her physical attachment to Jude. Going back to Phillotson, to be governed and sexually possessed by him, is a form of her already existing commitment to Jude, but one perverted by denial.

As well as voicing Hardy's disagreement with Sue's idealism, Arabella also characterizes the future in the novel. Her physical mobility coincides with her sexual freedom and both accompany her self-aware understanding of sexual need and of the human need for other people, as sexual partners and mutual supports. Phillotson's independence is made possible by his inhabiting a native place. In the succeeding generation this possibility has disappeared because of the change to a more fluid, homogeneous society. Christminster, which seems to offer a stable, idealistic alternative to London and the shapelessness of its commercial life, is actually worse. Its conventionality is absolute and it makes obedience to convention into an absolute value. Like Wintonchester in the final chapter of *Tess*, Christminster's ruralist medievalism disguises a tyrannical, national power. In the final chapters of *Jude*, nonetheless, a form of independence can be seen reasserting itself.

Jude dies alone in a garret while the streets of Christminster are packed with people, celebrating the 'Remembrance games' – that is, Commemoration Day in June. Arabella joins the crowds, knowing that Jude has already died and telling no-one about it. It looks a heartless thing to do but Hardy combines it with hints of Arabella's continuing attachment to her husband. Amidst the fun and games by the river 'she would have laughed heartily' but does not because 'the imprint on her mind's eye' of Jude's dead face had 'sobered her a little'; Vilbert, the quack doctor pursuing her, crops up again but Arabella 'shan't talk of love today'. There are other examples in the passage, each of them suggesting that, rather than being indifferent, Arabella cannot afford to dwell on her sorrows. She has said as much at the end of the previous chapter and it seems habitual – a way of life and a means of survival. Jude dies thinking of Sue and still loving her. His continuing attachment is less surprising and more obvious than Arabella's. The deep fidelity of his romantic feeling seems contrasted with Arabella's unfeeling promiscuity and this is the reading of her which Sue has made. Hardy suggests a likeness within the difference: though Jude's may be the nobler feeling, Arabella's is genuine too. Both characters behave according to their 'character and environment', so that Arabella's way of loving accords with the urban society she inhabits. On her way back from the riverside, she is caught up in the crush: 'At the narrow gangway [. . .] the crowd was literally jammed into one hot mass – Arabella and Vilbert with the rest.' This is a different Christminster from the one Jude imagines from Marygreen and one that lies closer to the working-class people he later meets there, with their 'palpitating' life. It is Christminster 'in a local sense' insofar as the local survives in a world of rapid communications, itinerant labour and internal tourism: the Remembrance games are for town and gown, residents and visitors, working-class and upper-class. This crowded mixture is the modern world which Jude cannot come to terms with. Within it and content with it, Arabella shows that a 'local sense' continues – in her unillusioned but consistent desire to be with one other person, Jude.[15]

Conclusion: Hardy's regionalism

The importance of personal attachment to the novel is made all the more clear by the presence in it of Father Time, Arabella's child by Jude. He was born in Australia and left behind with his grandparents when Arabella returned to England; his grandparents send him back once Arabella is settled and can look after him. Arabella, though, asks Jude to take him instead and sends him on from London to Aldbrickham where Jude is living with Sue. From Aldbrickham station, Father Time walks to Jude's house on the outskirts:

> He followed his directions literally, without an inquiring gaze at anything. It could have been seen that the boy's ideas of life were different from those of the local boys. Children begin with detail, and learn up to the general; they begin with the contiguous, and gradually comprehend the universal. The boy seemed to have begun with the generals of life, and never to have concerned himself with the particulars. To him the houses, the willows, the obscure fields beyond, were apparently regarded not as brick residences, pollards, meadows; but as human dwellings in the abstract, vegetation, and the wide dark world.
>
> (Hardy, *Jude*, Part 5, ch.3, p.278)

Hardy seems in this haunting passage to be directly recalling the ideals for geography espoused by Geikie, Huxley and even Mackinder. He both endorses the view that the contiguous leads to an understanding of the universal, that the local is a point of access to 'obscure fields beyond', and at the same time states that for Father Time particulars cannot be found at all. Moved around so often and so far, he does not have access to detailed particulars of anything and, analogously, he finds it very difficult to want or be attached to any other person or even himself. Hardy seems both to be supporting the belief that attention to geographical particulars may be of importance to the development of a personality and to feel that 'particulars' may be emotional or personal even more than geographical, given a social structure which deracinates and mobilizes.

Jude is similarly homeless as a boy so that the son exhibits a worsening of the condition that afflicted the father. Father Time's walk through Aldbrickham echoes his father's experience of the 'obscure fields' at Marygreen, fog-bound and isolated, where he is set scaring birds. Father Time's emotional emptiness shows the psychological need which lies behind Jude's devotion to Christminster and even the support it lends him. That place is the particular from which he starts, albeit a dangerous and misleading one because not close enough to be 'contiguous' and fully inspected.

The lack which Christminster fills is suggested in the first chapter. Soon after Phillotson has driven away, Jude resumes his task of drawing water from the well:

> The boy returned to the draw-well at the edge of the greensward [. . . .] There was a quiver in his lip now, and after opening the well-cover to begin lowering the bucket, he paused and leant with his forehead and arms against the framework [. . . .] The well into which he was looking was as ancient as the village itself, and from his present position appeared as a long circular perspective ending in a shining disk of quivering water at a distance of a hundred feet. There was a lining of green moss near the top, and nearer still the hart's-tongue fern.
>
> (Hardy, *Jude*, Part 1, ch.1, p.11)

Jude stares down, recalling 'in the melodramatic tones of a whimsical boy', Phillotson's doing the same. 'A tear rolled from his eye into the depths of the well.' Hardy briefly observes, before beginning a new sentence on a different, rather banal topic: 'The morning was a little foggy' and adding a moment later 'His thoughts were interrupted by a sudden outcry' – that of his aunt urging him to get on with his work. Elsewhere, this opening chapter sardonically emphasizes how Marygreen has been modernized, the old church torn down and the graves in its churchyard 'obliterated',[16] and here Hardy wants to establish the indifference which the novel's world shows to personal feelings as much as to historical associations.

As much as comfort is denied and Jude's instinctive act of mourning is curtailed, the incident shows also his desire that places should have personal associations. He wants the place to recall the people who have left; the well's 'shining disk of quivering water' offers that hope for a moment. It feels like a glimpse of a better world in which a precarious sense of reciprocity can be found because the 'quivering' water echoes 'the quiver' on Jude's lip. The glimmer of light, seemingly at the end of a tunnel, has the same allure as Christminster will have when Jude sees it from the ridgeway a little later and, as is true of Christminster as well, the light is a reflection. Both suggest that Jude, a homeless person, is looking for a home – not only a place to go to but somewhere to start from. The absence of such a starting-point is brought out by the remoteness of the shining disk, set by Hardy with neutral clarity 'at a distance of a hundred feet'. Jude's eye and mind then draw back from the unattainable towards objects closer and closer to hand, the moss and 'nearer still' the fern. Looking beyond these, however, all that can be seen is the foggy morning and his own breath 'unfurling itself as a thicker fog upon the still and heavy air'.

Jude has complained that Marygreen is 'a small sleepy place' where someone as clever as Phillotson could not possibly stay. Its confinement and isolation, the impossibility of connecting it with a wider world and of moving mentally from the contiguous to the universal – all these are suggested by the moss, the fern and the fog all around.[17] The well conveys the difficulty for Jude of establishing his place in and relation to the world beyond – of making the move from local to general which would create a geography for him. One reason for this is that the village, though marginal, is not remote: the church has been rebuilt by someone down from London.

In Mary Russell Mitford's account of village life, ponds and pools depict in miniature the secludedness, the idyllic and pristine qualities of villages, showing them to be 'islets of wilderness amidst cultivation'. In Mary Elizabeth Braddon's sensation fiction, wells and pools are the focus for a world-forgetting reverie; they become emblems of the rural, aristocratic stillness which may choke or suppress selfhood, particularly that of women, but may also provide a refuge from the bustle of urban modernity and the wear on the self it produces.[18] Jude's well, like the village altogether, provides no such refuge; the surrounding distractions and the remoteness of its depths work against Jude's hopes, against those embodied by Mitford's ponds and against the more ambivalent feelings presented through Braddon's wells and pools. Through the scene at the well, it is clear that the ruralist view of how town and country should relate cannot apply to Marygreen and its England; similarly, whether seductive, oppressive or self-affirming, the reveries of sensation fiction, their moments of stillness and escape, are unavailable.[19]

Instead of these optimistic pictures, Hardy presents a character caught between miniature particulars and surrounding amorphousness, between localism and anomie. In Hardy's earlier novels, generally speaking, 'the eye of imagination' has belonged to visitors and strangers, who create idylls out of the rural world's ordinary, complex realities. In *Jude*, it is an uprooted rustic who confers the same, idyllic quality on a city, Christminster. Hardy, though, sees imagination as integral to perception – people confer qualities on things; even 'the small and ordinary ones among mankind', such as Fanny Robin or Jude, possess 'poetical power'.[20] Father Time appears not to do so and the result is a decline in his powers of simple recognition: houses become 'human dwellings in the abstract', willows are reduced to 'vegetation', not even to trees. He lives in an objectless world, full of categories lacking instances.

Jude has an object, Christminster, and it fills the gap between the local and the universal – fills it by obscuring it. That is to say, Christminster's cultural identity links it to 'Englishness', a nationalist perspective which expands into the rural by imitating it. It is also the centre of a regional geography, the Oxford school, which restricts regionality to secluded, antiquated, rural districts and, simultaneously, sees southern England as in many respects a single region. It thus excludes from its self-description the urban and rootless, like Arabella. It also robs remote districts of their connections with other places – their cosmopolitanism, one might say – as well as denying them their separate centres and distinctiveness. Marygreen's position makes it especially vulnerable to this homogenizing influence; it has no centre of its own or point of reference that distinguishes it from other villages in southern England. Jude, finding himself there and lacking a source of identity in a previous home, attaches himself to Christminster because there is nothing else. He cannot help it and his impulsive fixation with the place expresses the 'beginning with the contiguous' that Hardy sees as natural to children.

Christminster, however, declares itself to be both the contiguous and the universal; it occupies the middle ground in such a a way as to deny the presence of anything smaller or larger. It lies at the centre of a regional England which does not form part of any larger unit, being autonomous and self-contained; at the same time, everywhere within that England is identical, indistinguishably rural. Consequently, Christminster gives the 'inquiring gaze' nowhere further to go, so creating obsessiveness and frustration. These malign mental effects parallel its restriction of advancement and ambition: Jude cannot enter the university in the same way that he is denied the opportunity to 'gradually comprehend the universal' and leave Christminster behind.

Hardy's novel is mounting, therefore, a critique of Englishness and of the regional geography which is one of its manifestations. Father Time is a prophecy that, if the natural powers – imaginative, synthesizing and analytical – which Geikie's form of geography cultivates, are neglected, they will atrophy and perish, leaving damaged people behind. Arabella, with her self-centredness and determination, hints at a mode of resistance to the homogenizing ambitions of Christminster's Englishness. She sticks with the contiguous, whoever or whatever that might be at a given moment. By having so little interest in the larger significance of events, she reaches, on a few subjects, a sound comprehension of what is universally true – sounder than Sue's grasp of these things, perhaps better than Jude's as well. She is Hardy's regionalism surviving in unfavourable conditions.

Hardy's regionalism displays itself more happily in earlier novels: in Sally Hall's independence and *A Laodicean*'s eclecticism; in Henchard's distant circling of Casterbridge, as he yearns after Elizabeth-Jane; in *Far from the Madding Crowd*'s sense of social groups as constellations; and in a Wessex geography conceived throughout in opposition to ruralist assumptions. His use of dialect and his maps deny that Wessex lies either outside the world or within it. It cannot be homogenized or hived off, not least because these two actions are fundamentally the same: both allow the reader to impose his or her assumptions about such a place, making it either home or away. Wessex claims equality and independence instead. In the same way that the language of *The Return of the Native* shifts the reader 'unendingly between microscopic and telescopic', so Hardy's geography leads his reader from the contiguous to the universal and back again. It is determined to show how places are connected to other places and still particular unto themselves. It is concerned to engender an expansion of awareness beyond the parochial that also situates the parochial more clearly – an expansion Geikie and his fellow geographers sought to bring about through their teaching of geography and the sense of region that it created.

Notes

1   Introduction

1. Michael Irwin, *Reading Hardy's Landscapes* (Basingstoke and New York: Macmillan – now Palgrave/St Martin's, 2000), pp.4, 6, 14.
2. Simon Gatrell, 'Wessex', *The Cambridge Companion to Thomas Hardy*, edited Dale Kramer (Cambridge: Cambridge University Press, 1999), p.19.
3. Simon Gatrell, *Hardy the Creator: A Textual Biography* (Oxford: Clarendon Press, 1988), p.129.
4. K.D.M. Snell, *Annals of the Labouring Poor: Social Change and Agrarian England, 1660–1900*, Cambridge Studies in Population, Economy and Society in Past Time (Cambridge: Cambridge University Press, 1985), p.392. Snell is using a model of the regional novel in which the genre is defined by topographical specificity and the accurate transcription of local customs and dialect. Hardy's work falls short when that model is applied to it. As I discuss below (Chapter 3), this model misrepresents a various group of novels and Hardy's novels work towards a new and distinctive kind of regional fiction (see Chapters 5 and 6).
5. Peter Widdowson, *Hardy in History: A Study in Literary Sociology* (London and New York: Routledge, 1989), p.56.
6. For Hardy's women, see Penny Boumelha, *Thomas Hardy and Women: Sexual Ideology and Narrative Form* (Brighton: Harvester, 1982), Rosemarie Morgan, *Women and Sexuality in the Novels of Thomas Hardy* (London: Routledge, 1988) and Patricia Ingham, *Thomas Hardy*, Feminist Readings (Hemel Hempstead: Harvester Wheatsheaf, 1989); for his subversiveness and innovativeness, see John Goode, *Thomas Hardy: The Offensive Truth* (Oxford: Blackwell, 1988) and Joe Fisher, *The Hidden Hardy* (Basingstoke and London: Macmillan – now Palgrave Macmillan, 1992); for his relations to popular fiction, see Richard Taylor, *The Neglected Hardy: Thomas Hardy's Lesser Novels* (London: Macmillan – now Palgrave Macmillan, 1982); for Hardy and Victorian learning, see Dennis Taylor, *Hardy's Literary Language and Victorian Philology* (Oxford: Clarendon Press, 1993).
7. Hardy, *Far from the Madding Crowd*, preface to 1912 edition. The wording in 1895 was 'merely realistic dream-country'; see Gatrell, 'Wessex', *Cambridge Companion to Hardy*, p.30. Compare also 'both what they half create, / And what perceive', William Wordsworth, 'Lines Composed a Few Miles above Tintern Abbey', ll.106–7. I discuss the similarities between Hardy's imaginative geography and Wordsworth's in Chapter 2.
8. 'Mrs Hardy' here is Hardy's second wife, Florence.
9. See *Geography and Education*, Education Pamphlet no. 39 (London: HMSO, 1961). On geography's development as a separate subject during the 1840s and 1850s, see J.N.L. Baker, *The History of Geography: Papers* (Oxford: Blackwell, 1963), pp.61ff.

10. The phrase is from A. Holt-Jensen, *Geography: Its History and Concepts: A Student's Guide* (London: Harper & Row, 1980), p.4.

11. T.W. Freeman, *A History of Modern British Geography* (London and New York: Longman, 1980), pp.34–5. Freeman quotes these words from the *Proceedings of the Royal Geographical Society* (1879). On imperial expansion and geography, see David Faulkner, 'The Birth of Culture from the Spirit of Cartography', *The Victorian Newsletter*, 81 (Spring 1992), pp.45–7.

12. Archibald Geikie, *The Teaching of Geography: Suggestions Regarding Principles and Methods for the Use of Teachers* (London and New York: Macmillan, 1887), p.vii. Freeman, *History of Modern British Geography*, p.35, states that Rev. Edward Hale put forward similar arguments in an address to the British Association in 1873.

13. Geikie, *Teaching of Geography*, p.149.

14. Geikie, *Teaching of Geography*, p.138.

15. Geikie, *Teaching of Geography*, pp.112ff.

16. Geography, Arnold said in 1842 'stretches out on one hand to history, and the other to geology and physiology' (quoted in Baker, *History of Geography*, p.35); Galton wrote in 1855 that the subject 'links the scattered sciences together, and gives to each of them a meaning and a significance of which they are barren when they stand alone' (quoted in Freeman, *History of Modern British Geography*, p.34).

17. T.H. Huxley, *Physiography: An Introduction to the Study of Nature*, first published 1877 (London: Macmillan, 1887), pp.vii–viii. The book was reprinted ten times in the ten years after publication. Huxley's work is discussed by Holt-Jensen, *Geography: History and Concepts*, pp.22ff.

18. Holt-Jensen, *Geography: History and Concepts*, p.27. Vidal saw this regional autonomy collapsing as he described it.

19. H.J. Mackinder, *Democratic Ideals and Reality: A Study in the Politics of Reconstruction* (London: Constable & Co., 1919), pp.244–67; C.B. Fawcett, *Provinces of England: A Study of Some Geographical Aspects of Devolution*, The Making of the Future Series (London: Williams & Norgate, 1919).

20. Fawcett, *Provinces of England*, p.185.

21. See *Thomas Hardy: The Critical Heritage*, edited R.G. Cox (London and New York: Routledge & Kegan Paul and Barnes & Noble, 1970), pp.347, 395–6, 433–4, articles published 1904, 1910 and 1914.

22. See George Wing, 'Hardy and Regionalism', *Thomas Hardy: The Writer and His Background*, edited by Norman Page (London: Bell & Hyman, 1980), pp.76–101 for a representative account. Peter Widdowson, *Hardy in History: A Study in Literary Sociology* (London and New York: Routledge, 1989) gives a history of Hardy's reception and his portrayal as the historian of Wessex.

23. There is, naturally enough, continuity between the earlier geographers and the regional school and no radical break. Mackinder, for example, opposes rote learning too and recommends that 'physical facts . . . must be taught concretely in the first instance, and only when they are known may they be built into general statements' (*Distant Lands: An Elementary Study in Geography* (London: G. Philip & Son, 1910), p.v). His emphasis on region creates, nonetheless, a different perspective from Huxley's or Geikie's.

24. Widdowson, *Hardy in History*, p.61.

25. For a summary of these developing connections, see John Kerrigan, 'The country of the mind', *TLS*, 11/9/1998, pp.3–4.
26. David Simpson, *The Academic Postmodern and the Rule of Literature: A Report on Half-Knowledge* (Chicago and London: The University of Chicago Press, 1995), p.117.
27. Ernesto Laclau, *Reflections on the Revolution of Our Time* (London: Verso, 1990), p.190; Doreen Massey, *Space, Place, and Gender* (Cambridge: Polity Press, 1994), p.154. Simpson explains localism's dominance in postmodernism as the result of a slippage between ethical terms and epistemological ones: a liberal desire to do justice to minority communities mistakenly espouses doubts about the possibility of knowing 'the other', except as a projection of self. See Simpson, *Academic Postmodern*, p.118; see also pp.131–2.
28. Raymond Williams, *The Country and the City* (London: Chatto & Windus, 1973), pp.208–9, 213.
29. Hardy, *Tess*, chapter 43, p.286.
30. John Goode, 'William Morris and the Dream of Revolution', *Literature and Politics in the Nineteenth Century*, edited by John Lucas (London: Methuen & Co., 1971), p.23; see also p.222. The essay is reprinted in *The Collected Essays of John Goode*, edited by Charles Swann, with an introduction by Terry Eagleton (Keele: Keele University Press, 1995), pp.272–320.
31. Celebrating labour has been seen as characteristic of the regional novel generally. F.W. Morgan, in his 1939 essay, 'Three Aspects of Regional Consciousness', describes literary regionalism as producing 'a living picture of the unity of place and people, through work', quoted in W.J. Keith, *Regions of the Imagination: The Development of British Rural Fiction* (Toronto, Buffalo, London: University of Toronto Press, 1988), p.5. I discuss the development of the regional novel in Chapter 3.
32. John Barrell, 'The Geographies of Hardy's Wessex', *Journal of Historical Geography*, 8:4 (1982), pp.347–61. Page references are to K.D.M. Snell, *The Regional Novel in Britain and Ireland, 1800–1990* (Cambridge: Cambridge University Press, 1998), pp.99–118 where the essay is reprinted. The essay appears almost complete in *Tess of the d'Urbervilles*, New Casebooks, edited by Peter Widdowson (Basingstoke: Macmillan, 1993), pp.157–71.
33. Barrell presents Tess as someone who loses her authenticity through partial education. She originally possessed 'concrete experience'; now she has and is nothing. If Hardy is teaching his reader to withdraw from local knowledge and confining characters within one world or the other, as Barrell suggests, then Tess is made into a kind of Other or, in Spivak's terms, a 'muted subaltern', 'spoken for' in an advocacy which tacitly assimilates her. See Gayatri Chakravorty Spivak, 'Can the Subaltern Speak?' (1988), *Colonial Discourse and Post-Colonial Theory: A Reader*, edited by Patrick Williams and Laura Chrisman (Harlow: Pearson Education, 1993), pp.66–111.
34. Hardy, *Tess*, chapter 44, pp.286–7.
35. Quoting Hardy, *Tess*, chapter 44, p.288.
36. Though 'avoiding inns' and eating at cottages instead, Tess's choice of route is not deliberately furtive; she knowledgeably follows the most convenient route. The contrast between 'transverse lane' and 'high road' or 'straight and deserted Roman road' recalls the end of 'The Three Strangers' in *Wessex Tales* and Henchard's journeys. See below, Chapters 2 and 5, for discussions of these.

37. Hardy, *Tess*, chapter 55, p.366. The stone pillar is a miniature Stonehenge, perhaps.
38. Barrell's essay makes alot of Tess's likeness to the 'birds of passage' that arrive at Flintcomb-Ash, 'gaunt spectral creatures with tragical eyes'. Hardy concludes his description of them by emphasizing their indifference: 'with dumb impassivity they dismissed experiences which they did not value for the immediate incidents of this homely upland' (Hardy, *Tess*, chapter 43, p.280). Coping and getting on, dismissing the irrelevant and concentrating on the immediate, are skills Tess is acquiring too.
39. Hardy, *Tess*, chapter 44, pp.288–9.
40. The phrase echoes *Great Expectations* where the 'marshes' of Pip's childhood is pronounced 'meshes'. It also recalls Tess earlier in the novel 'examining the mesh of events in her own life [. . .] her father's pride; the gentlemanly suitor awaiting herself in her mother's fancy' (Hardy, *Tess*, p.36).
41. Tess's position between local dialect and standard English, between indigenous socioeconomic structures and capitalist ones, suggests comparisons with the post-colonial subject. Hardy's own writing – not employing dialect outright and subversively employing educated forms and generic conventions – can be seen too as analogous to post-colonial writing. Ania Loomba, 'Overworlding the "Third World"', *Colonial Discourse and Post-Colonial Theory: A Reader* (1991), pp.305–23 provides a concise summary and brilliant analysis of current accounts of such 'hybridity'.
42. Simpson, *The Academic Postmodern*, p.133. Esther Schor, in *Bearing the Dead: The British Culture of Mourning from the Enlightenment to Victoria*, Literature in History Series (Princeton: Princeton University Press, 1995), remarks that in her work 'figurative language' is seen as neither reducible to nor independent of the 'social and ideological reality' uncovered by new historicist criticism (p.13). Adela Pinch, in *Strange Fits of Passion: Epistemologies of Emotion, Hume to Austen* (Stanford, California: Stanford University Press, 1996), states that her work 'includes a plea for a contextualized, gender-sensitive formalism' (p.12).
43. Massey, *Space, Place, and Gender*, p.134.
44. Massey, *Space, Place, and Gender*, pp.120–22, 154.
45. bell hooks, *Yearning: Race, Gender and Cultural Politics* (London: Turnaround, 1991), p.147; quoted in Massey, *Space, Place, and Gender*, pp.171–2.
46. The phrase she remembers here ('live and move and have our Being') comes from St Paul's sermon to the Athenians, Acts 17: 28.
47. Massey, *Space, Place, and Gender*, p.154. Conceiving society as a constellation is one of Hardy's concerns in *Far from the Madding Crowd*, as I discuss further in Chapter 5.
48. Derek Gregory, 'Lacan and Geography: the Production of Space Revisited', *Space and Social Theory: Interpreting Modernity and Postmodernity*, edited by Georges Benko and Ulf Strohmayer, The Royal Geographical Society with the Institute of British Geographers Special Publications Series, no. 33 (Oxford and Malden, MA: Blackwell, 1997), pp.216, 218, 219, quoting Henri Lefebvre, *The Production of Space*, first published in French, 1974, translated by Donald Nicholson-Smith (Oxford and Cambridge, MA: Blackwell, 1991), pp.5, 296.
49. Gregory, 'Lacan and Geography', p.216.
50. 'The insinuation is that only out of the dialectic of practice and reflection, that is, at the intersection of language and social action, will a true (read

revolutionary) spatial understanding be generated' (Julie Kathy Gibson-Graham, 'Postmodern Becomings: From the Space of Form to the Space of Potentiality', *Space and Social Theory*, pp.306–23 (p.308).) Lefebvre's hostility to theoreticians suggests the restrictions which his emphasis on practice places upon 'reflection'.

51. Ed Soja, 'Planning in/for Postmodernity', *Space and Social Theory: Interpreting Modernity and Postmodernity*, pp.236–49 (p.248).

52. Brian Jarvis, *Postmodern Cartographies: The Geographical Imagination in Contemporary American Culture* (London: Pluto Press, 1998), p.46. Jarvis commends, by contrast, Mike Davis's work on Los Angeles which 'manages to combine an analysis of macrogeographical process with a meticulously researched attention to local detail' (p.47).

53. Soja, *Postmodern Geographies: The Reassertion of Space in Critical Social Theory* (London: Verso, 1989), p.25.

54. Jarvis, *Postmodern Cartographies*, p.48.

55. Gibson-Graham, 'Postmodern becomings', *Space and Social Theory*, pp.319, 320, 320–1. I discuss Hardy's interest in and account of Impressionism below.

56. See Edward Soja and Barbara Hooper, 'The Spaces that Difference Makes: Some Notes on the Geographical Margins of the New Cultural Politics', *Place and the Politics of Identity*, edited by Michael Keith and Steve Pile (London and New York: Routledge, 1993), pp.183–205. Gibson-Graham quotes this essay (*Space and Social Theory*, p.321).

57. Massey, *Space, Place, and Gender*, p.154. Compare Patrick Wright's argument in favour of 'society', not 'nation', as the term in which to understand England: 'accepting the existence of society [. . .] implies at the very least an acceptance of [. . .] an open-ended multiplicity of traditions and histories rather than the artificial severity of a single and already completed national lineage' (Patrick Wright, *On Living in an Old Country: The National Past in Contemporary Britain*, with drawings by Andrzej Krauze (London: Verso, 1985), p.129). Neil Smith and Cindi Katz discuss the relation between spatial metaphors and material study in 'Grounding Metaphor: Towards a spatialized politics', *Place and the Politics of Identity*, pp.67–83, attacking both a tacit reliance among geographers on 'traditional realist assumptions' and their use of 'metaphors out of control', a spatial language which never inquires into the nature of the space employed in metaphor (pp.70, 80).

2 The Imaginative Geography of the West Country

1. Hardy, *Madding Crowd*, p.393, Preface to 1912 edition.

2. I discuss Hardy's maps further below. Maps are a feature of children's literature, perhaps particularly that designed for boys. A map is printed in Robert Louis Stevenson's *Treasure Island* (1883), Richard Jefferies's *Bevis: The Story of a Boy* (1882) and Rider Haggard's *King's Solomon's Mines* (1886). Tolkien's Middle-Earth and C.S. Lewis's Narnia are similarly presented via maps and, in all these, using and drawing maps, finding one's way with a compass or a set of instructions are essential to the experience of adventure. Arthur Ransome's *Swallows and Amazons* series shares this feature. By contrast, Hardy's map of Wessex offers no destination, no 'X marks the spot' or con-

sequent primary narrative. Where the map is centred and who centres it seem open to question. See Diana Loxley, *Problematic Shores: The Literature of Islands* (New York: St Martin's Press, 1990), p.95 for her discussion of maps and adventure narratives, particularly Captain Marryat's *Masterman Ready* (1841).

3. Hardy described his poem 'Domicilium' as 'Wordsworthian lines' (*Life*, p.8); see also *'Studies, Specimens &C'*, pp.3, 6, 31–2. Hardy's allegiance to Fielding is well summarized by Björk in *Literary Notebooks*, II, p.372. Hardy thought his portrayal of rustic characters owed more to Fielding and Shakespeare than to George Eliot; see *Life*, p.100.

4. J.G.A. Pocock, *Virtue, Commerce, and History: Essays on Political Thought and History, Chiefly in the Eighteenth Century* (Cambridge: Cambridge University Press, 1985), p.129; see also p.241. Pocock points out that country-party ideology had political consequences in the American Revolution and few, if any, in Great Britain itself: it was 'of vast importance in the history of thought [but] of very little importance in the history of English practice' (p.79).

5. William Gilpin, *Observations on the Western Parts of England, Relative Chiefly to Picturesque Beauty. To which are added, A Few Remarks on the Picturesque Beauties of the Isle of Wight* (London: T. Cadell and W. Davies, 1798), p.124. The tower was erected in 1772, stands 160 feet high and affords views of Wiltshire and the adjoining counties. Hardy refers to it as 'Stourton Tower' in his poem,'Channel Firing' (*Poems*, p.306).

6. This trend reaches its natural conclusion in Sarah Hamilton, *Alfred the Great, A Drama in Five Acts* (London: Longman, Rees, Orne, Brown, and Green, 1829), where Alfred retreats to a generic wilderness without any specified location. Hamilton's play continues the traditional link between Alfred and restored 'concord' between the races of Great Britain. Compare *Alfred: A Tragedy* (Dublin: Byrn & Son, 1777), p.35: 'The English and the Danes / Have fought too long, for this contested land, / Whose spacious kingdom can, with ease, contain, / The rival nations.'

7. Hardy's use of Saxon names, clearest in *The Hand of Ethelberta*, recalls the clash between native and invader figured by Alfred literature through the wars of Saxon and Dane. Ethelberta's dominance over Lord Mountclere at the close of Hardy's novel, with the severity and 'will of iron' (Hardy, *HE*, p.403) it demands, can be read in terms of local versus national, native versus metropolitan. Characteristically in Hardy, winning out over the foreign invader involves becoming like him.

8. These incidental references in map and place-names correspond to the multi-layered quality Hardy attributes to traditions visible in the landscape: 'The ashes of the original British pyre [. . .] lay fresh and undisturbed in the barrow [. . . .] Festival fires to Thor and Woden had [. . .] duly had their day [. . .] such blazes as this the heathmen were now enjoying are rather the lineal descendants from jumbled Druidical rites and Saxon ceremonies than the invention of popular feeling about Gunpowder Plot' (Hardy, *Return*, Book 1, chapter 3, p.20). I discuss these qualities further below, in Chapter 6.

9. 'Alfred: A Masque', *The Plays of James Thomson: 1700–1748: A Critical Edition*, edited by John C. Greene, 2 vols (New York and London: Garland Publishing, 1987), II, pp.321, 378, 380.

10. See, for instance, Thomas Cooke (1703–56), *The Bays Miscellany, or Colley Triumphant* (London: A. Moore, n.d.), p.20, where the character 'Flail' stoutly declares, 'Whoy, I'm but a West-country thresher, but I heard volk were a making Varses vor a Place at Court, zo I come to zhow my Zel; for an Rhiming be all, I'ze rhime as thick as Hail, I warrant ye.' The West Country farmer is a stock figure in Restoration drama and reappears as Squire Western in Fielding's *Tom Jones*. Defoe remarks about Yeovil, 'when we are come this length from London, the dialect of the English tongue, or the country way of expressing themselves is not easily understood, it is so strangely altered [. . .] it is so in many parts of England besides, but in none so gross a degree as in this part' (Defoe, *A Tour through the Whole Island of Great Britain*, 1724–6, abridged and edited by Pat Rogers (Harmondsworth: Penguin, 1971) pp.215–16).

11. *Plays of Thomson*, II, pp.363, 365.

12. See John Barrell, *English Literature in History, 1730–80: An Equal, Wide Survey* (London: Hutchinson, 1983). Pocock observes that the 'shrinkage of local influence' was a perception 'widely shared by observers and critics of the Hanoverian regime' even though it 'has been challenged by twentieth-century research' (*Virtue, Commerce, and History*, p.239). Linda Colley notices and challenges the assumption made by left- and right-wing historians that eighteenth-century 'national awareness was a functionalist creed, exploited by and invariably supportive of an unreformed and oligarchical state' ('Whose Nation? Class and National Consciousness in Britain 1750–1830', *Past and Present*, 113 (November 1986), pp.97–117 (p.104).)

13. *CARY'S New Itinerary; or, An Accurate Delineation of the GREAT ROADS, Both Direct and Cross, throughout England and Wales [. . .] From an Actual Admeasurement made by command of His Majesty's Postmaster General, for Official Purposes* (London: John Cary, 1798); Daniel Paterson, *A New and Accurate Description of all the Direct and Principal CROSS ROADS in Great Britain [. . .]* (T. Carnan: London, 1771). These are the first editions, many others followed: *CARYS New Itinerary* had reached a seventh edition by 1817; *Paterson's Roads*, a sixteenth by 1822.

14. Gilpin, *Western Parts of England*, p.152. See *Alfred, An Historical Tragedy, To which is added A Collection of Miscellaneous Poems* (Sheffield, privately printed, 1789), p.23: 'Not far from here, / In a rude place, surrounded by a large morass, / And hid from public eye by bush and brier, / The faithful friends of Alfred lie conceal'd'; and *Science Revived, or The Vision of Alfred. A Poem in Eight Books* (London: J.A. Gemeau & Co., 1802), pp.3–4.

15. Gilpin quotes from Thomson frequently (for instance, *Western Parts of England*, pp.150, 292). Ann Bermingham views Gilpin as instrumental in the construction of a landscape that represents ancient English liberties (see Ann Bermingham, 'System, Order, and Abstraction: The Politics of English Landscape Drawing around 1795', *Landscape and Power*, edited by W.J.T. Mitchell (Chicago and London: University of Chicago Press, 1994), pp.77–101).

16. See Henry Fielding, *The History of Tom Jones, a Foundling* (1749), book 6, chapter 2.

17. See Ralph Allen, *Bye, Way and Cross-Road Posts*, documents edited by A.M. Ogilvie (London: W.P. Griffith & Son Ltd, 1898).

18. See Fielding, *Tom Jones*, book 9, chapter 2: 'they had no sooner gained the

summit, than one of the most noble prospects in the world presented itself to their view, and which we would likewise present to the reader; but for two reasons. *First*, we despair of making those who have seen this prospect, admire our description. *Secondly*, we very much doubt whether those, who have not seen it, would understand it' (edited R.P.C. Mutter (Harmondsworth: Penguin, 1966), p.440).

19. Tom Jones, book 1, chapter 4, p.58.

20. Celia Fiennes, *The Journeys*, edited by Christopher Morris (London: The Cresset Press, 1949), p.243. She notices too the appearance of a distinctive, foreign-seeming dress: 'all sorts of country women wrapped up in the manteles called West Country rockets'. Daniel Defoe mentions the Lower Way and the Upper Way from Bridgwater to Bristol; the former is 'not always passable, being subject to floods, and dangerous inundations, I mean, dangerous to travel through, especially for strangers' (Defoe, *Whole Island*, p.255). W.G. Hoskins states that the levels 'were mostly drained between the tenth and fourteenth centuries by the marshland abbeys' (*The Making of the English Landscape*, 1955 (Harmondsworth: Penguin, 1985), p.99).

21. Defoe evidently regrets Monmouth's defeat as well, though he glosses over it: 'The rest I need not mention'. Defoe's hopes for peace and national stability lie in commercial activity, where for Fielding they require explicit allegiance to the Protestant settlement. Accordingly, Defoe emphasizes each region's contribution to London's wealth or food-supply, presenting the country as tied together by these economic links whatever the historical divisions may be (Defoe, *Whole Island*, p.254 and *passim*). Hardy refers obliquely to Judge Jefferies in *Mayor*, chapter 8, p.51.

22. See Nigel Leask, *The Politics of Imagination in Coleridge's Critical Thought* (London: Macmillan, 1988), p.3: 'The poetry of both Coleridge and Wordsworth in the productive years of 1797–1805 was a sophisticated, if somewhat socially marginalised attempt to promote the civic values of an egalitarian commonwelath, and not the product of a conservative reaction to the failure of French and English radicalism'.

23. Stephen Gill (ed.), *The Salisbury Plain Poems of William Wordsworth*, The Cornell Wordsworth (Ithaca and London: Cornell University Press, 1975), ll, 37, 298ff, pp.22, 31; Pocock, *Virtue, Commerce, and History*, p.79.

24. William Crowe, *Lewesdon Hill*, 1788 (Oxford: Woodstock Books, 1989), p.15.

25. The 'statesmen' of the Lake District, 'small independent *proprietors* of land', gain social feeling, 'domestic affections' and a power 'inconceivable by those who have only had an opportunity of observing hired labourers, farmers, and the manufacturing Poor' (Wordsworth to Charles James Fox, 14/1/1801, Ernest de Selincourt, *The Letters of William and Dorothy Wordsworth: The Early Years, 1787–1805*, 2nd rev. edn. (Oxford: Oxford University Press, 1967), pp.314–15). Wordsworth admired similar independence in other parts of the country; see his 1807 sonnet, 'Vanguard of Liberty, ye men of Kent'.

26. This was the same day that John Wordsworth joined the party.

27. S.T. Coleridge, *Collected Letters*, edited by E.L. Griggs, 6 vols (Oxford: Oxford University Press, 1956–71), I, p.299.

28. *Home at Grasmere*, MS B, ll, 827, 466–8, *Home at Grasmere: Part First, Book First of 'The Recluse'*, edited by Beth Darlington, The Cornell Wordsworth

(Ithaca and London: Cornell University Press, 1977; repr. with corrections, 1989), pp.68, 90.

29. In the later manuscript, a more explicit reminder of the Saxons occurs: 'That very voice – which in some timid mood / Of superstitious fancy might have seemed / Awful [. . .] as the Norman Curfew's regular beat / To hearths when first they darkened at the knell' (MS D, ll, 335–7, 339–40, *Home at Grasmere*, p.65).

30. On *Home at Grasmere*, see Kenneth R. Johnston, *Wordsworth and the Recluse* (New Haven and London: Yale University Press, 1984) pp.219–24; Jonathan Wordsworth, *William Wordsworth: The Borders of Vision* (Oxford: Oxford University Press, 1982), pp.125–7; and Richard Bourke, *Romantic Discourse and Political Modernity: Wordsworth, the Intellectual and Cultural Critique* (Hemel Hempstead: Harvester Wheatsheaf, 1993), pp.94–116.

31. I discuss westerly journeys further below, Chapter 4. Wordsworth's 'Stepping Westward' again finds a '*heavenly* destiny' located in the west and reminds one of *Home at Grasmere* even though it is set in Scotland.

32. In *Romantic Geography: Wordsworth and Anglo-European Spaces* (Basingstoke and New York: Palgrave Macmillan, 1998), Michael Wiley sees Wordsworth's Salisbury Plain and Grasmere as both offering 'sustainable critical alternatives to the social and political world as it was represented institutionally in Britain' (p.37). His readings concentrate on Wordsworth's use of pastoral utopias to counter institutional authority; he thinks about Wordsworth's different kinds of space without reference to their geographical location.

33. Lucille Herbert, 'Hardy's Views in "Tess of the D'Urbervilles"', *ELH*, 37 (1970), pp.77–94 (p.79).

34. Herbert, 'Hardy's Views', pp.92, 94. See my discussion of John Barrell, above.

35. See *Paterson's Roads* (1771), pp.3–4; and Pigot & Co., *British Atlas, comprising the Counties of England [. . .]*, 1840, facsimile reprint (London: Salamander Books, 2000), pages unnumbered. The same route is followed by William George Maton, according to his *Observations Relative Chiefly to [. . .] Western Counties of England, Made in the Years 1794 and 1796* (Salisbury: J. Easton, 1797).

36. Defoe, *Whole Island*, p.209.

37. Charles G. Harper, who published books on *The Hardy Country* (1904) and *Wessex* (1911), typifies this exaggeration when he claims that the preferred eighteenth-century route into the southwest was the one via Bath and Somerset. The contemporary record shows several possible routes. Harper is attempting to make the remoteness of 'the Hardy country' an ahistorical, fundamental truth. See Charles G. Harper, *The Exeter Road: The Story of the West of England Highway* (London: Chapman & Hall, 1899), pp.3–6.

38. J.H. Lucking, *Railways of Dorset: an Outline of their Establishment, Development and Progress from 1825* (Lichfield: The Railways Correspondence and Travel Society / Dorset Natural History and Archeological Society, 1968), p.21. I rely on Lucking's study throughout this section.

39. Charles Lock, 'Hardy and the Railway', *Essays in Criticism*, 50:1 (2000), pp.44–66 (pp.48ff) intelligently discusses the impact of railways on Casterbridge.

40. The railway network in Dorset is shown fully in Fig. 1.

41. David St John Thomas discusses 'the devastating effect on main-road villages by-passed by the trains' which, he states, was especially bad in Dorset. 'Old-established markets faded as new ones were opened nearer the railway; public houses once thronged with travellers [. . .] were left dependent on the local population, itself declining and impoverished' (*The West Country*, A Regional History of the Railways of Great Britain, vol.1 (London: Phoenix House, 1960), p.137). See Hardy, *DR*, vol.1, chapter 8, section 3, p.124: the Three Tranters Inn (in 'Carriford', based on the actual West Stafford) declined because the railway 'had absorbed the whole stream of traffic which formerly flowed through the village'; see also the short story, 'The Waiting Supper', section 6 (first published 1888, collected in *A Changed Man* (1913).)

42. The description of Weymouth contrasts with that of Dorchester (emphasizing links to Oxford and Cambridge), that of Poole (emphasizing commercial routes to London and Portsmouth) and that of Blandford Forum (emphasizing gentlemanly elegance); see Hutchins, *Dorset*, I, pp.1, 215; II, p.335.

43. See John K. Walton, *The English Seaside Resort: A Social History 1750–1914* (Leicester and New York: Leicester University Press/St Martin's Press, 1983), pp.52ff.

44. Pigot & Co., *British Atlas*, 'Dorsetshire'.

45. The 1822 edition of *Paterson's Roads* provides a series of maps, starting in Kent and following the south coast as far as Southampton and the New Forest. The 1817 edition of *CARY'S Itinerary* gives detailed descriptions not only of Bath, Oxford and Cambridge but, in addition, maps of the 'Environs of Ramsgate and Margate', 'Environs of Bognor, Worthing and Brighton'. Both guidebooks increasingly aim at the tourist market that develops along the south coast.

46. Hardy, *Mayor*, notes, p.327. Wilson's notes do not mention the cutting out of 'western'.

47. Hardy, *Mayor*, chapters 40, 43, 44; pp.281, 304, 312.

48. Falmouth is a striking choice in this context, given that 'London to Falmouth' is the name of the coach route passing through Dorchester in Pigot & Co.'s *British Atlas* of 1840.

49. David St John Thomas refers to this route as taken by 'seamen crossing by land from Weymouth to Bristol to save going round the Cornish coast' (Thomas, *The West Country*, p.137).

50. Hardy, *Mayor*, chapters 4, 18, 44, 45; pp.27–8, 115, 312, 317. Hardy may be remembering Wordsworth's 'Michael'(first published in *Lyrical Ballads* (1800)) when he places Henchard in this 'utter solitude', 'alone / With a few sheep' (ll, 13, 10–11). It suits the feeling that Farfrae's success is, in some lights, an act of filial betrayal.

51. The novel is set during the 1830s and 1850s (the opening chapters 18 years earlier than the main story). The railway extended as far as Dorchester in 1847; Hardy specifies, however, an anomalous moment: 'the railway had stretched out an arm towards Casterbridge at this time, but had not reached it by several miles as yet' (*Mayor*, chapter 37, p.261). This remark is made resonant by its place in the narrative, a little before Henchard's and Lucetta's exposure by the skimmity-ride. Railways loom, threatening Henchard; the main story takes place as railways are arriving, as Farfrae is establishing himself.

52. Hardy, *Mayor*, chapter 44, revised version, p.373. Hardy cut this chapter from the serial for the 1886 edition and restored it in 1895.
53. '"Well, well – never mind – it is all over and past," said Newson good-naturedly. "Now, about this wedding again"' (Hardy, *Mayor*, chapter 43, p.311). These are his last words in the book: their prospectiveness balances kindliness to Elizabeth-Jane and a forgiving spirit towards Henchard with a rejection of the past whose ease can seem callous.
54. See *Life*, p.20.
55. Hardy, *Mayor*, chapter 44, p.313. Compare this passage and the discussion which follows with Hardy's poem 'I Was the Midmost': the first stanza opens 'I was the midmost of my world', the second 'She was the midmost of my world', and the third and last, 'Where now is midmost in my world?' (*Poems*, p.666).
56. See, for instance, 'Yell'ham-Wood's Story', 'I Looked Up from My Writing', 'Growth in May', 'Waiting Both' (*Poems*, pp.298, 551, 626, 701).
57. Hardy, *Mayor*, chapter 45, pp.318–19. 'Ramification' derives from the Latin *ramus*, a branch; in *OED*, quotations (under definition 2) suggest the subdivision of a main structure to the point of indistinguishability: 'From the small rivers [. . .] the far-extending ramifications are innumerable' (1776), 'The root [. . .] terminating in minute ramifications and filaments' (1813), 'All feathers are subdivided until the ultimate ramifications are exceedingly minute' (1834).
58. Hardy, *Mayor*, p.321.
59. For Warton, see: 'The ripen'd orchard [. . .] azure skies, / The cheerful sun [. . .] all, all conspire, / To raise, to sooth, to harmonize the mind, / To life on wings of praise, to the great Sire / Of being and of beauty' ('The Enthusiast or the Lover of Nature', ll. 158–63, *The Three Wartons: A Choice of their Verse*, edited by Eric Partridge (London: Scholartis, 1927), p.78); see also Ann Radcliffe, *The Mysteries of Udolpho*, vol.1, chapter 3; James Thomson, *Spring* (1746 text), ll. 882–903, 950–62.

3 Ruralism and Provincialism in the Victorian Novel: North and South

1. E.P. Thompson points out that 'So far from extinguishing local traditions, it is possible that the early years of the Industrial Revolution saw a growth in provincial pride and self-consciousness' (*The Making of the English Working Class*, revised edition with new preface (London: Penguin, 1980), p.448). Robin Gilmour, 'Regional and Provincial in Victorian Literature', *The Literature of Region and Nation*, edited by R.P. Draper (Basingstoke: Macmillan – now Palgrave Macmillan, 1989), p.53 gives several examples of how provincial England began to be seen. See also Philip S. Bagwell, 'The Decline of Rural Isolation', *The Victorian Countryside*, edited by G.E. Mingay, 2 vols (London, Boston & Henley: Routledge & Kegan Paul, 1981), I, pp.30–42. Changes in the perception of provincial areas intersect with the other cultural transformations brought about by social change in the period, notably, redefinitions of class and the emergence of an urbanised personality. See Elizabeth Deeds Ermarth, *The English Novel in History 1840–1895*, The Novel

in History Series, gen. ed. Gillian Beer (London and New York: Routledge, 1997), which reads the period's novels as 'experimental laboratories for defining and exploring a new construction of corporate order' (p.vii). See also the more Foucauldian study, Mary Poovey, *Making A Social Body: British Cultural Formation, 1830–64* (Chicago and London: University of Chicago Press, 1995) which reads the period's novels as helping to put forward 'the idea that individuals were alike in being responsible (economic and moral) agents [. . .] as a substitute for the tutelary role that the metaphor of the social body had initially assigned to the state' (p.22).

2. Hilary M. Schor, *Scheherazade in the Marketplace: Elizabeth Gaskell and the Victorian Novel* (New York and Oxford: Oxford University Press, 1992), p.24.

3. William Howitt, *The Rural Life of England*, 1838. Quotations are from the third edition, corrected and revised (London: Longman, Brown, Green and Longmans, 1844). The Howitts also produced *The Book of the Seasons* (1831), *Sketches of Natural History* (1834), *The Boy's Country Book* (1839), *Homes and Haunts of England* (1847) and *The Year-Book of the Country* (1850). Elizabeth Gaskell's description of Stratford appeared in their volume *Visits to Remarkable Places* (1840, second series 1842) and she contributed stories to their weekly journal, *Howitt's Journal* (published in volume form, 1847). William Howitt helped her publish *Mary Barton*. See Schor, *Scheherazade in the Marketplace*, pp.24–5. An alignment between ruralism and colonialism is suggested by William Howitt's *Colonization and Christianity: A Popular History of the Treatment of the Natives by the Europeans in all their Colonies* (1838).

4. Elizabeth K. Helsinger, *Rural Scenes and National Representation: Britain, 1815–1850*, Literature in History Series (Princeton NJ: Princeton University Press, 1997), p.121. This is one of very few discussions of Mitford or the Howitts; even here, the Howitts are little more than referred to. Merryn Williams, *Thomas Hardy and Rural England* (London and Basingstoke: Macmillan, 1972), pp.17–20, 59–62, discusses the Howitts. P.D. Edwards, *Idyllic Realism from Mary Russell Mitford to Hardy* (Basingstoke: Macmillan, 1988) charts the use Tennyson, Gaskell and others made of the 'gentle idyllic realism, or realistic idyll' (p.3) invented by Mitford. The Howitts are not mentioned. George Levine, *The Realistic Imagination: English Fiction from Frankenstein to Lady Chatterley* (Chicago and London: University of Chicago Press, 1981) discusses nineteenth-century novels' rural scenery by contrast with sublime, romantic landscapes; ruralism becomes an aspect of Victorian realism's support for moderation. See also Gillian Beer, 'Charles Kingsley and the Literary Image of the Countryside', *Victorian Studies*, 8 (1965), pp.243–54.

5. Edward Bulwer-Lytton, *England and the English*, 2 vols (London: Richard Bentley, 1833), p.86; *Eugene Aram*, 1832, one-volume edition (London: Richard Bentley, 1832), pp.2, 5. Lytton's essay, 'On the Differences between the Urban and Rural Temperament', published in *Caxtoniana* (1863) is consistent with his views and feelings in the 1830s.

6. 'Those young men, whom it is a pleasure to see with their knapsacks on their backs ranging over moor and mountain, by lake or ocean, in Scotland or Wales' (Howitt, *Rural Life*, p.81). The use of 'picturesque' in 'The poetry and the picturesque of rural life' suggests continuity between Howitt's landscape and that of the picturesque, a generation earlier. Gilpin's love of pictorially harmonious vistas overlaps with a preference for signs of human activity,

taming the wilderness (see Gilpin, *Observations on Western Parts of England*, pp.29, 81–3, 149–50, 192–8). Howitt refers to Gilpin in his chapter on the New Forest (*Rural Life*, p.375). Gilpin was Vicar of Boldre in the New Forest and his *Remarks on Forest Scenery* (1791) are '*Illustrated by Scenes of New-Forest in Hampshire*'.

7. Alun Howkins, in 'The Discovery of Rural England', *Englishness: Politics and Culture 1880–1920*, edited by Robert Colls and Philip Dodds (Beckenham, North Ryde, New South Wales, and New York: Croom Helm, 1986), pp.63–4, has dated the emergence of this characteristic landscape later, around 1870, as a response to social and economic crisis. Howitt's depiction can be used for such ends but originates in a more optimistic ambition in which economic progress benefits the countryside by 'improving' it. Simultaneously, the countryside provides images of 'humble sociality' that will be useful in tempering the excesses of industrial capitalism.

8. Rydal Mount, where Wordsworth moved in 1813, was a sizeable house. By contrast with Dove Cottage, it illustrates the leisured and cultured quality of Howitt's 'rural life'. 'Mrs Southey' refers to Robert Southey's second wife, Caroline Anne Bowles, whom he married in 1839. Buckland lies just north of Lymington and close to Boldre.

9. Levine, *Realistic Imagination*, pp.204, 216.

10. Frances Milton Trollope, *The Vicar of Wrexhill*, 3 vols (London: Richard Bentley, 1837) opens with an apology for sketching once more 'The beauties of an English village'; Wrexhill, however, is worth describing: 'not even England can show many parts of greater beauty than this oak-sheltered spot can display. Its peculiar style of scenery, half garden, half forest in aspect, is familiar to all who are acquainted with the New Forest, although it has features entirely its own. One of these is an overshot mill' (p.1). Watermills are very common in ruralist literature throughout the century, probably because they represent a form of industrial development which harmonized with and animated the agricultural world.

11. Helsinger, *Rural Scenes and National Representation*, pp.122, 123, 132.

12. *Rural Scenes and National Representation*, pp.128, 132.

13. Christiana Payne, 'Rural Virtues for Urban Consumption: Cottage Scenes in Early Victorian Painting', *Journal of Victorian Culture*, 3:1 (Spring 1998), pp.45–68 (pp.47, 58). Helsinger's work tends to neglect the morally instructive aspects of paintings; Constable's rustic pictures 'show us what should have been but never was – certainly not for Constable, nor for the consumers of his work'; they 'project an idea of local, rural England as the enabling space of both careless boyhood and the bourgeois family' (Helsinger, *Rural Scenes and National Representation*, p.63). According to this, Constable's pictures falsify; they are another instance of how the relations of power are ignored in the most popular Victorian art. Payne's work suggests by contrast that relations of moral – if not economic – power are addressed in such work. On these issues, see Ann Bermingham, *Landscape and Ideology: The English Rustic Tradition* (Berkeley and Los Angeles: University of California Press, 1986) and her 'System, Order, and Abstraction: The Politics of English Landscape Drawing around 1795', *Landscape and Power*, edited by W.J.T. Michell (Chicago and London: University of Chicago Press, 1994), pp.77–109.

14. Helsinger, *Rural Scenes and National Representation*, pp.128, 218. This point of view depends on arguments in Martin J. Wiener, *English Culture and the Decline of the Industrial Spirit, 1850–1980* (Cambridge: Cambridge University Press, 1981). Edwards, *Idyllic Realism*, places Hardy at the end of a ruralist tradition which he sees as lasting, largely unchanged, from the 1830s to the 1870s.

15. See Wiener, *Industrial Spirit*, pp.52–3, 57, and Peter Brooker and Peter Widdowson, 'A Literature for England', *Englishness*, pp.116–63 (p.120). Hardy's relation to Englishness is discussed below, Chapter 6.

16. Thomas Hardy, *The Woodlanders*, 1887, chapter 1 (Oxford: Oxford University Press, 1996), p.8.

17. See K.D.M. Snell, *The Regional Novel in Britain and Ireland, 1800–1900* (Cambridge: Cambridge University Press, 1998), pp.5–8, where the history of the genre is summarized; see also *Literature of Region and Nation*, p.2: Regionalism 'seems to have been a growth of the late eighteenth century – a response to the Industrial Revolution'. W.J. Keith, *Regions of the Imagination: The Development of British Rural Fiction* (Toronto, Buffalo, London: University of Toronto Press, 1988), pp.19–20, refers to Edgeworth but places her second to Scott as the primary source of regional writing; so too does James Reed in *Sir Walter Scott: Landscape and Locality* (London: The Athlone Press, 1980), especially pp.2–9. How one defines the regional and the provincial novel influences where one locates its origins; see below.

18. 'Between the allegorical territories of Bunyan and the precisely delineated localities of Scott, most of the action in novels is played out in a topographical vacuum, conventionally contained by Town and Country' (Reed, *Scott: Landscape and Locality*, p.6). For a discussion of Fielding's topographical specificity, see above.

19. W.J. Keith is aware of overlap between genres (historical novel, romance, regional fiction) but he argues for a quite narrow definition: regional fiction means novels that 'present a locality distinctive in character and related [. . .] to a corresponding countryside identifiable on a map of the United Kingdom' (Keith, *Regions of the Imagination*, p.10); Snell asserts at the outset: 'By "regional novel" I mean fiction that is set in a recognisable region, and which describes features distinguishing the life, social relations, customs, language, dialect, or other aspects of the culture of that area and its people' (Snell, *The Regional Novel*, p.1). Snell identifies a descriptive project, aligned with local history; Keith is more interested in writing that celebrates nature, organizing the genre around the aims and sensibility of Richard Jefferies' work; regional fiction is elided, as his subtitle suggests, with '*British Rural Fiction*'. In my view, novels with regional/provincial elements have in common neither the survey nor celebration of rural life but disputes over both of these.

20. Harold Bloom's work on influence has drawn attention to the rivalry and psychological dialectic which usually governs relations between successive writers within a tradition. See his *The Anxiety of Influence: A Theory of Poetry* (London, Oxford, New York: Oxford University Press, 1973).

21. Gilmour, 'Regional and Provincial in Victorian Literature', *Literature of Region and Nation*, pp.51–60, summarizes received histories of the genre. Glen Cavaliero, *The Rural Tradition in the English Novel 1900–1939* (London and

Basingstoke: Macmillan – now Palgrave Macmillan, 1977) remains the best study of the later sub-genre.

22. Katie Trumpener, *Bardic Nationalism: The Romantic Novel and the British Empire*, Literature in History Series (Princeton, NJ: Princeton University Press, 1997), pp.17, 141–2 is illuminating about intertextual relations in Romantic period fiction while the main thrust of her argument aims to show this writing's indebtedness to other texts (antiquarian and commercial) and its responsiveness to social and political change. This seems the right balance to strike.

23. Ferrier's notes are mostly very brief; I discuss one example below. Lady Morgan's are longer, more effusive and combine rational clarity with chatty ardour. Jane Porter's *The Scottish Chiefs* (1810) is extensively annotated; Mary Brunton's *Discipline* (1814) provides notes to chapters 22–8 when the story moves to Scotland. Marilyn Butler discusses annotation of novels in connection with annotated Romantic poems in Maria Edgeworth, *Castle Rackrent and Ennui*, edited by Marilyn Butler (Harmondsworth: Penguin, 1992), pp.16–17.

24. Trumpener, *Bardic Nationalism*, p.33. On cosmopolitan versus nationalist forms of travel writing, see Seamus Deane, 'Virtue, Travel, and the Enlightenment', *Nations and Nationalisms: France, Britain, Ireland and the Eighteenth-Century Context*, edited by Michael O'Dea and Kevin Whelan (Oxford: Virtue Foundation, 1995), pp.275–95.

25. Trumpener, *Bardic Nationalism*, pp.60–61.

26. Discussion of Edgeworth's politics has been considerable; see, particularly, Esther Wohlgemut, 'Maria Edgeworth and the Question of National Identity', *Studies in English Literature, 1500–1900*, 39:4 (Autumn 1999), pp.645–58, both for its argument, showing how Edgeworth 'reinterpreted both cosmopolitan and national definitions of belonging' (p.645) and for her assessment of the current literature (pp.645–7, 657). On Edgeworth as colonialist, see E. Kowaleski-Wallace, *Their Fathers' Daughters: Hannah More, Maria Edgeworth, and Patriarchal Complicity* (Oxford and New York: Oxford University Press, 1991); on the political aspect of the genre of national tale, see Gary Kelly, *English Fiction of the Romantic Period, 1789–1830* (London: Longman, 1989), pp.86–98 and Ina Ferris, 'Narrating Cultural Encounter: Lady Morgan and the Irish National Tale', *Nineteenth-Century Literature*, 51:3 (December 1996), pp.287–303.

27. On differences between the political and colonial context of Irish and Scottish regional writing, see J.Th. Leerssen, 'Fiction Poetics and Cultural Stereotype: Local Colour in Scott, Morgan, and Maturin', *Modern Language Review*, 86 (1991), pp.273–84. On Scott's various and subtle uses of annotation, see Jane Millgate, *Scott's Last Edition: A Study in Publishing History* (Edinburgh: Edinburgh University Press, 1987).

28. For a useful discussion of accuracy and fantasy in Scott's historical novels, see Gillian Beer, *The Romance*, Critical Idiom Series (London: Methuen, 1970), pp.64–8. For a more hostile account of Scott's practice (both as novelist and annotator), see James Kerr, *Fiction against History: Scott as Story-Teller* (Cambridge: Cambridge University Press, 1989), pp.21, 128–30.

29. 'Introduction', Edgeworth, *Castle Rackrent and Ennui*, p.23.

30. Susan Ferrier, *Marriage*, 1818, vol. I, chapter 7 (Oxford and New York: Oxford University Press, 1986), p.36.

31. *OED* states that 'stirk' means either bullock or heifer and in Scottish usage is 'chiefly applied to the male' bullock; 'stot' in northern usage may mean either 'young castrated ox' or 'heifer'; a Scottish usage is not distinguished.

32. Edgeworth's approach is similar to Ferrier's in being explicitly justificatory – giving details of actual cruelty to wives in Ireland, she observes: 'These circumstances may appear strange to an English reader; but there is no danger in the present times, that any individual should exercise such tyranny.' In a lengthy endnote, Edgeworth argues that strange customs and superstitions have a rational basis: 'Some remote origin for the most superstitious or romantic popular illusions may often be discovered.' When the Irish custom of fostering children is referred to, she directs the reader to several other texts, establishing its frequency (Edgeworth, *Castle Rackrent and Ennui*, pp.30n, 107, 159). Jane Millgate shows Scott glossing Gaelic phrases and Scottish proverbs while also providing detailed antiquarian notes (*Scott's Last Edition*, p.86). Scott's enthusiastic antiquarianism differs in tone from Edgeworth's cooler analyses of local custom; both writers, along with Ferrier, are responding in different ways to difficulties inherent in the mediating role each has taken up.

33. Emily Brontë, *Wuthering Heights*, 1847, chapter 1 (Oxford: Oxford University Press, 1981), p.3.

34. *Wuthering Heights*, chapter 1, p.1.

35. The word is usually applied to smaller objects than legs – fruit, especially grapes, or flowers – or to larger objects made smaller by distance or point of view – islands and nebulae are both quoted in the *OED*. Applied to joints of meat, the word suggests Lockwood's attempt to prettify and to shrink the objects while appearing to give a simple, helpful description; the clash of register shows the legs' obstinately disconcerting presence. For a fuller discussion of how a scientific vocabulary bears on travel writing and the beginnings of anthropology, see Mary Louise Pratt, *Imperial Eyes: Travel Writing and Transculturation* (New York and London: Routledge, 1992).

36. '[F]laishion tuh', meaning 'have the face to', and 'war', meaning 'worse', are candidates for glossing. See *Wuthering Heights* (Oxford: Oxford University Press, 1976), Appendix VII for a fuller discussion of Brontë's dialect. Patricia Ingham, 'Dialect in the Novels of Hardy and George Eliot', *Literary English Since Shakespeare*, edited by George Watson (London, Oxford and New York: Oxford University Press, 1970), pp.347–63 perceptively discusses the consequences of both novelists' use of dialect and forms a helpful introduction to the subject more generally. I discuss Hardy's use and presentation of dialect in Chapter 6.

37. Nancy Armstrong, in her insightful article, 'Emily's Ghost: The Cultural Politics of Victorian Fiction, Folklore, and Photography', *Novel: A Forum on Fiction*, 25 (Spring 1992), pp.245–67, discusses the novel in similar terms as a response to internal colonization. She reads the narrative as showing that 'Yorkshire culture belongs to the past' (p.251) and is gradually being assimilated and homogenized – by the end of the book, 'Anyone who cannot assume a role within the modern nuclear family has passed or will soon pass away' (p.260). Armstrong admits, however, that the novel also remains inconclusive: 'Does [Lockwood's dream] ask us to contemplate something that someone like Lockwood can never feel or know because his experience

is narrower and more homogeneous than that encoded in the British culture he confronts?' (p.251).

38. George Eliot, *Adam Bede*, chapters 41, 48, edited by Stephen Gill (Harmondsworth: Penguin, 1980), pp.424, 468. The phrase may be not only proverbial but an allusion to Charles Reade's novel, *It is Never Too Late to Mend* (1856). Hardy mocks the phrase when Arabella resolves to remarry Jude: 'It is – hic – never too late – hic – to mend!' (Hardy, *Jude*, part 6, ch.6, p.376).

39. This relatively little-discussed but moving story, fundamental to an understanding of George Eliot, is the third of the *Scenes of Clerical Life*. See David Carroll, ' "Janet's Repentance" and the Myth of the Organic', *Nineteenth-Century Fiction*, 35:3 (December 1988), pp.331–48.

40. Steve Bamlett, ' "A Way-Worn Ancestry Returning": The Function of the Representation of Peasants in the Novel', *Peasants and Countrymen in Literature*, edited by Kathleen Parkinson and Martin Priestman (Roehampton Institute, 1982), pp.153–82, argues that Eliot's realism is governed by the belief that peasant life offered a means of harmonizing country and city, a belief she took from Riehl's *Natural History of German Life*.

41. Henry Auster, *Local Habitations: Regionalism in the Early Novels of George Eliot* (Cambridge, MA: Harvard University Press, 1970), p.30. Auster is quoting from Phyllis Bentley's pioneering study, *The English Regional Novel* (London: George Allen & Unwin, 1941); on p.39n, Auster cites Lord David Cecil commenting to similar effect about Eliot's localities. Graham Handley, *George Eliot's Midlands: Passion in Exile* (London: Allison & Busby, 1991) identifies Eliot's locations very thoroughly but remarks of *Middlemarch*, 'the physical identification of place is subordinate to the moral and spiritual concerns of character' (p.9).

42. The prologue to *Felix Holt* is the clearest instance of this technique; see also *Adam Bede*, chapter 2, setting up the contrast between Loamshire and Stonyshire.

43. Michael Squires, *The Pastoral Novel: Studies in George Eliot, Thomas Hardy, and D.H. Lawrence* (Charlottesville: University Press of Virginia, 1974), precisely locates *Adam Bede* and *Silas Marner* within the pastoral genre. Stability becomes a virtue in itself, increasingly so as Eliot's career continued, as is indicated by the much-quoted passage from chapter 2 of *Daniel Deronda* (1876): 'A human life, I think, should be well rooted in some spot of native land' and in the essay, 'Looking Backward', published in *Impressions of Theophrastus Such* (1879). These sentiments have been linked to Riehl's *Natural History of German Life*, but were present also in the English ruralist tradition. See Mrs. Craik, *Olive*, 3 vols (London: Chapman & Hall, 1850), p.6: 'It is sweet to say, "Those are *my* mountains," or "This is *my* fair valley;" and there is a delight almost like that of a child who glories in his noble or beautiful parents, in the grand historical pride which links us to the place where we were born.'

44. This opposition is particularly marked in *Adam Bede*, which presents Loamshire and Stonyshire as north and south.

45. For a discussion of this view and its limitations, see Pearl L. Brown, 'The Pastoral and Anti-Pastoral in Elizabeth Gaskell's *Cousin Phyllis*', *The Victorian Newsletter*, 82 (Fall 1992), pp.22–7.

46. Henry Fothergill Chorley, *Athenaeum*, 7 (April 1855), quoted in Elizabeth Gaskell, *North and South*, edited by Jenny Uglow (London and Vermont: Everyman, 1993), p.442.
47. The phrases quoted are from *Mary Barton*, chapter 37. Helen M. Jewell, *The North–south divide: The origins of northern consciousness in England* (Manchester and New York: Manchester University Press, 1994) gives a helpful survey of the historical background to the divide; D.F. Pocock, 'North and South in the Book of Genesis', *Studies in Social Anthropology: Essays in Memory of E.E. Evans-Pritchard by his former Oxford Colleagues*, edited J.H.M. Beattie and R.G. Lienhardt (Oxford: Clarendon Press, 1975), pp.273–84 suggests symbolic resonances (the south is luxurious, the north austere) which may have crossed into English culture.
48. John Lucas, *The Literature of Change: Studies in the Nineteenth-Century Provincial Novel* (Brighton: Harvester Press, 1977), p.18.
49. Joseph Kestner, *Protest and Reform: The British Social Narrative by Women, 1827–67* (London: Methuen, 1985), quoted *North and South*, pp.465–6.
50. Gaskell, *North and South*, ch.52, p.440.
51. Elizabeth Gaskell, *Wives and Daughters*, 1866, ch.10, edited by Angus Easson (Oxford and New York: Oxford University Press, 1987), p.117.
52. Similarly, at the close of *Mary Barton*, we learn that it is 'Dear Job Legh' who plans to visit, 'to try and pick up a few specimens of Canadian insects' (ch.38). Tess Cosslett, *The 'Scientific Movement' and Victorian Literature* (Brighton and New York: Harvester and Barnes & Noble, 1982) helpfully summarizes different versions of scientific inquiry available in the period. Matthew Arnold's *On the Study of Celtic Literature* (1867) raises the same issues as emerge here from provincial novels' striving for scientific accuracy. He argues that the Welsh language should be replaced by English (in order to expedite the 'fusion of all the inhabitants of these islands into one homogeneous, English-speaking whole') and, secondly, that studying Celtic literature reveals an underlying kinship between Celt and Saxon. 'And this new, reconciling sense has, I say, its roots in science.' The Celts can be 'known as they are' once they have been brought into the fold and their language eradicated (*The Complete Prose Works of Matthew Arnold*, vol.2, edited by R.H. Super (Ann Arbor: University of Michigan Press, 1962), pp.296–302).
53. Gaskell, *Wives and Daughters*, ch.10, pp.116–17.
54. See *North and South*, ch.37, titled 'Looking South', where Margaret describes the life of the agricultural labourer as in many ways worse than that of a factory worker, and ch.46, where Margaret revisits Helstone with her father's Oxford friend, Mr Bell, and disabuses him of his idyllic picture of rural ways. Lucas draws attention to Sylvia's need, in *Sylvia's Lovers*, for the countryside when she moves into town after her marriage (*Literature of Change*, p.24) and W.A. Craik points out as characteristic of Gaskell an 'unostentatiously Wordsworthian enthusiasm [for] the seasons, weather and physical activity' (*Elizabeth Gaskell and the English Provincial Novel* (London: Methuen & Co., 1975), pp.257–8).
55. In her earlier works, the similarity to the Howitts appears more obviously: old fields surviving amid industrial development offer refreshment and redemptive peace to harassed workers; see *Mary Barton*, ch.1 and her early story 'Libbie Marsh's Three Eras', first published by the Howitts, with

its idyllic depiction of 'Dunham' (Dunham Massey Hall, southwest of Manchester).

56. This quality draws Gaskell close to Charlotte Brontë. Rosemarie Bodenheimer, *The Politics of Story in Victorian Social Fiction* (Ithaca: Cornell University Press, 1988), pp.37–57, identifies a comparable dividedness in Brontë who defies paternalist order while also submitting to it. Tim Dolin reads *Shirley* (1849) as an exemplary provincial novel because it resists the centre, being 'never silently complicit in internal colonization'; he concludes again, however, that though 'a confrontational book' it is also 'an appeasing one' ('Fictional Territory and a Woman's Place: Regional and Sexual Difference in *Shirley*', *ELH*, 62 (1995), pp.197–215 (pp.211–12).) On this subject, see also the excellent article by Pam Morris, 'Heroes and Hero-Worship in Charlotte Brontë's *Shirley*', *Nineteenth-Century Literature*, 54:3 (December 1999), pp.285–307.

57. Thomas Hardy, *A Pair of Blue Eyes*, 1873, ch.13. Knight calls the view from the window of his chambers into the gaslit street outside, his 'Humanity Show' and Hardy links it to the acquarium, suggesting that science has helped create in him an unfeeling detachment from other people.

58. See Cosslett, *The 'Scientific Movement'*, pp.159–62, for a perceptive discussion of Fitzpiers, the dilettante scientist.

59. Gaskell, *North and South*, chs 2 and 46, pp.15, 386, 402. After *North and South*, 'Helstone' becomes a name that means rural England: Mrs Henry Wood's *The Channings* (1862) is set in 'Helstonleigh', a rural cathedral city probably modelled on Worcester; in Daphne du Maurier's *Jamaica Inn* (1936), 'Helston' (referring to the real Helston between Falmouth and Penzance) is presented as an idyllic, rural place the heroine must leave.

60. Hardy may have connected Hampshire with the novelist Charlotte Mary Yonge who lived her whole life at Otterbourne, a few miles south of Winchester. Yonge's tractarianism and conservatism accompany a conventional delight in English rurality, particularly that of her home and of Devon; see *Abbeychurch, or Self Control and Self Deceit* (1844) set in 'Abbeychurch St. Mary's', recognizably Otterbourne, and *Beechcroft at Rockstone* (1888), set in unspoilt Devonshire. Hardy would have been familiar with the author of the best-selling, *Heir of Redclyffe* (1853) and out of sympathy with her religious and political views.

61. Pinion, *Hardy Companion*, p.246. In this final stage of her journeying, as earlier, Hardy draws on Hetty's 'Journey in Despair' (*Adam Bede* (1859) Book 5, ch.37), northwards from Windsor back towards Hayslope – a journey during which she looks for somewhere to hide in the field paths of Warwickshire and its lanes enclosed by high hedgerows.

62. Hardy, *Tess*, chs 11, 57, and 58, pp.75, 374, 376. Alec calls it the oldest wood and may be talking for effect, mimicking a frequent claim. In Charlotte Brontë's *Shirley*, ch.12, Nunnwood is celebrated as 'the sole remnant of antique British forest in a region whose lowlands were once all sylvan chase'.

63. Hardy mentions in passing that Alec's father comes from 'the North' and 'decided to settle as a county man in the South of England', partly to lose his identity as 'the smart tradesman of the past'. This detail suggests that he is thinking in terms of north and south and, even, writing *North and South*

in reverse. On country houses in the period, see Michael Hall, *The English Country House: From the Archives of Country Life 1897–1939* (London, Auckland, Melbourne, Singapore and Toronto: Mitchell Beazley, 1994), esp. pp.7–12, and Clive Aslet, *The Last Country Houses* (New Haven and London: Yale University Press, 1982).

64. The conventional associations of the forest can be illustrated from Mary E. Braddon, *Vixen* (1879), set in the New Forest, especially ch.17, 'Where the Red King was Slain'. The forest offers beauty, seclusion and a panorama showing 'a vast champaign, stretching far away to the white walls, tiled roofs, and ancient abbey-church of Romsey; here a glimpse of winding water, there a humble village [. . .] nestling among the trees' (Mary E. Braddon, *Vixen* (Stroud and New Hampshire: Alan Sutton, 1993), p.158). The Red King is William Rufus, son of William the Conqueror. His death was often read as a Saxon attack on Norman tyranny and lends the New Forest a patriotic meaning, being the place where a (foreign) tyrant was executed. Hardy's poems, 'Last Look round St. Martin's Fair' and 'Throwing a Tree: New Forest', *Poems* nos. 730, 837, confirm his wariness of the 'Great Forest'.

65. Thomas Hardy, 'Lady Mottisfont', *A Group of Noble Dames*, 1891 (London and New York: Macmillan and St Martin's, 1968), p.132. The sentence runs '[Her husband] repaired and improved the old highway running from Wintonchester south-westerly through the New Forest – and in the heart of this [. . . .]'. He seems the refuge, by contrast with the forest; secondly, his road improvements open up the forest and in the same way he releases one of its prisoners, his wife.

66. It 'may have been originally conceived as a story in *A Group of Noble Dames*' (Martin Ray, *Thomas Hardy: A Textual Study of the Short Stories* (Aldershot and Brookfield, Vermont: Ashgate, 1997), p.313.

67. Thomas Hardy, *Tess*, ch.55, p.363; *The Well-Beloved*, Part 3, ch.8; *The Pursuit of the Well-Beloved*, chs 30–32 (Hardy, *Well-Beloved*, pp.153ff, 335); Hardy, *Jude*, Part 3 ch.4, p.148. Many of *The Hand of Ethelberta*'s early scenes are placed in Sandbourne, 'a coast town and watering-place not many miles from Anglebury'. In 1896, Hardy rephrased this introductory description, once again highlighting contrast: 'a modern coast town and watering-place not many miles from ancient Anglebury' (Hardy, *HE*, ch.2 and note, pp.24, 427).

68. Hardy, *Tess*, ch.58, p.378.

69. See *Life*, p.126. Bernard Jones, 'William Barnes, the Philological Society up to 1873 and the *New English Dictionary*', *Speech Past and Present: Studies in English Dialectology in Memory of Ossi Ihalainen*, edited by Juhani Klemola, Merja Kytö and Matti Rissanen (Frankfurt am Main: Peter Lang, 1996), pp.80–100, suggests Barnes was more cosmopolitan, being a comparative philologist of great range who was 'demeaned to the level of a local parson glossarist' by the academic establishment (p.98). See also, Gillian Beer, *Open Fields: Science in Cultural Encounter* (Oxford: Clarendon Press, 1996), p.44, for a similar view of Barnes.

70. See John Prest, *Liberty and Locality: Parliament, Permissive Legislation, and Ratepayers' Democracies in the Nineteenth Century* (Oxford: Clarendon Press, 1990), pp.44–7, 208–20. See also R.J. Lambert, 'Central and Local Relations in Mid-Victorian England: the Local Government Act Office, 1858–71',

Victorian Studies, 6 (1962), pp.121–50. See Geoffrey Best, in *Mid-Victorian Britain* (London: Weidenfeld & Nicolson, 1971, rep. 1979): 'from the forties until the seventies, the urban local authorities of Britain were, *vis-à-vis* Whitehall, more independently active than ever before [. . .] or since' (p.55) and W.L. Burn in *The Age of Equipoise: A Study of the Mid-Victorian Generation* (London: Unwin University Books, 1964): '[the mid-sixties saw] a lessening of the reaction against "centralization", a greater disposition to accept authoritative and even authoritarian action' (p.82).

71. John Burrow, *A Liberal Descent: Victorian Historians and the English Past* (Cambridge: Cambridge University Press, 1981), p.140. Thinkers as widely different in their opinions as John Stuart Mill and Lord Acton were both arguing against a powerful central government in the 1860s – Mill in his essay 'Centralisation', *Edinburgh Review*, 105 (April 1862), pp.327–58, Lord Acton in his reviews in the *Home and Foreign Review* (reprinted in Lord Acton, *Essays on Church and State*, edited by Douglas Woodruff (London: Hollis and Carter, 1952), pp.398ff). Mill's position is similar to that put forward in his *Principles of Political Economy* (1848), Book 5, ch.11; in 1862, he sees it beginning to be adopted even by Frenchmen.

72. See below, Chapter 7.

73. Hardy, *Tess*, ch.59, p.383. The *Mothers' Union* was founded in the 1870s by the wife of Rev. Sumner, whose parish and home were near Winchester.

74. J.B. Bullen, 'The Gods in Wessex Exile: Thomas Hardy and Mythology', *The Sun is God: Painting, Literature and Mythology in the Nineteenth Century*, edited by J.B. Bullen (Oxford: Clarendon Press, 1989), pp.181–98 (p.197).

75. Jeff Nunokava, '*Tess*, tourism and the spectacle of the woman', *Rewriting the Victorians: Theory, history, and the politics of gender*, edited by Linda M. Shires (New York and London: Routledge, 1992), pp.70–86, notices Hardy's closeness to tourist language when describing both Wintonchester and Sandbourne, citing a contemporary Baedeker in support. He reads these similarities as making the novel 'a generic handbook for the tourist' (p.78), without an ironic or parodic angle on this rhetoric and the vantage-point it creates.

76. Jean Jacques Leclercle makes the same point about the word 'hanging' here in 'The Violence of Style in "Tess of the d'Urbervilles"', *Alternative Hardy*, edited by Lance St John Butler (Basingstoke: Macmillan – now Palgrave Macmillan, 1989), p.1.

77. Hardy, *Withered Arm*, pp.352, 354–5. See *Life*, pp.32–3, for Hardy's accounts of witnessing hangings.

4   Ruralism and Provincialism in the Victorian Novel: East and West

1. 'Domicilium', Hardy's first poem, begins 'It faces west'; see also 'I Found Her Out There' and 'The Woman who Went East' (*Poems*, pp.3, 342, 916). It has been pointed out before that this departure recalls the end of *Paradise Lost*, when Adam and Eve are driven from Paradise; they leave, however, in the opposite direction, by the 'eastern gate', and 'looking back, all th'eastern side beheld / Of Paradise' (Book 12, ll. 638, 641–2).

2. On Devon, see Sam Smiles and Michael Pidgley, *The Perfection of England: Artist Visitors to Devon c. 1750–1870* (Plymouth: University of Plymouth, 1995). The phrase 'the perfection of England' was coined by Henry James in 'North Devon', *The Nation* (1872), repr. in *Transatlantic Sketches* (1875) and *English Hours* (1905). On Cornwall, see Philip Dodds's valuable essay, 'Gender and Cornwall: Charles Kingsley to Daphne du Maurier', *The Regional Novel in Britain and Ireland, 1800–1900* (Cambridge: Cambridge University Press, 1998), edited by K.D.M. Snell, pp.119–35. One reason for the difference between the two counties was the absence from Cornwall of railways until the construction of the Tamar bridge in May 1859; thereafter, the difference became gradually less absolute. Mary E. Braddon, *Only a Clod* (1865), employs the standard contrast between Cornwall and the Thames Valley, whereas her later *Wyllard's Weird* (1885) presents a Cornwall accessible by railway and closer to the ruralist image of the countryside.

3. Christopher GoGwilt, *The Invention of the West: Joseph Conrad and the Double-Mapping of Europe and Empire* (Stanford, California: Stanford University Press, 1995), is one of the few studies to consider the rise in importance of the term. GoGwilt sees 'the West' as a means after 1880 of defining European identity by contrast with Slavs and colonized natives in the east. He does not discuss the term within a specifically English geography. Franco Moretti, *An Atlas of the European Novel, 1800–1900* (London and New York: Verso, 1998), pp.124ff and Robert Mighall, *A Geography of Victorian Gothic Fiction: Mapping History's Nightmares* (Oxford: Oxford University Press, 1999), pp.27–77 both discuss mid-nineteenth-century London in relation to Dickens (see below).

4. 'Northern Metaphor' and 'Southern Metaphor' are used by Donald Horne, *God is an Englishman* (Sydney, Australia, 1969) in his account of Victorian imaginative geographies, the northern being industrial and the southern rural, even though much industry was situated in southern England. Compare Martin J. Wiener, *English Culture and the Decline of the Industrial Spirit, 1850–1980* (Cambridge: Cambridge University Press, 1981), pp.41–2. On the dominance of the southeast in the nineteenth century, see C.H. Lee, 'The Service Sector', *Journal of Historical Geography*, 10 (1984), pp.139–55.

5. See Roger Simpson, *Camelot Regained: The Arthurian Revival and Tennyson, 1800–1849* (Cambridge: D.S. Brewer, 1990), especially pp.55–113. James Douglas Merriman, *The Flower of Kings: A Study of Arthurian Legend in England between 1485 and 1835* (Lawrence, Manhattan, Wichita: University of Kansas Press, 1973), pp.137ff stresses the period's need to create a symbol out of Arthur. On nineteenth-century Arthurianism more generally, see Mark Girouard, *The Return to Camelot: Chivalry and the English Gentleman* (New Haven and London: Yale University Press, 1981).

6. Glastonbury's nearness to Athelney made it easy to connect Alfred and Arthur; John Parker's poem, 'The Celtic Annals' (1831) did so explicitly. Tennyson's *Idylls of the King* (1859–84) contributed to the increasing link between Arthur and Cornwall. On nineteenth-century Arthurian literature, see Beverly Taylor and Elizabeth Brewer, *The Return of King Arthur: British and American Arthurian Literature since 1800* (Cambridge and Totowa, NJ: D.S. Brewer and Barnes & Noble, 1983). Arthur's eclipse of Alfred shadows the period's tendency to replace the opposition of Saxon and Norman with that

of Saxon and Celt. See David Alderson, *Mansex fine: Religion, manliness and imperialism in nineteenth-century British culture* (Manchester and New York: Manchester University Press, 1998), pp.112–19.

7. See *Life*, pp.66, 280 and *Literary Notebooks*, II, p.387.

8. Two novels, *John Halifax, Gentleman* (1857) and *Agatha's Husband* (1853), by the highly successful Dinah Craik, can be used to illustrate this pervasive feature. John Halifax is consoled when prevented from marrying the woman he loves by the sight of a beautiful sunset and dies looking westward at evening. The setting promises eternal life for him. In the earlier novel, Agatha's courtship takes place in London as gleams of moonlight peep into city-squares from the west. Her husband has made his money in Canada and his family lives in Dorset; the couple travel there together when first married. Light from the west peeps into London like the prospect of this new life.

9. George Meredith, *The Ordeal of Richard Feverel: A History of Father and Son*, vol.2, ch.4, edited by Edward Mendelson (Harmondsworth: Penguin, 1998), pp.166–7. Mendelson's edition reprints the 1859 text which Meredith revised considerably in later life, changing the chapter numbering. This passage comes from ch.19 of Meredith's 1900 revised edition. Compare a later passage: 'Over the pine-hills beyond the station a last rosy streak lingered across a green sky. Richard eyed it as they flew along. It caught him forward: it seemed full of the spirit of his love, and brought tears of mournful longing to his eyelids' (vol.2, ch.7, p.205; 1900, ch.22).

10. Meredith, *Ordeal of Richard Feverel*, pp.61, 82, 124–5. Both Charles Reade's *It is Never Too Late to Mend* (1856) and his *Hard Cash* (1863) employ the romance of Thames valley settings. See also Simon Schama, *Landscape & Memory* (London: Fontana, 1996), pp.328–31, 359–64, on the importance of the Thames to Elizabethan national identity and in nineteenth-century painting, especially Turner.

11. See J.B. Bullen on the sun in *Tess* (Chapter 3, note 74, above). Stonehenge and Winchester are both connected with Arthur. Merlin was said to have magically transported the stone circle from Ireland; the round table was thought by some antiquarians to survive in Winchester (see Simpson, *Camelot Regained*, pp.59–60). Possibly these associations are at work in the final chapters of *Tess*.

12. F.M.L. Thompson, *The Rise of Respectable Society: A Social History of Victorian Britain, 1830–1900* (London: Fontana, 1988); John Summerson, *The London Building World of the Eighteen Sixties* (London: Thames & Hudson, 1973), p.8. London's economic and cultural centrality meant its geography was most influential but nearly all Victorian cities divided into poorer easterly quarters and more affluent western suburbs. Maurice Beresford, *East End, West End: The Face of Leeds During Urbanisation, 1684–1842* (Leeds: Thoresby Society, 1988) argues that preference for the west did not initially or necessarily arise from a desire to be the windward side of the smoke but may have more complex cultural roots.

13. William Cobbett, *Rural Rides*, edited by George Woodcock (Harmondsworth: Penguin, 1967), pp.66–71. On 'Home Counties' see *OED*.

14. Moretti, *Atlas of the European Novel*, p.123. Similar criticisms of Moretti's work have been made by Jacqueline Guy in her review of the book, *Nineteenth-Century Literature*, 54:3 (December 1999), pp.401–4.

15. Charles Dickens, *Bleak House*, 1853, ch.64 (1868 text), edited by Norman Page (Harmondsworth: Penguin, 1971), p.912. The whole paragraph confirms the ruralism of the scene. George Gissing remarked of Dickens: 'Among his supreme merits is that of having presented in abiding form one of the best of our national ideals – rural homeliness' (quoted in John Goode, *George Gissing: Ideology and Fiction* (London: Vision Press, 1978), p.20).

16. *Little Dorrit*, Book 1, ch.16, pp.235, 244; ch.17, p.252. Thompson, *Rise of Respectable Society*, points out that, as railways made commuting easier, it became 'virtually impossible to tell apart a house in the country and a fringe villa'. Similarly, 'large and grand houses standing in grounds of several acres' were built on the edges of cities and often lasted 'no more than a single generation before having their grounds and gardens carved up into building plots' (pp.166–7).

17. *Little Dorrit*, p.254. Jane Austen, *Emma* (1816) contrasts the vulgar Mrs Elton, from 'Maple Grove', with Mr Knightley's care for his native trees (vol.3, ch.6). In Fanny Burney's *The Wanderer; or, Female Difficulties* (1814), an unpleasant, socially ambitious woman is named Mrs Maple. Compare too Dinah Craik, *Olive*, 3 vols (London: Chapman & Hall, 1850), pp.10–11: Brierley Hall's 'two lines of patriarchal elms' contrast with 'modern villas starting up around us so fatally fast, snug and smug [. . .] with newly-painted palisades, and araucarias and deodaras stuck here and there in the fresh-made lawn'. Araucarias are monkey-puzzles, deodaras a species of cedar imported from the Himalayas. Hardy's 'evergreen oaks' screening the jail in Wintonchester have similar connotations (Hardy, *Tess*, ch.59, p.397).

18. The route follows a Roman road, Watling Street, connecting the Kentish coast to Chester, via London. John Richard Green, in his nation-building history, *The Making of England* (London: Macmillan & Co., 1885) draws special attention to this road: 'the route which crossed the downs of Kent from Richborough to the Thames linked the roads that radiated from London over the surface of the island with the general network of communications along which flowed the social and political life of the Roman world' (p.3).

19. The running title is 'War Against Donkeys'; its meaning of 'a stupid or silly person' was current in Dickens's day.

20. 'I am David Copperfield, of Blunderstone, in Suffolk,' David tells his aunt when first introducing himself (*David Copperfield*, ch.13). The recent BBC film version (broadcast Christmas 1999) gave David's first novel the title *Blunderstone*. In the original, David writes 'a Story, with a purpose growing, not remotely, out of my experience' (ch.58); no title is given for it. The title supplied in the film is chosen presumably to indicate this element of autobiography; it suggests an account, however, which is more nostalgic than Dickens whose own autobiographical novel, *David Copperfield*, brackets together mobility, moral development and self-betterment.

21. The county boundaries were slightly altered in 1974 but, even beforehand, Blundeston was a remote place, out on a limb of its county.

22. The east is connected in Dickens with the east wind which he found peculiarly depressing; one of the earlier titles for *Bleak House* was 'Bleak House and the East Wind'; Pip complains in *Great Expectations* that 'Day after day, a vast heavy veil had been driving over London from the East, and it drove

still, as if in the East there were an Eternity of cloud and wind' (ch.39). Charlotte Brontë also connected the east wind with misery and disease; see *Villette* (1853), ch.4, edited by Margaret Smith and Herbert Rosengarten (Oxford and New York: Oxford University Press, 1990), p.46 and note.

23. See *Great Expectations*, edited by Angus Calder (Harmondsworth: Penguin, 1965), pp.495–6.

24. E.M. Forster's *Howards End* again opposes Shropshire and the 'English' countryside, on the fringes of London, repeating Dickens's geography and reversing his preferences. Shropshire is seen as too wild and remote, 'Howards End', located in a ruralist landscape in Hertfordshire, makes possible a middle way, temperate and tolerant.

25. This belief comes through most clearly in *The Private Papers of Henry Ryecroft* (1903); it is foreshadowed at the close of *The Odd Women* (1893) and throughout *The Year of Jubilee* (1894).

26. George Gissing, *The Nether World*, edited by Stephen Gill (Oxford and New York: Oxford University Press, 1992), pp.164–5. This edition reprints the text of the 1890 one-volume edition.

27. George Gissing, *New Grub Street*, edited by Bernard Bergonzi (Harmondsworth: Penguin, 1968), ch.3, p.58.

28. Anthony Trollope, *Australia and New Zealand*, 2 vols, 1873, edited by P.D. Edwards and R.B. Joyce (St. Lucia: University of Queensland Press, 1967), p.441.

29. Anthony Trollope, *Doctor Thorne*, 1858, ch.1 (London: Oxford University Press and Humphrey Milford, 1926), p.1.

30. R.A. York, *The Rules of Time: Time and Rhythm in the Twentieth-Century Novel* (Madison and London: Fairleigh Dickinson University Press and Associated University Presses, 1999), pp.21–35, discusses the rhythms in the structure of *The Warden*, relating these to its feelings about progress. One may easily suppose, York concedes, 'that this is a book in praise of inertia. But the recognition of change is emphatic. It is, in fact, a book about the destruction of the past' (p.23).

31. Trollope, *Doctor Thorne*, ch.1, p.1.

32. See, for instance, Frances Milton Trollope, *The Vicar of Wrexhill*, 3 vols (London: Richard Bentley, 1837), discussed above, Chapter 3, note 10. Bullhampton, in Trollope's *The Vicar of Bullhampton* (1870), is similarly an 'altogether agricultural' and 'altogether conservative' place, situated with apparent but actually deceptive precision, somewhere in western Wiltshire on the edges of Salisbury Plain (ch.1 (Oxford and London: Oxford University Press, 1924), pp.1–2).

33. P.D. Edwards, *Anthony Trollope: His Art and Scope* (Brighton: Harvester, 1978), p.44. In *An Eye for an Eye* (1879, though 'written as early as 1870'), Trollope pictures Dorset as possessing typical Gothic features – remoteness, aged, autocratic nobles, a village dominated by a gloomy mansion. He connects both the absence of links to the centre and an excess of such links with aristocracy, old and new; somewhere in the social, economic and geographical middle there is an old balance to be restored.

34. The name 'Barset' evidently recalls Dorset and 'Barsetshire' recalls Devonshire or Somersetshire; Dorset is referred to as Dorsetshire more rarely. Barchester's cathedral and clergy suggests Salisbury or Winchester, possibly

Wells; train journeys in the novels give the impression of somewhere closer to London certainly than the last of these. These vaguenesses and multiple reference points suggest that Barsetshire epitomizes a large area of the south and southwest.

35. *The Perpetual Curate* (1863) opens in plainly Trollopian style: 'Carlingford is, as is well known, essentially a quiet place. There is no trade in the town, properly so called. [...] In Carlingford proper there is no trade, no manufactures, no anything in particular, except very pleasant parties and a superior class of people [....] But in every community some centre of life is necessary. This point, round which everything circles, is, in Carlingford, found in the clergy' (Margaret Oliphant, *The Perpetual Curate*, 3 vols (Edinburgh and London: W. Blackwood & Sons, 1863), I, ch.1, pp.1–2).

36. Penelope Fitzgerald, in her introduction to Margaret Oliphant, *The Rector and The Doctor's Family* (London: Virago, 1986) cautiously identifies Carlingford with Aylesbury, because of the Chiltern connections; Aylesbury is unlikely, however, because it would not be reached via Didcot.

37. Margaret Oliphant, *Salem Chapel*, 2 vols (Edinburgh and London, W. Blackwood & Sons, 1861), chs 1 and 2, pp.1, 24–5.

38. Margaret Oliphant, *Miss Marjoribanks*, edited by Elisabeth Jay (Penguin: Harmondsworth, 1998), pp.345, 361.

39. The point is made when the estate comes back into the story: 'Tom [Miss Marjoribanks's cousin and fiancé], too, could remember Marchbank, and his uncle's interest in it, and the careful way in which he explained to the ignorant that this was the correct pronunciation of his own name' (Oliphant, *Miss Marjoribanks*, p.484).

40. Oliphant too married her cousin, keeping her maiden name. Trollope's *An Eye for an Eye* (1879) is warier of the same ambition: 'They were and always had been Mellerbys of Mellerby, – the very name of the parish being the same as that of the family' (ch.3 (Harmondsworth: Penguin, 1993), p.52). Charlotte Brontë's *Villette* begins in the stability of the Bretton household, 'Bretton of Bretton', that 'clean and ancient town' (ch.1, p.1).

41. This political argument is, arguably, the least interesting part of the book and the events that form this neat conclusion are allowed to appear lucky rather than meant. The novel keeps its distance from the perfect appropriateness of its ending and similar distance is consistently maintained in its treatment of the heroine. Events are allowed to take place in such a way that they appear providential and, at the same time, as the result of private self-interest. It is no surprise, therefore, that Miss Marjoribanks has studied 'political economy' (p.90).

42. Mrs Oliphant, *Phoebe, Junior*, 1876, with an introduction by Penelope Fitzgerald (London: Virago Press, 1989), p.336.

43. Phoebe reads one of 'Mr Stuart Mill's "Dissertations"', rather as Miss Marjoribanks reads political economy; she is also, however, steeped in Charlotte Yonge (*Phoebe, Junior*, chs 5, 19, 23, pp.36, 141, 175).

44. The novel's full title is *Phoebe, Junior. A Last Chronicle of Carlingford*, echoing Trollope's *The Last Chronicle of Barset* (1867) and its sub-plot concerning Mr May bears a close resemblance to Mr Crawley's financial problems in that novel. And, as in Trollope's *An Eye for an Eye*, Dorset is linked to an antiquated world-order.

45. *Phoebe, Junior*, chs 4 and 12, pp.26, 81.
46. Mary Elizabeth Braddon, *Lady Audley's Secret*, 1862, ch.1.
47. Wilkie Collins, *No Name*, 1862, edited by Mark Ford (Harmondsworth: Penguin, 1994), pp.266–7.
48. Wilkie Collins, *Armadale*, 1866, Book the Second, chs 4 and 9, edited by Catherine Peters (Oxford and New York: Oxford University Press, 1989), pp.236, 308.
49. Similarly perhaps in his *The Awkward Age* (1899), Nanda's acceptance of Mr Longdon is more troubling because the house he offers lies in Suffolk.
50. Collins published *Rambles Beyond Railways: Notes in Cornwall Taken A-Foot* (London: Richard Bentley, 1851).
51. Collins, *No Name*, 'The First Scene', ch.11, pp.82, 90.
52. Wolfgang Schivelbusch, *The Railway Journey: The Industrialization of Time and Space in the 19th Century* (Leamington Spa, Hamburg, New York: Berg, 1986), pp.129–49, presents a valuable discussion of how railway accidents were perceived in the period and what physiological and psychological effects they had.
53. Recognizable though altered names recur in Collins: the Norfolk scenes take place in the environs of 'Thorpe-Ambrose', reminiscent of the actual Thorpe St. Andrew, a few miles east of Norwich. The relation between real name and novelistic one is similar to that in Hardy's novels and may indicate Collins's influence on Hardy's construction of a geography.
54. Wilkie Collins, *The Moonstone* (1868) continues these associations and develops a connection between eastern England and the dubious imperial east. Anthea Trodd points out the importance of this orientalist component to detective fiction written in the wake of Collins's novel (Wilkie Collins, *The Moonstone*, edited by Anthea Trodd (Oxford and New York: Oxford University Press, 1982), pp.xvii–xviii).
55. Collins, Ar*madale*, The Story, Book the First, ch.3, pp.136–8.
56. The Isle of Wight, part of Hampshire and an increasingly important holiday location, features in these novels as a retreat, like Hampshire, of ambiguous purity. Magdalen's virtuous sister, Norah, in *No Name*, settles there; Lady Audley moves between her dishonest life at Audley Court and her roots at Ventnor, Isle of Wight, and in Meredith, Richard Feverel's virginal wife, Lucy, is despatched to the Isle of Wight while her husband struggles with her father. Hardy's story 'An Imaginative Woman' (first published 1894) makes use of these associations.
57. See her *Aurora Floyd* (1863), the follow-up to the highly successful, *Lady Audley's Secret*. Braddon employs throughout the familiar geography to less worrying effect than in either her own earlier novel or Collins's work. Via Talbot Bulstrode, the west of England is linked to qualities of resilience and integrity which Aurora needs. Without irony, true Englishness is located there and made the property of the landed gentry.
58. See Stephen Knight, 'Location and Dislocation in the British Mystery', *Peripheral Visions: Images of Nationhood in Contemporary British Fiction*, edited by Ian A. Bell (Cardiff: University of Wales Press, 1995), pp.29–31 and Nicholas Daly, 'Sensation Fiction and the Modernization of the Senses', *ELH*, 66:2 (Summer 1999), pp.461–87 (p.473).
59. Gillian Beer, 'Can the Native Return?', *Open Fields: Science in Cultural Encounter* (Oxford: Oxford University Press, 1996), pp.45, 47, 53.

60. Hardy, *Return*, pp.10–11, 88. Beer discusses the allusions to Arctic exploration in *Open Fields*, pp.46–8.
61. Hardy, *Return*, pp.69–70. Eustacia asks Wildeve to help her escape by driving her to Budmouth; her last journey goes in a southerly direction, from Mistover to Blackbarrow and then down the hill to Shadwater Weir.
62. Thomasin and Diggory leave at the novel's close to live 'About two miles to the right of Alderworth [. . .] where the meads begin' (Bk. 6, ch.1, p.375); that is, off the heath in a southerly direction, in a more fertile area. Diggory's farm is also referred to as 'North Shadwater' (Bk. 6, ch.4, p.391), partly because it lies on the northerly side of the river valley. This destination though contrasts with 'Southerton', where Wildeve plans to take Thomasin (Bk. 5, ch.5, p.335). Though leaving the heath, Diggory and Thomasin are not headed for the fashionable 'south' of Wildeve and Eustacia. Hardy named Diggory's farm 'Stickleford' in later editions, giving it the Wessex name for the village of Tincleton, four miles east of Stinsford.
63. J. Hillis Miller, 'Heidegger and Hardy', *Topographies* (Stanford, California: Stanford University Press, 1995), pp.21–56.
64. Miller, *Topographies*, p.45.
65. Hardy revises some of his distances and changes names between editions but the eastward location of the Alderworth cottage is understood from the outset. See Hardy, *Return*, Bk. 3, ch.6, p.206.
66. See Hardy, *Return*, Bk. 1, ch.10, p.95.
67. Clym's relation to his mother has often been read autobiographically; the novel's geography ties in with this because Hardy's birthplace in Higher Bockhampton 'faces west' ('Domicilium', l, 1, *Poems*, p.3). Turning the house round gives an increased sense of fixed opposition and claustrophobia to the relations between mother and son; it adds as well to the insularity and inward-looking quality of Egdon.
68. Compare Richard Jefferies, *After London; or, Wild England*, 1885 (Oxford and New York: Oxford University Press, 1980), p.16: 'Hitherto the stream of human life had directed itself to the westward, but when this reversal of magnetism occurred, a general desire arose to return to the east.'
69. Compare the opening of *A Laodicean*: 'The graveyard being quite open on its western side, the tweed-clad figure of the young man, and the tall mass of antique masonry [. . .] were fired to a great brightness by the uninterrupted solar rays, that crossed the neighbouring mead like a warp of gold threads, in whose mazes groups of equally lustrous gnats danced and wailed incessantly' (Bk. 1, ch.1, p.1).
70. Autobiography informs the geography again here because Hardy often thought of himself as having brought his first wife Emma from her native place in the west to an easterly dwelling-place where she was unhappy. See 'The Woman Who Went East' and 'I Found Her Out There', *Poems*, pp.342–3, 916–17. Eustacia on Egdon looking back nostalgically to Budmouth resembles Emma before her marriage, living in St. Juliot, North Cornwall and remembering a more glamorous life in Plymouth.
71. Venn camps on Egdon out of concern for Thomasin; his trade takes him away from the district because he sells reddle to sheep-farmers and 'the downs where most [. . .] were to be found lay some to the north, some to the west of Egdon' (Hardy, *Return*, Bk. 2, ch.7, p.147).
72. Hardy, *Return*, Bk. 1, ch.2 and Bk. 6, ch.1, pp.13, 374.

73. Compare Diggory with Jennifer Gribble's perceptive remark that, 'If Egdon begins as a landscape on which time makes but little impression, it comes most memorably alive not as brooding presence but as a living record of immediate sensation': 'The Quiet Woman of Egdon Heath', *Essays in Criticism*, 46 (1996) pp.234–57 (p.237).
74. On Hardy's map for the novel, east rises and west falls while Diggory's routes, unlike those of the rest of the characters, are often unmarked. Diggory, who had 'business of his own to attend to', 'bowed in manner of his own invention' when taking his leave of Thomasin (Hardy, *Return*, Bk. 4, chs 3, 4, pp.261, 262).

5   Rural Encounters

1. The name 'Carriford' was probably chosen partly to suggest West Stafford, a village on the railway line near Hardy's home. The resemblance to 'carry forward' may be deliberate, as may be a link to the French, 'carrefour', a crossroads. Echoes of this kind fit with the novel's interest in agency and upward mobility. The name may also be related to Margaret Oliphant's Carlingford.
2. Hardy's first short story, 'Destiny and a Blue Coat', published in October 1874, does constrast rail and road and it takes place in the northwestern part of Dorset which was so personally resonant for Hardy. Characters in the story travel from a village near Beaminster to Weymouth and back again; they begin and end in the horse-drawn carrier from Maiden Newton to Beaminster and take the train between Maiden Newton and Weymouth. In a story of sexual jealousy, the train offers apparent freedom while travelling in the carrier leads to being overheard and found out. The passionate watchfulness exhibited by the old ways of life contrasts with new mobility and the opportunities it offers. The story and its location in some ways prefigure 'Interlopers at the Knap', first published May 1884, discussed later in Chapter 6.
3. Hardy, *DR*, vol.1, ch.8, s.3, p.124.
4. Hardy *DR*, vol.1, ch.5, s.1, pp.60–61 and vol.2, ch.2, s.1, p.171.
5. 'Gradfield' recalls 'Gradgrind' from Dickens's *Hard Times*, perhaps suggesting the grind of routine architectural work – copying drawings, making surveys and so on; a mechanical, uncreative task similar to Gradgrind's. 'Gradfield' also suggests grading (even grinding) fields, regularizing and flattening the natural. A joke about Hardy's impatience with his architectural labour is joined perhaps to a feeling that the work is inherently destructive.
6. Owen's is comparable to Hardy's own experience when arriving in London and looking for work as an architect; see *Life*, p.41.
7. Hardy, *DR*, vol.1, ch.6, s.3, p.94.
8. *Life*, pp.88, 97.
9. Hardy, *Madding Crowd*, back cover blurb. This edition reprints Hardy's manuscript. Chapter numbers differ from other editions because what became chapter 16, 'All Saints' and All Souls'' was added between manuscript and first publication.
10. See John Goode, *Thomas Hardy: The Offensive Truth* (Oxford and New York: Blackwell, 1988), pp.14–33; Marjorie Garson, *Hardy's Fables of Integrity:*

Woman, Body, Text (Oxford: Clarendon Press, 1991), pp.47–50, and Joe Fisher, *The Hidden Hardy* (Basingstoke: Macmillan – now Palgrave Macmillan, 1992), pp.38–62. Pamela Dalziel, ' "She matched his violence with her own wild passion": Illustrating *Far from the Madding Crowd*', *Reading Thomas Hardy*, edited by Charles P.C. Pettit (Basingstoke and New York: Macmillan – now Palgrave Macmillan, 1998), pp.1–32, convincingly suggests that a pastoral reading of the novel was established by its first illustrations in the *Cornhill*.

11. Hardy, *Madding Crowd*, ch.21, p.127. Altered to 'these Wessex nooks' in the 1895 edition and thereafter.
12. See Rosemarie Morgan, *Cancelled Words: Rediscovering Thomas Hardy* (London and New York: Routledge, 1992), p.170. The opening of chapter 11 reads in 1874, 'For dreariness nothing could surpass a prospect in the outskirts of the city of Melchester'; it was later changed to 'the outskirts of a certain town and military station, many miles north of Weatherbury'. In chapter 10, the regiment is reported in 1874 to have left 'for Melchester'; later this is changed to 'for Melchester and onwards'.
13. Hardy, *Madding Crowd*, chs 1, 31, 39 and appendix 3, pp.4, 185, 229, 413–14.
14. See ch.33, p.200, about Boldwood: 'there is a breadth of vision in the free man which in the lover we vainly seek. Where there is much bias there must be some narrowness'. Compare Mrs Yeobright's commitment to Clym in *The Return of the Native* (Hardy, *Return*, Bk. 3, ch.7 and Bk. 4, ch.6, pp.213, 282.
15. Hardy, *Madding Crowd*, ch.3, p.16, 'Gabriel's face rising like the moon' and chs 16, 27, pp.102, 162.
16. Gabriel has a long memory for slights; when offered 'Cain Ball' as an assistant in chapter ten, he agrees despite the boy's unfortunate name. ' "O I don't mind names," said Gabriel' (p.71). This assertion sounds pointed because of Bathsheba's coquettish refusal to tell him her name in ch.3.
17. Hardy, *Madding Crowd*, ch.55, p.348.
18. Wordsworth may have been influential here; 'Michael' and *The Excursion*, Bk. 5, ll. 670ff both memorably draw comparisons between stars and lights shining from distant houses.
19. Hardy makes an important change to chapter 2. Watching the stars gives Gabriel an 'impression of riding along' with them, an 'epic form' of the 'poetry of motion'; Hardy ends the paragraph in 1874: 'After such a nocturnal reconnoitre among these astral clusters, aloft from the customary haunts of thought and vision, some men may feel raised to a capability for eternity at once' (Hardy, *Madding Crowd*, p.9). Hardy later rewrote the sentence: 'After such a nocturnal reconnoitre, it is hard to get back to earth, and to believe that the consciousness of such majestic speeding is derived from a tiny human frame' (Thomas Hardy, *Far from the Madding Crowd*, edited S.B. Falck-Yi (Oxford and New York: Oxford University Press, 1993), p.14). Though both versions express some ambivalence about this feeling, the second increases the sense of delusion.
20. Fanny's separateness is borne out by Hardy's added chapter, 'All Saints' and All Souls'' which describes her abortive wedding to Troy; in its absence the ms. narrative is perfectly intelligible.
21. This discussion is informed by conversations with Hester Jones and by her work, 'Some Literary Treatments of Friendship' (unpublished doctoral thesis, University of Cambridge, 1992).

22. Christian Cantle in *The Return of the Native* is comparably though more definitely asexual. Timothy Fairway comments about him: 'Wethers must live their time as well as other sheep, poor soul' (Hardy, *Return*, Bk. 1, ch.3, p.30).

23. Herbert Spencer, 'The Social Organism', *Essays, Scientific, Political, and Speculative*, 2nd edn, 2 vols (London and Edinburgh: William Norgate, 1868), I, p.402. The second edition is a reprint of the first American edition in which the essays are unrevised but printed in a different order and with one added.

24. Ch.27, pp.161–2; see also ch.14, p.87: like the 'solid black spot' of bees, 'the large red seal' of Bathsheba's valentine to Boldwood becomes 'as a blot on the retina of his eye'.

25. Spencer, 'The Nebular Hypothesis', *Essays*, I, pp.240–1. The essay was first published in the *Westminster Review*, July 1858; 'The Social Organism' appeared in the same place in January 1860.

26. Spencer, 'Nebular Hypothesis', *Essays*, I, pp.245, 250–1.

27. Spencer, 'Social Organism', *Essays*, I, p.252.

28. Spencer, 'Social Organism', *Essays*, I, p.396.

29. Hardy, *PBE*, pp.129, 133. In a moment of emotional crisis, Manston gazes down into a 'rain-water-butt' where 'Hundreds of thousands of minute living creatures sported and tumbled' (Hardy, *DR*, vol.2, ch.4, s.3, pp.221–2). Mrs Yeobright as she crosses the heath sees 'the maggotty shapes of innumerable obscene creatures [. . .] heaving and wallowing' in mud (Hardy, *Return*, Bk. 4, ch.5, p.270).

30. Doreen Massey, *Space, Place and Gender* (Cambridge: Polity Press, 1994), p.154.

31. Michael Rabiger, 'Hardy's Fictional Process and his Emotional Life', *Alternative Hardy*, edited by Lance St John Butler (Basingstoke: Macmillan – now Palgrave, 1989), pp.88–109 (p.104).

32. For Hardy's impressionism, see, among several studies, Penelope Vigar, *The Novels of Thomas Hardy: Illusion and Reality* (London: The Athlone Press, 1974). For an account of pictorialism in the Victorian novel more widely, see Murray Roston, *Victorian Contexts: Literature and the Visual Arts* (Basingstoke: Macmillan – now Palgrave Macmillan, 1996). On Hardy's 'series of seemings', see the excellent work by Ian Gregor, 'Hardy's World', *ELH*, 38 (1971), pp.274–93, and Michael Irwin and Ian Gregor, 'Either Side of Wessex', *Thomas Hardy after Fifty Years*, edited by Lance St John Butler (London and Basingstoke: Macmillan – now Palgrave Macmillan, 1977), pp.104–15.

33. Hardy, *DR*, vol.1, ch.3, s.2, pp.48–50. The novel has attracted comparatively little attention; my discussion here and of Hardy generally is often in response to Joe Fisher's perceptive and original book, *The Hidden Hardy*.

34. The straight line expresses decisiveness and decisiveness seems the result of being in love. Compare 'The History of the Hardcomes', one of the stories in the linked sequence, 'A Few Crusted Characters' (first published 1891, then in *Life's Little Ironies*, 1894). A pair of lovers row out from the Esplanade at Budmouth: 'Stephen and Olive shrank smaller and smaller as they shot straight out to sea' and 'disappeared while still following the same straight course away from the world of land-livers' (*Life's Little Ironies*, edited Alan Manford (Oxford and New York: Oxford University Press, 1996). pp.174, 176.

35. Hardy places Palchurch 'ten or twelve miles north of Creston, and about half

that distance from Carriford' (Hardy, *DR*, p.293). Bincombe or Broadmayne are possible places Hardy had in mind, though the topography of the novel is unspecific.

36. Manston, approaching the village and seeing a fire in the distance, encounters difficulties: 'the excessive winding of the roads misled him as to its direction, not being an inhabitant of the district, or a countryman used to forming such judgments' (Hardy, *DR*, p.182). Locals are referred to as 'natives' several times; see p.401.

37. John Newman and Nikolaus Pevsner, *Dorset*, The Buildings of England Series (Harmondsworth: Penguin, 1972), pp.159, 402. (Hereafter, Pevsner, *Dorset*.) Both buildings are small; Pevsner mentions the 'naturalistic foliage' of the chancel arch in Stour Row and describes West Compton as 'a hardly inhabited combe'.

38. In Hardy, *Tess*, ch.16, p.101, Tess travels south-eastwards through 'Stourcastle' (Sturminster Newton) by road and 'onward to a junction of highways, where she could await a carrier's van that ran to the south-west; for the railways which engirdled this interior tract of country had never yet struck across it'. Hardy is probably thinking of a crossroads north of Okeford Fitzpaine; the road Tess joins leads northwards to Manston.

39. In 1872–3, Crickmay built the church of St Margaret's in Margaret Marsh, a village lying between Manston and Stour Row (Pevsner, *Dorset*, p.269). Hardy was working for Crickmay until spring 1872 and may have been involved here again, though by then the novel was finished. He got to know the area better from 1876 to 1878 when he lived in Sturminster Newton and, later still, chose Marnhull (a few miles north of Hinton St. Mary) for 'Marlott' in *Tess*. An earlier familiarity with the district would help account for his choosing to move to Sturminster in 1876, a decision which seems unexpected otherwise.

40. *Hardy: A Biography*, pp.84, 112, 118. Millgate suggests that locations in the unpublished novel are connected to Hardy's girlfriend in the 1860s, Eliza Nicholls; that is, to the south Dorset coast and to Findon in Sussex where Eliza's parents lived.

41. Hardy, as a boy, 'did not want at all to be a man' but when successful was pressed to join the Rabelais Club 'as being the most virile writer of works of the imagination then in London' (*Life*, pp.28, 136). Martin Seymour-Smith, *Hardy* (London: Bloomsbury, 1994), pp.33–6, ably discusses the question of Hardy's late puberty and arguments that he was sexually impotent.

42. It may be too fanciful to point out that Hinton St. Mary and Manston are likewise twin: the villages stand on alternative routes from Sturminster Newton north, either of which Hardy could have taken on his way to Stour Row.

43. Hardy recurs to family place-names more bleakly in *Tess of the d'Urbervilles*: Parson Tringham tells Jack Durbeyfield, 'Branches of your family held manors over all this part of England' (Hardy, *Tess*, ch.1, p.8). On Hardy's sources and techniques for choosing names, see Ralph W.V. Elliott, *Thomas Hardy's English* (Oxford and London: Basil Blackwell and André Deutsch, 1984), pp.289–95.

44. The exceptions to this rule come in mid-career: *The Return of the Native* (1878) is set near Bockhampton but was written at Sturminster Newton – Hardy

draws attention to this fact in the *Life*, p.120; *The Trumpet-Major* (1880) and *A Laodicean* (1881) were both written in London, the first being set in southern Dorset, the second in an undefined western county (which became 'Outer Wessex', that is, Somerset, in the Wessex edition of 1895–6). I discuss this sequence of novels in Chapter 6.

6   Wessex, Elusive and Independent

1. Norcombe Hill has also been identified with a hill near Eggardon between Dorchester and Bridport. I cannot find it on the Ordnance Survey maps; F.B. Pinion, *A Hardy Companion: A Guide to the Works of Thomas Hardy and their Background*, pp.424–5, gives the Toller Down location.
2. *The Place-Names of Dorset*, edited A.D. Mills, 3 vols (Nottingham: English Place-Names Society, 1977–89), I, p.130; II, pp.146, 149. Andrew Hamer, 'Marygreen', *KM 80: A Birthday Album for Kenneth Muir: Tuesday, 5 May, 1987* (Liverpool: Liverpool University Press, 1987), pp.62–5 is the best discussion I have come across of the significance Hardy generates from his place-names.
3. Denys Kay-Robinson, *Hardy's Wessex Reappraised* (Newton Abbot: David & Charles, 1972), p.131; F.B. Pinion, 'The Country and Period of *The Woodlanders*', *Thomas Hardy Year-Book*, no. 2 (1971), pp.46–55 (p.50).
4. *Life*, p.224, 'Becky S.' is probably Rebecca Swetman, married to John Swetman of Melbury Osmund. Hardy's maternal grandmother was a member of the Swetman family which, according to Hardy, had owned land in Melbury 'when the Ilchesters were at plow' (*Hardy: A Biography*, p.12). Compare the Chickerels and the Durbeyfields. Lois Deacon, 'Tess's Walk to Beaminster', *Thomas Hardy Year-Book*, 3 (1972–3), pp.27–31) points out how Tess's journey from Flintcomb-Ash to Emminster crosses this area that was so important to Hardy.
5. Martin Ray, *Thomas Hardy: A Textual Study of the Short Stories* (Aldershot and Brookfield, Vermont: Ashgate, 1997), pp.49–54, 318–22, provides a comprehensive account of Hardy's alterations.
6. See Ray, *Short Stories*, p.50: 'Pinion correctly observes that the topography of the story in the serial was more accurate than in later versions.'
7. 'Enter ye in at the strait gate; for wide is the gate, and broad is the way, that leadeth to destruction, and many there be which go in thereat: Because strait is the gate, and narrow the way, which leadeth unto life, and few there be that find it.' (Matthew 7: 13–14, King James Bible). Hardy's 'straight' echoes both the 'strait', narrow way and the 'broad' one. In their language and relationship, Japheth and Darton also recall the Porter and Macduff of *Macbeth*, Act III, scene 2.
8. The 'directing-post' recalls those of Wordsworth's poetry, notably of the Salisbury Plain poems and of *The Prelude*. The 'blank arms' of the signpost strangely echo one of Hardy's much later poems about his first wife, 'Near Lanivet, 1872', where Emma accidentally and ominously appears crucified when she leans against a 'stunted handpost' (*Poems*, p.436).
9. Hardy, *Withered Arm*, p.161. The story was first published in March 1883. Hardy altered the contents of *Wessex Tales* in 1896 and again in 1912; 'The Three Strangers' came first in each edition.

10. Hardy, *Withered Arm*, pp.88–9. As 'The Distracted Young Preacher', the story first appeared in April 1879 and is the earliest written of *Wessex Tales*; it was placed last in each edition; in 1912, Hardy added a postscript stating that the marriage to the preacher was required by the taste of magazine readers and he would himself have preferred to give the truer account of events in which Lizzy marries the leading smuggler instead and emigrates to America. *The Return of the Native*, published November 1878, is similar both in providing a marriage and in Hardy's later repudiation of that ending.

11. Hardy, *Withered Arm*, p.355. The story was first published January 1888. 'The Melancholy Hussar' was first published in 1890 and added to *Wessex Tales* in 1912; Hardy, *PBE*, vol.2, ch.4 and vol.3, ch.13, pp.157, 375–6. See the discussion of 'Wintonchester' in *Tess* above, Chapter 3. Jean Jacques Leclercle in a valuable essay addresses the wider issue raised here (in 'The Violence of Style in *Tess of the d'Urbervilles*', *Alternative Hardy*, edited by Lance St John Butler (Basingstoke: Macmillan – now Palgrave, 1989), pp.1–25, For him, the oppressive power of language is part of Hardy's condition, reflected in Tess's destruction and Hardy's styleless style. He does not discuss Hardy's projection of a world beyond oppressive language or of a way of speaking/writing which might reflect or approach that condition – the voice of a child or a 'faltering Phrase' (used of Elfride in the title to vol.2, ch.4 of *A Pair of Blue Eyes*). See also Jo Devereux, 'Thomas Hardy's *A Pair of Blue Eyes*: The Heroine as Text', *The Victorian Newsletter*, 81 (Spring 1992), pp.20–23.

12. See Sigmund Freud, 'The Uncanny', *Art and Literature*, edited by Albert Dickson, The Penguin Freud Library, general editor James Strachey, vol.14 (London: Penguin, 1990), p.356: doubling leads to a 'dividing and interchanging of the self' so that someone confronted by their double 'is in doubt as to which his self is, or substitutes the extraneous self for his own'.

13. Hardy, *Withered Arm*, p.279. Hardy writes the story in the first half of 1884, a little after hearing the story in December 1882 of a woman who refused to marry and be 'made respectable'. See *Life*, pp.162–3.

14. Though the collected edition in which this title was first given to the novels did not appear until 1895–6, the use of *Wessex Tales* as Hardy's title suggests that he was beginning to think in 1888 of 'Wessex' as a way of unifying his work. The location of 'The Three Strangers' cannot be securely identified; places a few miles northwest and south of Dorchester have been suggested (Ray, *Short Stories*, p.13; Kay-Robinson, *Wessex Reappraised*, p.137). Neither does it recall his other work. Instead, placed at the head of the collection, it asserts the distinctive genre of what is to follow.

15. For the novel's connections with Corfe Castle and places nearby, see C.J.P. Beatty, 'When is a Castle not a Castle?', *Proceedings of the Dorset Natural History and Archaeological Society*, 90 (1969), pp.258–60 and 'Colonel Waugh and *A Laodicean*', *Thomas Hardy Year-Book*, 1 (1970), pp.19–21. References to Casterbridge were replaced by 'Toneborough' in 1895–6, that being the Wessex name for Taunton.

16. See *Life*, p.106: 'The beginning [of *The Hand of Ethelberta*] appeared in the *Cornhill* for May, when Hardy had at last the satisfaction of proving, amid the general disappointment at the lack of sheep and shepherds, that he did not mean to imitate anybody.'

17. Architecture is a constant preoccupation; see especially Hardy, *Laodicean*,

Book 1, chs 1 and 9, pp.5, 58–61. Colonialism and Empire are touched on
via Dare's multiple origins, De Stancy's time in India and Abner Power's
trading links with South America. Hardy's 'Literary Notes' from the time
when he was writing the novel show his reading Matthew Arnold closely,
including his essay, 'Pagan and Medieval Religious Sentiment', and Karl
Hillebrand's article, 'Familiar Conversations on Modern England', *Nineteenth
Century*, 7 (June 1880), pp.995ff. See *Literary Notebooks*, pp.127–35, 363–70.

18. Pinion, *Hardy Companion*, p.39, states that Hardy consulted Collinson's
History of Somerset in the British Museum for its account of Dunster Castle,
quoted in Book. 1, ch.13.

19. 'Enthusiasm' has overtones of religious fervour, especially that of dissenters
like the Baptists. See Susie I. Tucker, *Enthusiasm: A Study in Semantic Change*
(Cambridge: Cambridge University Press, 1972). Arnold connected provincialism with what he saw as a dreary dissenting culture, lacking eloquence
as much as naturalness. See Valentine Cunningham, *Everywhere Spoken
Against: Dissent in the Victorian Novel* (Oxford: Clarendon Press, 1975),
pp.21ff, for the accusation and the non-conformist responses to it.

20. 'Power is perhaps modelled on the successful Baptist railway-builder and
Liberal MP, Samuel Morton Peto' (Hardy, *Laodicean*, editor's notes, p.388).
The name may also have a secret autobiographical resonance: 'Will Strong'
and 'Egbert Mayne' are both partly autobiographical characters and Hardy
may have been thinking as well of Thomas Power O'Connor (1848–1929),
the famous editor of *T.P.'s Weekly*.

21. Hardy, *HE*, 'Sequel', pp.398–406; Thomas Hardy, *Two on a Tower*, edited by
Suleiman M. Ahmad (Oxford and New York: Oxford University Press), chs.
39–41, pp.254–81.

22. Hardy, *Laodicean*, Book. 6, ch.5, p.375. Numerous convents and orders of
Anglican nuns were founded in the mid-nineteenth century, most of them
connected with the Tractarian movement. 'By the eighteen-seventies sister-
hoods appear to have attained to a certain popularity even in fashionable
circles' and are 'frequently mentioned in Miss Yonge': Margaret More and
Alicia C. Percival, *Victorian Best-seller: The World of Charlotte M. Yonge*
(London, Sydney, Toronto: Harrap & Co., 1948), p.111.

23. '[English Gothic] had again returned to silence; indeed – such is the surprising instability of art "principles" as they are facetiously called – it was
just as likely to sink into the neglect and oblivion which had been its lot in
Georgian times' (Hardy, *Laodicean*, Book. 1, ch.1, p.6).

24. Hutchins, *Dorset*, II, p.316. Hardy mentions (*Life*, p.120) that Eustacia Vye's
name was chosen out of Hutchins, *Dorset*, indicating that, although he made
greatest use of the work in composing *Tess* and *A Group of Noble Dames*, he
also employed it as early as 1877.

25. See J.H. Lucking, *Railways of Dorset: an Outline of their Establishment,
Development and Progress from 1825* (Lichfield: The Railways Correspondence
and Travel Society/Dorset Natural History and Archaeological Society,
1968), pp.16–21 and Hardy, *Laodicean*, Book. 1, ch.12, pp.80–85. Samuel
Morton Peto, the model for John Power, built the Dorset section of
the London and South Western Railway which went through Buckhorn
Weston.

26. See Figs. 2b and 2c. Unusually, Hutchins mentions that Powerstock church

has recently been restored and that, in Buckhorn Weston, 'The church is now (1870) undergoing substantial repairs and enlargement' (Hutchins, *Dorset*, II, p.320, and IV, p.117). Hardy read reviews of his novels carefully and was vulnerable to them; he may have felt similarly about accounts of the buildings he was involved in and so checked through Hutchins's volumes looking for comments. If so, this would have drawn him to Powerstock and Buckhorn Weston.

27. Peter Widdowson, *Hardy in History: A Study in Literary Sociology* (London and New York: Routledge, 1989), pp.16–17; Martin J. Wiener, *English Culture and the Decline of the Industrial Spirit, 1850–1980* (Cambridge: Cambridge University Press, 1981), pp.51–3.

28. Wiener, *Industrial Spirit*, p.52; Widdowson, *Hardy in History*, pp.62–4; see also Peter Brooker and Peter Widdowson, 'A Literature for England', *Englishness: Politics and Culture 1880–1920*, edited by Robert Colls and Philip Dodds (Beckenham, North Ryde, New South Wales, and New York: Croom Helm, 1986), pp.116–63: 'in the period 1900–14, Thomas Hardy, the "poet" of Wessex, was emphatically shaped into the English rural annalist *par excellence*' (p.120). George Wing, 'Hardy and Regionalism', in *Thomas Hardy: The Writer and His Background* (London: Bell & Hyman, 1980), pp.76–101, is a good example of Wessex's being read as uncomplicatedly integral to Hardy's project.

29. Robert Colls, 'Englishness and the Political Culture', *Englishness*, pp.29–61. On geography in the period, see above, Chapter 1.

30. See Patrick Wright, *On Living in an Old Country: The National Past in Contemporary Britain* (London: Verso, 1985), both for its criticisms of Wiener and for its account of the 'English national consciousness' which 'makes an exclusive principle of a well-rehearsed imagination of history, race, place and belonging' (p.128). Compare Eve Kosofsky Sedgwick's subtle reading of nationalism in the period in her essay, 'Nationalisms and Sexualities in the Age of Wilde', *Nationalisms & Sexualities*, edited by Andrew Parker, Mary Russo, Doris Sammer and Patricia Yaeger (New York and London: Routledge, 1992), pp.235–45.

31. Joe Fisher, *The Hidden Hardy* (Basingstoke: Macmillan – now Palgrave, 1992), pp.2–3.

32. The map may have been included in 1895–6 because other maps were appearing at the time. See *Hardy: A Biography*, p.361.

33. The rivers are not named in 1895–6; names are added for 1912–13.

34. Kingsbere comes up incidentally in several of the novels and stories; Sandbourne features in *The Hand of Ethelberta* and is mentioned in *The Well-Beloved* and *Jude*. There is a single mention of Trantridge outside the novel, in one of the stories in *Life's Little Ironies*, and to Marlott in *A Group of Noble Dames*.

35. Hardy drew a sketch-map for the novel, with the title 'Tess's Country'. Real and Wessex place-names are written together and the region is defined by its network of railway lines. (Roads, rivers and other physical features are all absent.) This suggests how important railways were to Hardy's understanding of Wessex geography – that proximity to or distance from a railway line played a major role in defining place. It highlights too how railways were deliberately not included in the maps Hardy published.

36. Although fictitious, the Wessex names for the counties are written in capital letters.
37. As Hardy writes beside his own sketch-map of Wessex: 'It is to be understood that this is an imaginative Wessex only, & that the places described under the names here given are not portraits of any real places, but visionary places which may approximate to the real places more or less.'
38. This again is a change from 1895–6, where places are marked by small circles. On conventions of mapping and their implications, see Richard Helgerson, *Forms of Nationhood: The Elizabethan Writing of England* (Chicago and London: University of Chicago Press, 1992).
39. As early as the 1860s, the first series Ordnance Survey maps were recognized as combining out-of-date information, from surveys carried out during the Napoleonic wars, with some up-to-date detail, particularly railway lines which were engraved onto the old plates that remained otherwise unchanged. See Matthew Arnold's comments in 'Ordnance Maps', published December 1862, *The Complete Prose Works*, edited by R.H. Super, vol.2 (Ann Arbor: University of Michagan Press, 1962), pp.252–6, 364–6.
40. Hutchins, *Dorset*, celebrates the variety of remains to be found in the county; Charles Warne's work was more detailed and more enthusiastic – see his *Ancient Dorset. The Celtic, Roman, Saxon, and Danish Antiquities of the County [. . .]* (Bournemouth: D. Sydenham, 1872). Warne's map accompanying *Dorsetshire: Its Vestiges, Celtic, Roman, Saxon, and Danish [. . .]* (London: D. Sydenham and John Camden Hotten, 1865) similarly shows remains from all historical periods overlaying one another on a single sheet. A magazine article about Hardy, published in 1886 and probably ghosted by him, shows his sense of a historically composite landscape in which 'the immense ramparts of Maiden Castle' are visible from the same window as 'the monument to Sir Thomas Hardy, Nelson's captain' (reprinted *IR*, pp.20–23).
41. *Thomas Hardy: The Critical Heritage*, edited by R.G. Cox (London and New York: Routledge & Kegan Paul and Barnes & Noble, 1970), pp.46, 56.
42. *Personal Writings*, pp.91–3; the comments date from 1878 and 1881.
43. 'The Dorsetshire Labourer' (1883), *Personal Writings*, p.170; Hardy, *Tess*, ch.3, p.21.
44. *Hardy: The Critical Heritage*, p.46.
45. Hardy, *Mayor*, p.337; *Tess*, p.lxiv. Compare Hardy, *Madding Crowd*, p.xxxvii: '[Hardy] also continued to work on minute details of dialect, changing *you* to *ye* and *ye* to *'ee* and vice versa [. . .] never fully satisfied that he had achieved precisely the right balance between standard and dialectal forms'.

7   Wessex and Elsewhere

1. Hardy, *Jude*, Part 2, ch.1, Part 4, ch.1, p.78, 199. Until 1974, the county boundary between Berkshire and Oxfordshire followed the Thames between Henley and Oxford and further west as far as Lechlade; Berkshire corresponds to North Wessex so that this passage is accurate about the border of Hardy's Wessex.
2. Charles Lock, 'Hardy and the Railway', *Essays in Criticism*, 50:1 (2000), p.64.

3. John Goode, *Thomas Hardy: The Offensive Truth* (Oxford: Blackwell, 1988), pp.141, 146.

4. Goode, *Offensive Truth*, p.141. See also Philip M. Weinstein, *The Semantics of Desire: Changing Models of Identity from Dickens to Joyce* (Princeton and London: Princeton UP, 1984): 'The landscape of *Jude the Obscure*, unlike that of *Tess of the d'Urbervilles*, is overwhelmingly cultural. The landmarks within it comprise the range of human institutions and conventions by which the journeying spirit finds itself stymied rather than fulfilled.'

5. Hardy mentions that the atmosphere in the valley is 'bluer, moister' than that of Jude's upland world, recalling Tess's view into the Vale of Blackmoor from the high ground near Flintcomb-Ash; see Hardy, *Tess*, ch.44, p.297; ch.16, p.103.

6. Marjorie Garson, *Hardy's Fables of Integrity: Woman, Body, Text* (Oxford: Clarendon Press, 1991), p.169. See also Andrew Enstice, *Thomas Hardy: Landscapes of the Mind* (London and Basingstoke: Macmillan – now Palgrave Macmillan, 1979), p.6 for Christminster's similarities to Casterbridge seen by Henchard and to the Great Barn at Weatherbury.

7. Hardy, *Jude*, Part 1, ch.3, p.19; Goode, *Offensive Truth*, p.152.

8. See Hardy, *Jude*, Part 2, ch.3, p.93–4; *Well-Beloved*, p.56, 68.

9. See particularly the account of the 'Great Wessex Agricultural Show' held at Stoke-Barehills and crowded with Londoners (Part 5, ch.5, pp.289–90). Ease of movement here contrasts with Jude's earlier journey from Christminster to Kennetbridge, to visit the composer he admires, which has to be made 'by a series of crooked railways' (Part 3, ch.10, p.194).

10. The first instalment of the serial of the novel was entitled, *The Simpletons*. The second instalment had the title, *Hearts Insurgent*. *Jude the Obscure* was settled on when the manuscript was complete.

11. Hardy, *Jude*, Part 6, ch.5, p.366

12. It is a neat irony that, in moving to Marygreen to marry and live with Phillotson, Sue is returning to her birthplace (which she left as a child when her parents' marriage broke down, moving with her mother to London). Both the adoptive Londoners of the novel – Arabella and Sue – think that Christminster is slightly ridiculous. Jude seems, consequently, more 'behind' than ever. Sue's collapse into Tractarian self-punishment stresses how powerful and destructive Christminster remains, how its dead hand crushes personal idealism as well as aspirations towards self-betterment. It also implies that Jude's apparently provincial desire to be part of a larger unit also governs the citizens of the world like Sue.

13. John R. Doheny observes how little critical attention has been paid to Arabella in 'Characterization in Hardy's *Jude the Obscure*: The Function of Arabella', *Reading Thomas Hardy*, edited by Charles P.C. Pettit (Basingstoke and New York: Macmillan – now Palgrave Macmillan, 1998), pp.57–82.

14. Hardy, *Jude*, Part 5, ch.8, p.316; Part 6, ch.11, p.408. The editor notes the more aggressive reading deleted in the manuscript: ' "never found peace since she left my man's arms," said Arabella triumphantly' (p.465).

15. Hardy, *Jude*, Pt. 2, ch.11, pp.404–6.

16. The churchyard is now in the process of being restored by the present-day residents.

17. John Goode discusses this incident very well; see *Offensive Truth*, p.146.

18. Elizabeth K. Helsinger, *Rural Scenes and National Representation, 1815–1850*, Literature in History Series (Princeton N.J.: Princeton University Press, 1997), pp.124–6 analyses most intelligently Mitford's use of pools. See Mary Elizabeth Braddon, *Lady Audley's Secret*, edited by David Skilton (Oxford and New York: Oxford University Press, 1987), ch.1, p.2: 'A glorious old place – a place that visitors fell into raptures with; feeling a yearning wish to have done with life, and to stay there for ever, staring into the cool fish-ponds, and counting the bubbles as the roach and carp rose to the surface of the water – a spot in which Peace seem to have taken up her abode, setting her soothing hand [. . .] on the still ponds and quiet alleys [. . .] ay, even upon the stagnant well, which, cool and sheltered as all else in the old place, hid itself away in a shrubbery behind the gardens, with an idle handle that was never turned.' And see above, Chapter 4.
19. Jude discovers that, as a little girl, Sue played 'down the long slide on yonder pond, with her little curls blowing, one of a file of twenty' (Part 2, ch.6, p.112) but this idyllic scene feels very much in the past.
20. Hardy, *Madding Crowd*, ch.39, p.233.

Select Bibliography

This list aims to be introductory and representative. It focusses on secondary material. The notes provide fuller referencing. Items in the list of abbreviations are not given and well-known primary texts are included only when a particular edition is of particular help.

Armstrong, Nancy, 'Emily's Ghost: The Cultural Politics of Victorian Fiction, Folklore, and Photography', *Novel: A Forum on Fiction*, 25 (Spring 1992), pp.245–67.

Baker, J.N.L., *The History of Geography: Papers* (Oxford: Blackwell, 1963).

Barrell, John, 'The Geographies of Hardy's Wessex', *Journal of Historical Geography*, 8:4 (1982), pp.347–61.

Beer, Gillian, *Open Fields: Science in Cultural Encounter* (Oxford: Oxford University Press, 1996).

Bell, Ian A. (ed.), *Peripheral Visions: Images of Nationhood in Contemporary British Fiction* (Cardiff: University of Wales Press, 1995).

Benko, Georges and Ulf Strohmayer (eds), *Space and Social Theory: Interpreting Modernity and Postmodernity*, The Royal Geographical Society with the Institute of British Geographers Special Publications Series, no.33 (Oxford and Malden, MA: Blackwell, 1997).

Bentley, Phyllis, *The English Regional Novel* (London: George Allen & Unwin, 1941).

Bermingham, Ann, *Landscape and Ideology: The English Rustic Tradition* (Berkeley and Los Angeles: University of California Press, 1986).

Bodenheimer, Rosemarie, *The Politics of Story in Victorian Social Fiction* (Ithaca: Cornell University Press, 1988).

Boumelha, Penny, *Thomas Hardy and Women: Sexual Ideology and Narrative Form* (Brighton: Harvester, 1982).

Burrow, John, *A Liberal Descent: Victorian Historians and the English Past* (Cambridge: Cambridge University Press, 1981).

Butler, Lance St John (ed.), *Thomas Hardy after Fifty Years* (London and Basingstoke: Macmillan – now Palgrave Macmillan, 1977).

Butler, Lance St John (ed.), *Alternative Hardy* (Basingstoke: Macmillan – now Palgrave Macmillan, 1989).

Cavaliero, Glen, *The Rural Tradition in the English Novel 1900–1939* (London and Basingstoke: Macmillan – now Palgrave Macmillan, 1977).

Colls, Robert and Philip Dodd (eds), *Englishness: Politics and Culture, 1880–1920* (Beckenham and North Ryde, New South Wales: Croom Helm, 1986).

Cosslett, Tess, *The 'Scientific Movement' and Victorian Literature* (Brighton and New York: Harvester and Barnes & Noble, 1982).

Cox, R. (ed.), *Thomas Hardy: The Critical Heritage* (London and New York: Routledge & Kegan Paul and Barnes & Noble, 1970).

Craik, W.A., *Elizabeth Gaskell and the English Provincial Novel* (London: Methuen & Co., 1975).

Daly, Nicholas, 'Sensation Fiction and the Modernization of the Senses', *ELH*, 66:2 (Summer 1999), pp.461–87.

Darby, H.C., 'The Regional Geography of Hardy's Wessex', *Geographical Review*, 38 (1948), pp.426–43.

Duncan, Craig, Kelvyn Jones and Graham Moon, 'Do Places Matter? A Multi-level Analysis of Regional Variations in Health-Related Behaviour in Britain', *Social Sciences and Medicine*, 37 (1993), pp.725–33.

Edgeworth, Maria, *Castle Rackrent and Ennui*, edited by Marilyn Butler (Harmondsworth: Penguin, 1992).

Edwards, P.D., *Idyllic Realism from Mary Russell Mitford to Hardy* (Basingstoke: Macmillan – now Palgrave Macmillan, 1988).

Elliott, Ralph W.V., *Thomas Hardy's English* (Oxford and London: Basil Blackwell and André Deutsch, 1984).

Entrikin, J. Nicholas, *The Betweenness of Place: Towards a Geography of Modernity* (Basingstoke: Macmillan – now Palgrave Macmillan, 1991).

Fawcett, C.B., *Provinces of England: A Study of Some Geographical Aspects of Devolution*, The Making of the Future Series (London: Williams & Norgate, 1919).

Fisher, Joe, *The Hidden Hardy* (Basingstoke and London: Macmillan – now Palgrave Macmillan, 1992).

Freeman, T.W., *A History of Modern British Geography* (London and New York: Longman, 1980).

Garson, Marjorie, *Hardy's Fables of Integrity: Woman, Body, Text* (Oxford: Clarendon Press, 1991).

Gatrell, Simon, *Hardy the Creator: A Textual Biography* (Oxford: Clarendon Press, 1988).

Gatrell, Simon, 'Wessex', *The Cambridge Companion to Thomas Hardy*, ed. Dale Kramer (Cambridge: Cambridge University Press, 1999).

Geikie, Archibald, *The Teaching of Geography: Suggestions Regarding Principles and Methods for the Use of Teachers* (London and New York: Macmillan – now Palgrave Macmillan, 1887).

Gilmour, Robin, 'Regional and Provincial in Victorian Literature', *The Literature of Region and Nation*, ed. R.P. Draper (Basingstoke: Macmillan – now Palgrave Macmillan, 1989).

Girouard, Mark, *The Return to Camelot: Chivalry and the English Gentleman* (New Haven and London: Yale University Press, 1981).

Goode, John, *Thomas Hardy: The Offensive Truth* (Oxford: Blackwell, 1988).

Green, John Richard, *The Making of England* (London: Macmillan & Co., 1885).

Gregor, Ian, 'Hardy's World', *ELH*, 38 (1971), pp.274–93.

Hechter, Michael, *Internal Colonialism: The Celtic Fringe in British National Development, 1536–1966* (London: Routledge & Kegan Paul, 1975).

Helsinger, Elizabeth K., *Rural Scenes and National Representation: Britain, 1815–1850*, Literature in History Series (Princeton, NJ: Princeton University Press, 1997).

Holt-Jensen, A., *Geography: Its History and Concepts: A Student's Guide* (London: Harper & Row, 1980).

hooks, bell, *Yearning: Race, Gender, and Cultural Politics* (London: Turnaround, 1991).

Howitt, William, *The Rural Life of England*, 1838, 3rd edn, corrected and revised (London: Longman, Brown, Green and Longmans, 1844).

Ingham, Patricia, 'Dialect in the Novels of Hardy and George Eliot', *Literary English Since Shakespeare*, ed. George Watson (London, Oxford and New York: Oxford University Press, 1970), pp.347–63.

Irwin, Michael, *Reading Hardy's Landscapes* (Basingstoke and New York: Macmillan – now Palgrave Macmillan, 2000).

Jarvis, Brian, *Postmodern Cartographies: The Geographical Imagination in Contemporary American Culture* (London: Pluto Press, 1998).

Jewell, Helen M., *The North–South Divide: The Origins of Northern Consciousness in England* (Manchester and New York: Manchester University Press, 1994).

Kay-Robinson, Denys, *Hardy's Wessex Reappraised* (Newton Abbot: David & Charles, 1972).

Kay-Robinson, Denys, 'Hardy's Wessex', *The Genius of Thomas Hardy*, ed. Margaret Drabble (London: Weidenfeld & Nicolson, 1976).

Keith, Michael and Steve Pile (eds), *Place and the Politics of Identity* (London and New York: Routledge, 1993).

Keith, W.J., *Regions of the Imagination: The Development of British Rural Fiction* (Toronto, Buffalo, London: University of Toronto Press, 1988).

Lambert, R.J., 'Central and Local Relations in Mid-Victorian England: the Local Government Act Office, 1858–71', *Victorian Studies*, 6 (1962), pp.121–50.

Lefebvre, Henri, *The Production of Space*, trans. Donald Nicholson-Smith (Oxford and Cambridge, MA: Blackwell, 1991).

Lock, Charles, 'Hardy and the Railway', *Essays in Criticism*, 50:1 (2000), pp.44–66.

Lucas, John, *The Literature of Change: Studies in the Nineteenth-Century Provincial Novel* (Brighton: Harvester Press, 1977).

Lucking, J.H., *Railways of Dorset: an Outline of their Establishment, Development and Progress from 1825* (The Railways Correspondence and Travel Society / Dorset Natural History and Archeological Society, 1968).

Mackinder, H.J., *Britain and the British Seas*, 1902, 2nd edn (Oxford: Clarendon Press, 1907).

Massey, Doreen, *Space, Place and Gender* (Cambridge: Polity Press, 1994).

Miller, J. Hillis, *Topographies* (Stanford, California: Stanford University Press, 1995).

Mingay, G.E. (ed.), *The Victorian Countryside*, 2 vols (London, Boston and Henley: Routledge & Kegan Paul, 1981).

Mitchell, W.J.T. (ed.), *Landscape and Power* (Chicago and London: University of Chicago Press, 1994), pp.77–101.

Moretti, Franco, *Atlas of the European Novel* (London and New York: Verso, 1998).

Morgan, Rosemarie, *Women and Sexuality in the Novels of Thomas Hardy* (London: Routledge, 1988).

Morgan, Rosemarie, *Cancelled Words: Rediscovering Thomas Hardy* (London and New York: Routledge, 1992).

Morris, Pam, 'Heroes and Hero-Worship in Charlotte Brontë's *Shirley*', *Nineteenth-Century Literature*, 54:3 (December 1999), pp.285–307.

Newman, John and Nikolaus Pevsner, *Dorset*, The Buildings of England (Harmondsworth: Penguin, 1972).

Payne, Christiana, 'Rural Virtues for Urban Consumption: Cottage Scenes in Early Victorian Painting', *Journal of Victorian Culture*, 3:1 (Spring 1998), pp.45–68.

Pettit, Charles P.C. (ed.), *Reading Thomas Hardy* (Basingstoke and New York: Macmillan – now Palgrave Macmillan, 1998).

Pigot & Co., *British Atlas, comprising the Counties of England [. . .]*, 1840, facsimile reprint (London: Salamander Books, 2000).

Pinion, F.B, *A Hardy Companion: A Guide to the Works of Thomas Hardy and their Background* (London, Melbourne, Toronto and New York: Macmillan – now Palgrave Macmillan, 1968).

Pocock, Douglas C.D., *Humanistic Geography and Literature: Essays on the Experience of Place* (London and Totowa, NJ: Croom Helm and Barnes & Noble, 1981).

Prest, John, *Liberty and Locality: Parliament, Permissive Legislation, and Ratepayers' Democracies in the Nineteenth Century* (Oxford: Clarendon Press, 1990).

Ray, Martin, *Thomas Hardy: A Textual Study of the Short Stories* (Aldershot and Brookfield, Vermont: Ashgate, 1997).

Schivelbusch, Wolfgang, *The Railway Journey: The Industrialization of Time and Space in the 19th Century* (Leamington Spa, Hamburg and New York: Berg, 1986).

Schor, Esther, *Bearing the Dead: The British Culture of Mourning from the Enlightenment to Victoria*, Literature in History Series (Princeton, NJ: Princeton University Press, 1995).

Shires, Linda M. (ed.), *Rewriting the Victorians: Theory, History, and the Politics of Gender* (New York and London: Routledge, 1992).

Simpson, David, *The Academic Postmodern and the Rule of Literature: A Report on Half-Knowledge* (Chicago and London: The University of Chicago Press, 1995).

Snell, K.D.M., *Annals of the Labouring Poor: Social Change and Agrarian England, 1660–1900*, Cambridge Studies in Population, Economy and Society in Past Time (Cambridge: Cambridge University Press, 1985).

Snell, K.D.M. (ed.), *The Regional Novel in Britain and Ireland, 1800–1990* (Cambridge: Cambridge University Press, 1998).

Soja, Ed, *Postmodern Geographies: The Reassertion of Space in Critical Social Theory* (London: Verso, 1989).

Summerson, John, *The London Building World of the Eighteen Sixties* (London: Thames & Hudson, 1973).

Taylor, Dennis, *Hardy's Literary Language and Victorian Philology* (Oxford: Clarendon Press, 1993).

Taylor, Richard, *The Neglected Hardy: Thomas Hardy's Lesser Novels* (London: Macmillan – now Palgrave Macmillan, 1982).

Thomas, David St John, *The West Country*, A Regional History of the Railways of Great Britain, vol.1 (London: Phoenix House, 1960).

Thompson, F.M.L., *The Rise of Respectable Society: A Social History of Victorian Britain, 1830–1900* (London: Fontana, 1988).

Thrift, Nigel, *Spatial Formations* (London, Thousand Oaks, CA and New Delhi: Sage Publications, 1996).

Tuan, Yi-Fu, *Topophilia: A Study of Environmental Perception, Attitudes, and Values* (Englewood Cliffs, 1974).

Vigar, Penelope, *The Novels of Thomas Hardy: Illusion and Reality* (London: The Athlone Press, 1974).

Walton, John K., *The English Seaside Resort: A Social History 1750–1914* (Leicester and New York: Leicester University Press/St Martin's Press, 1983).

Warne, Charles, *Dorsetshire: Its Vestiges, Celtic, Roman, Saxon, and Danish [. . .]* (London: D. Sydenham and John Camden Hotten, 1865).

Warne, Charles, *Ancient Dorset. The Celtic, Roman, Saxon, and Danish Antiquities of the County [. . .]* (Bournemouth: D. Sydenham, 1872).

Widdowson, Peter, *Hardy in History: A Study in Literary Sociology* (London and New York: Routledge, 1989).

Wiener, Martin J., *English Culture and the Decline of the Industrial Spirit, 1850–1980* (Cambridge: Cambridge University Press, 1981).

Wiley, Michael, *Romantic Geography: Wordsworth and Anglo-European Spaces* (Basingstoke and New York: Macmillan – now Palgrave Macmillan, 1998).

Williams, Merryn, *Thomas Hardy and Rural England* (London and Basingstoke: Macmillan – now Palgrave Macmillan, 1972).

Williams, Raymond, *The Country and the City* (London: Chatto & Windus, 1973).

Wing, George, 'Hardy and Regionalism', *Thomas Hardy: The Writer and His Background*, ed. Norman Page (London: Bell & Hyman, 1980), pp.76–101.

Wright, Patrick, *On Living in an Old Country: The National Past in Contemporary Britain*, with drawings by Andrzej Krauze (London: Verso, 1985).

Index

Acton, Lord, 216
Alderson, David, *Mansex fine*, 218
Alfred, King, 27–9, 36, 88
  literature, 27, 29–30, 34–5, 201, 202
  see also Athelney; country-party
Allen, Ralph, 31, 202
Armstrong, Nancy, 'Emily's Ghost', 211–12
Arnold, Matthew, 10, 161, 163, 184, 213, 230, 232
Arnold, Thomas, 6, 197
Arthur, King, 51, 88
  literature, 217–18
  see also Glastonbury
Athelney, 28–30, 33–5, 217
Austen, Jane, 93, 219
Auster, Henry, *Local Habitations*, 70, 212

Baker, J.N.L., *The History of Geography*, 196
Barker, Pat, 60
Barnes, William, 215
Barrell, John, 12–16, 45, 48, 198–9, 202, 204
Bayley, John, 1
Beer, Gillian, 113, 207, 210, 215, 222–3
Bentley, Phyllis, 70, 212
Beresford, Maurice, *East End, West End*, 218
Bermingham, Ann, 202, 208
Best, Geoffrey, *Mid-Victorian Britain*, 216
Blackmore, R.D., 111
Bloom, Harold, 209
Bodenheimer, Rosemarie, *The Politics of Story*, 214
Boumelha, Penny, 196
Braddon, M.E., 106, 110, 193, 215, 217, 222, 234
Brandon, Raphael, 167

Brontë, Charlotte, 76–7, 214, 220–1
Brontë, Emily, 59, 61, 65–9, 74, 128, 145, 176, 211
Brunton, Mary, 210
Bullen, J.B., 83, 216, 218
Bulwer-Lytton, Edward, 53, 207
Burke, Edmund, 10
Burn, W.L., *The Age of Equipoise*, 216
Burney, Fanny, 219
Burrow, John, *A Liberal Descent*, 216
Butler, Marilyn, 63–4, 210

Carlyle, Thomas, 10
Carroll, David, 212
Cary's New Itinerary, 30, 202, 205
Cavaliero, Glen, 209–10
Cecil, Lord David, 212
Clough, Arthur Hugh, 184
Cobbett, William, 56–7, 91, 218
Coleridge, Samuel Taylor, 32, 34, 203
Collins, Wilkie, 106–11, 122, 124, 222
  No Name, 106, 108–9, 124, 222
  Armadale, 106–7, 109, 222
  Woman in White, 107–8, 124
Colls, Robert and Philip Dodds, *Englishness*, 169–70, 208, 209, 231
  see also Dodds, Philip
Constable, John, 56–7, 208
Cookson, Catherine, 60
Cornwall, 86–7, 88, 111, 112, 217
  see also Devon
Cosslett, Tess, 213, 214
Cottle, Joseph, 34–5
  Alfred, an Epic Poem, 34–5
country-party, 27, 30, 33, 88
Craik, Dinah, 111, 212, 218, 219
Crickmay, G.R., 166, 217
  see also Hardy, Thomas, and architecture